S0-BDO-192

Guide to the Recommended
COUNTRY INNS
OF NEW ENGLAND

"A worthwhile addition to the library of inveterate New England Inn visitors."
—*Hudson Valley Magazine*

"More guests come to our inn with Elizabeth's book tucked under their arm than any other guidebook. They feel what we know—Elizabeth has been to her inns and she tells it as it is."
—*Paul and Louise Ebeltoft, innkeepers*
Copper Beech Inn, Ivoryton, Connecticut

"A look at the most charming way to spend your vacation."
—*Philadelphia Daily News*

"Spotlights pleasant houses where—as visitors to New England know—handcrafted quilts, antique furniture, home-cooked meals and spectacular mountain scenery are the norm . . ."
—*The Tampa Tribune, Florida*

"Truly the finest, most complete, legitimate book on country inns. Inns are listed because of their merit, not for payment of a fee or membership in a special organization."
—*Barbara and Charles Wallace, innkeepers*
Fitzwilliam Inn, Fitzwilliam, New Hampshire

"(You are) treated to personal observations of the author, who herself has visited every inn, and it is these often forgotten details that make each entry memorable . . ."
—*The New Haven Register, Connecticut*

"We like to recommend Elizabeth's book because it is one of the best. She makes sure she checks on each inn before a new edition is printed."
—*Sandy and Jack Allembert, innkeepers*
Four Columns Inn, Newfane, Vermont

"Not a guide you flip through lightly. Get comfortable in a cozy wing chair. . . . Just when you think you've found the perfect inn, you'll turn the page and discover another one."
—*Sunday Call-Chronicle*
Allentown, Pennsylvania

1

NINTH EDITION

Guide to the Recommended

COUNTRY INNS
OF NEW ENGLAND

by Elizabeth Squier
Illustrated by Olive Metcalf

The Globe Pequot Press

Chester, Connecticut 06412

Library of Congress Number: 73–83255
ISBN: 0-87106-867-2
Manufactured in the United States of America
Ninth Edition
Second Printing, October 1985

Contents

Dedicated to Yin,
my Bluepoint Himalayan,
and Yang,
my Maine Coon,
with love

How This Guide Is Arranged

The inns are listed by states, and alphabetically by towns within each state. The states are arranged by a peculiar whim of the publisher in the following order: Connecticut, Rhode Island, Massachusetts, Vermont, New Hampshire, and Maine. Before each state listing is a map and special index to help you in planning a trip, and on page 425 is a complete index of every inn in the book.

The abbreviations - The following abbreviations are used:

EP – European Plan—Room without meals.

EPB – European Plan—Room with full breakfast.

AP – American Plan—Room with all meals.

MAP – Modified American Plan—
Room with breakfast and dinner.

BYOB – Bring Your Own Bottle.

The pointing fingers - In the write-ups you will, from time to time, find some pointing fingers ☞ ☞ ☞ ☞ ☞. While I have not rated the inns, when I found something particularly outstanding or different, I inserted a ☞ as a special note.

And the E symbol - At the end of the write-ups you will find this symbol:

E - Stands for Elizabeth

This was to give me the opportunity to add an individual note on a special, personal delight.

How To Enjoy This Guide

When I first started writing THE GUIDE TO THE RECOM-MENDED COUNTRY INNS OF NEW ENGLAND back in 1973, country inns were relatively scarce. Since that time, however, the number of country inns has been rapidly grow-ing as more and more people have tired of the monotony of motels and thruway hotels and have begun searching for the infinitely more warming pleasure of a good country inn.

Therefore, as I have begun the research for each edition of this guide, it has become more and more difficult for me to wade through the volumes of mail from new country inns. I have had to be increasingly selective in choosing the best inns in each state. Do not be distressed if an inn you like is not in this guide. Please understand that my definition of a country inn is that it must have lodging as well as good food, and must have a certain ambience that appeals to me. I pre-fer that the inns I select serve at least two meals a day and be open most of the year, but I have made exceptions when an inn seems just too special to leave out of this guide.

By my descriptions and comments I have tried to indicate the type of atmosphere you can expect to find in an inn, whether it would be a fun place to bring your children, or whether it would be more appropriate to leave the children at home. Do not forget that the very reason you are passing up a motel or a hotel is for the bit of adventure and surprise you will find sit-ting in a weathered farmhouse, eating country cooking, chatting with a discovered friend, and finding new delight in a very old tradition.

Although I make every attempt to keep this guide up-to-date, please realize that prices and menus are subject to change, as are innkeepers. If you are planning to stay overnight, or even to have a special dinner out, I recommend that you call ahead for reservations so that you will not be disappointed. Many of the inns are quite small, and it would be a shame to travel a long distance and not get in.

With prices fluctuating so widely in today's economy, I quote an inn's current low and high rates only. This will give you a good indication, though not exact, of the price ranges you can expect. I have not included the tax rate, service charge, or tipping suggestions for any of the inns. Be sure to inquire about these additional charges when you make your reservations. Be prepared to pay a deposit when you make your reservation at most of the inns.

About pets: Most of the inns do not accept pets, but give an inn a call before you go. They may be able to make arrangements for you.

And a special note hopefully to dispel a rumor that has been going about. *There is no charge of any kind for an inn to be in this guide.*

So, enjoy! This GUIDE TO THE RECOMMENDED COUNTRY INNS OF NEW ENGLAND was compiled for you, fellow lovers of New England Country Inns.

Elizabeth

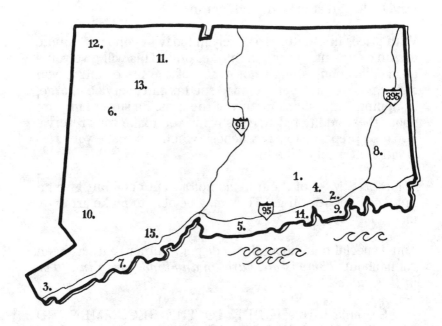

Numbers on map refer to towns numbered
on index on opposite page

Connecticut

The Inn at Chester
Chester, Connecticut
06412

Innkeepers: David and Elise Joslow
Telephone: 203-526-4961
Rooms: 47, all with private bath.
Rates: $80 per room, EP.
Facilities: Open all year. Breakfast, lunch, dinner, Sunday
   brunch, full license. Elevator, sauna, exercise room, tennis court, jogging track, billiard room, bicycles, three
   conference rooms. Lake nearby. All major credit cards
   accepted.

The years 1776–1778 were the beginning of the Inn at
Chester, but, of course, John B. Parmelee who owned the
house then had no idea that 200 years later it would become
a fine country inn.

All the guest accommodations are lovely. They were decorated by Elise, who is an author herself and a fine one. She
also writes the inn brochures. Some of the rooms have sitting
areas, and ☞ four have fireplaces. There is an elevator to

take you up and down from your room. This is a ☞ good inn for the handicapped. Twenty-six rooms are equipped for handicapped guests.

During the warm months the outside terrace is a perfect spot to enjoy fine dining or a cocktail. There are three private dining rooms and three that are open to the public. The largest dining room is in what was once a barn, a fantastic, high-ceilinged room with dark wood and a huge fireplace. A small greenhouse is attached to it. This makes a magnificent setting for the marvelous food.

An interesting breakfast selection is ☞ Bircher Muesli, a hearty alpine favorite made of oats, hazelnuts, and fresh fruits. My favorite lunch choice is the really good black bean soup with the proper accompaniments of chopped egg, minced onions, and sherry. At dinnertime the rooms are candlelit. For a starter, try the Mushroom Strudel. It is pure ambrosia. The inn also serves Rack of Lamb for one, which is done to perfection. The Pork with Plums also is outstanding. Leave some space for dessert; all of them are made here and each one is divine.

The inn has piano music seven nights a week, and on special holidays an a cappella choir sings from the balcory in the main dining room.

There are large and small conference rooms, a billiard room with a fireplace, and an exercise room. Have a massage or take a sauna. It's all right here for you.

How to get there: Take Exit 6 off Route 9 and turn west on Route 148. Go 3.2 miles to the inn. In a private plane, fly in to the Chester Airport.

☕

E: *Elise and I are both cat happy She has a Burmese named Arthur, a name I happen to love, and a flat-coated retriever called Raffles.*

The dog nuzzled my leg. The fire sent out a glow.
The drink was good. Only at an inn.

Griswold Inn
Essex, Connecticut
06426

Innkeepers: Bill and Victoria Winterer
Telephone: 203-767-0991
Rooms: 19, all with private bath; 4 suites.
Rates: $55, double occupancy; $65 to $75, suites; continental breakfast included.
Facilities: Open all year. Closed Christmas Eve and Christmas Day. Lunch, dinner, Sunday brunch, children's menu, bar. All major credit cards accepted.

Essex is a very special town right on the Connecticut River. Although it was settled long before the Revolution, Essex is still a living, breathing, working place, not a recreated museum of a town. The first warship of the Continental Navy, the *Oliver Cromwell,* was built and commissioned here in 1776.

"The Gris," as the inn is fondly called by everyone, is the highlight of anyone's trip to Essex. When you come in from the cold to the welcome of ☞ crackling fireplaces, you are doing what others have done before you for 200 years. You can lunch or dine in the cool dimness of the Library, or the Gun Room. A special spot is the Steamboat Room where the mural on the far wall floats gently, making you feel that you are really on the river. Their collection of ☞ Currier & Ives is museum-size and quality. ☞ There is music almost every night, old time banjoes, sea chanteys, Dixieland jazz, or just good piano; but never rock 'n' roll.

In the bar is a great, old-fashioned popcorn machine. Bill Winterer gives popcorn to all ☞ the children who come in. Do ask for some. It's one of many personal touches that make this nice kind of inn such a special place.

The Hunt Breakfast is the renowned Sunday brunch at the inn. This bountiful fare is worth a trip from anywhere. The selection is extensive, with enough good food to satisfy anyone's palate.

The guest rooms are old, but nice. The *Oliver Cromwell* suite is in the main building, with a woodburning fireplace, comfortable couches, a four-poster bed, and a lovely bar for your very own. There is a very nice view of Middle Cove from here.

Upriver in Middletown Bill has another inn, the Town Farms Inn. At this time there are no rooms, but the food is divine.

And down the river in Old Saybrook Bill owns the Dock, a fine seafood restaurant.

How to get there: Take the Connecticut Turnpike to Exit 69, and follow Route 9 north to Exit 3. Turn left at the bottom of ramp to a traffic light, turn right and follow this street right through town to the river. The inn is on your right, about 100 yards before you get to the river.

ℑ

E: *My favorite thing about The Gris? Love that popcorn machine in the bar.*

The Homestead Inn
Greenwich, Connecticut
06830

Innkeepers: Lessie Davison and Nancy Smith
Telephone: 203-869-7500
Rooms: 19, plus 6 suites, all with private bath, color television, clock radio, and telephone.
Rates: $73 single; $91 to $115, double; $135, suites; continental breakfast included.
Facilities: Inn open all year. Dining room closed Christmas, New Year's Day, and Labor Day. Lunch Monday through Friday, dinner seven days a week, bar. All major credit cards accepted.

There are very good reasons why this lovely Victorian inn has been chosen as the ☛ best country inn in the country. Jacques Thiebeult is the French chef who oversees the superb food served here. Richard (Dick) Perchak, the head maître d', makes you feel like royalty. I think we all need this kind of treatment once in a while.

The dining room is elegant in a rustic fashion; beams,

brick walls, fireplaces, skylights, and well spaced tables with comfortable chairs. A simple bunch of flowers is on each table.

The inn's rooms are beautifully refurbished and each has a name. William Inge wrote "Picnic" while staying at the inn in the 1950s, and the name of the room he stayed in is the Picnic Room. I stayed in this one too. The Poppy Room is a single with the smallest bathtub I believe was ever made. The Tassle Room has his and her desks, the Sleigh Room has old sleigh beds, and the Robin Room has delicate stencils on the walls. They were found under six layers of wallpaper dating back to 1860. The Bride's Room has a queen-sized canopy bed. All have the modern conveniences of electric blankets, televisions, clock radios, and phones.

La Grange is the dining room and the food is fabulous. Besides the extensive menus there are many specials. One that I had was ☞ poached fresh Dover sole, the best I have ever eaten. Another dinner offering is "Black Angus" Sirloin, Béarnaise. A real winner is Mélange de Fruits de Mer au Safrin—lobster, shrimp, scallops, and mussels in a creamy saffron sauce. The presentation of the food is so ☞ picture perfect, you could almost eat the plate.

One of the luncheon dishes is Escallops of Veal, served with chestnuts, cream, and cognac. Some of the hors d'oeuvres are fresh poached Arctic salmon or a pot of snails with cream, Pernod, and herbs. The desserts, needless to say, are spectacular.

Do I like it here! I just wish I lived a bit closer.

How to get there: Going north or south on I-95, take Exit 3. Go north about 200 yards to a light, turn left on Horseneck Road, go to the deadend, and turn left. Go under the turnpike and up a hill. The inn is on your right.

E: *The ironstone place settings in Wedgewood's Chinese Bird pattern and the beautiful stemware are for me.*

Copper Beech Inn
Ivoryton, Town of Essex, Connecticut
06442

Innkeepers: Paul and Louise Ebeltoft
Telephone: 203-767-0330
Rooms: 5, all with private bath.
Rates: $55 to $85, double occupancy, continental breakfast
 included.
Facilities: Open all year. Restaurant closed Mondays,
 Christmas Eve, Christmas Day, and New Year's Day.
 Lunch, dinner. Greenhouse cocktail lounge open Tues-
 day through Sunday in season, and Friday and Saturday
 out of season. All major credit cards accepted.

  The magnificent copper beech tree that shades the front
lawn of this wonderful inn was inspiration for the name.
  The rooms are charming, with antiques, comfortable
beds, and unbelievable old-fashioned bathrooms. Lots of soft
towels are a real plus.
  The four dining rooms have comfortable Chippendale or
Queen Anne chairs. The dining porch, which is my favorite,

is done in white wicker. The spacious tables are spread far apart for gracious dining. Fresh flowers are everywhere, and the waiters serving the excellent Four Star fare are friendly and efficient.

There are at least fifteen or sixteen appetizers to start the menu, each one better than the next. The soups that follow are superb. The lobster bisque has chunks of lobster in it, as it should. The chilled Billi-Bi is excellent. Lunch at the inn is fun and very good. Dinner by candlelight is perfection. The menu changes three or four times a year, but to give you an idea: salmon in puff pastry with sole mousse and a salmon sauce suprême, or medallions of veal, or one of my very favorites, Châteaubriand, tender tenderloin of beef surrounded by fresh vegetables.

And for dessert there are about sixteen choices, all made fresh here at the inn. Do try the white chocolate mousse. I like it here, as I think you can tell.

How to get there: The inn has recently added limousine service from open marinas, bus, trains, and local airports. If you're driving, the inn is located one mile west of Connecticut Route 9, from Exit 3 or 4. Follow the signs to Ivoryton. The inn is on Ivoryton's Main Street, on the left side.

E: *A turkey sandwich to go after a sumptuous dinner is my idea of a perfect Thanksgiving.*

> *One good night in a country inn*
> *can keep the mind in quiet order*
> *for many moons.*

olive Metcalf

Madison Beach Hotel
Madison, Connecticut
06443

Innkeepers: Betty and Henry Cooney, Kathleen and Roben
   Bagdasarian
Telephone: 203-245-1404
Rooms: 28, all with private bath; 4 suites; all with air condi-
   tioning and cable television.
Rates: In season, $75 to $85, single; $75 to $175, double; con-
   tinental breakfast included. Off season, $50 to $70, sin-
   gle; $60 to $150, double; continental breakfast included.
Facilities: Closed October 31 to April 15. Lunch, dinner, bar,
   lounge, conference room. Private beach on Long Island
   Sound. All major credit cards accepted.

   If you are fortunate enough to own a boat, do come to
Madison, drop your anchor, and row right in to the Madison
Beach Hotel. If you don't own a boat, you don't need to hesi-
tate to come here. The hotel is very easy to reach and should
not be missed.
   This Victorian beauty dates back to the 1800s. It has

had many uses and a lot of names, but it has never been better than it is today. The whole inn has been refurbished with an abundance of tender love and care.

Each of its rooms and magnificent suites has its own entrance and balcony overlooking the Sound and beach. The rooms are large and airy and furnished with antique oak bureaus and wicker and rattan furniture. Soft puffs cover the wicker so you just sink into comfort. The four suites are absolutely breathtaking; each has its own kitchen, and the views from all of them are just wonderful.

There is a distinct nautical flavor to the wharf dining room and the lovely crow's-nest dining room on the upper level. The luncheon menu is extensive. The lobster salad roll is huge and even I could not quite finish it. Several cold salad plates are offered. These are so nice on a hot day. For dinner they have queen- or king-sized cuts of roast prime ribs of beef, served with horseradish sauce. This is such a nice way to serve beef. The stuffed veal chop is different and very good. From the sea there are sixteen entrees, each one sounding more enticing than the next.

The beach is private, seventy-five feet of it. The water is clear with no undertow, so the children are safe. There is good fishing off the inn's pier. Or sit on the porch in one of the many wicker rockers and just enjoy where you are.

How to get there: From I-95 take Exit 61 onto Route 79. Go to Route 1 (Boston Post Road), turn right to West Wharf Road at the Madison Country Club. Go to the end of it, and here is the inn.

E: *There is good entertainment by a trio every Friday and Saturday night.*

olive Metcalf

Boulders Inn
New Preston, Connecticut
06777

Innkeepers: Carolyn and Jameson Woollen
Telephone: 203-868-7918
Rooms: 5, all with private bath, in the inn; 8 cottages with fireplaces.
Rates: $75, single; $120, double; MAP; EP rates available in the off season.
Facilities: Open all year. Breakfast, lunch, and dinner from Memorial Day to Labor Day. After Labor Day, breakfast, dinner Wednesday through Saturday, Sunday brunch. Bar. Swimming, boating, tennis, bicycling, hiking, and cross-country skiing nearby. MasterCard and Visa accepted.

The stone boulders from which the inn was made jut right into the inn, and so the name, Boulders Inn.

If you have the energy, take a hike up Pinnacle Mountain behind the inn. From the top of the mountain you'll be rewarded with a ☞ panorama that includes New York State to the west and Massachusetts to the north. The inn has a new dog, Zoara, who may be on hand to guide you along one of the mountain's hiking trails.

If you're not a hiker, you can enjoy the marvelous countryside right from the inn. There is an outside terrace where, in summer, you may enjoy cocktails, dinner, and ☞ spectacular sunsets. The Woollens have added on to the dining room, making it octagonal in shape, which affords a wonderful view of the lake. The spacious living room has large windows, and its comfortable chairs and couches make it a nice place for tea or cocktails. All the guest accommodations have a view either of the lake or of the woods and are tastefully furnished. ☞ There are eight cozy cottages, all with fireplaces.

The food is excellent with all baking done right here. The desserts are grand. Be sure to try the Chicken Cashew Crepe at Sunday brunch. Delicious. Dinner has several entrees. One favorite is Boeuf Bourguignon, morsels of beef sautéed in cognac and baked in a rich sauce of burgundy wine, fresh mushrooms, and herbs.

How to get there: From New York take I-84 to Route 7 in Danbury and follow it north to New Milford. Take a right onto Route 202 to New Preston. Take a left onto Route 45 and you will find the inn as you round onto the lake.

E: *Tweek is a black inn cat. Curl up in a chair with a book and Tweek will join you.*

In the autumn, especially as one ages,
a firelit tavern in an excellent inn cannot be bettered
by the smallest mansions in Christendom.

The Hopkins Inn
on Lake Waramaug
New Preston, Connecticut
06777

Innkeepers: Franz and Beth Schober
Telephone: 203-868-7295
Rooms: 9, 7 with private bath; one apartment.
Rates: $33 to $44, double occupancy, EP.
Facilities: Inn open May to November. Restaurant closed
  January through March. Breakfast for house guests
  only, lunch, dinner, bar, lounge. Private beach on lake.
  Golf, tennis, and horseback riding nearby. No credit
  cards accepted.

Overlooking lovely Lake Waramaug sits this inn surrounded by majestic trees on particularly beautiful grounds.
The inn has glorious, unmatched views of the lake.

In season there is ☞ dining under the magnificent
maple and horse chestnut trees, and dine you will. The inn
has a ☞ trout pond where you can pick the fish you fancy,

and next you have Trout Meunière; fresher fish would be hard to find.

Franz is the chef, and a few of his specials include Lamb Curry, Veal Piccata or Milanaise, and Boeuf Bourguignon. Those are for lunch. For dinner how about bay scallops in a special garlic sauce, and backhendl with lingonberries. And there is always a special or two.

The dining rooms are cheerful. The fireplace has ceramic square tiles across the mantle, and the decorations are wine racks full of wines from all over the world. Naturally their wine list is quite impressive and, pleasantly, fairly priced.

There is a private beach down at the lake for use by inn guests. Bicycling, hiking, horseback riding, golf, and tennis are available nearby.

The rooms are very clean, neat and country-inn comfortable. Almost all of the rooms have a view of the lake.

How to get there: Take I-84 to Route 202 East to Route 45 in New Preston. Turn left on Route 45 and follow it 2 miles past the lake. Take your first left after the lake. Then take the second right onto Hopkins Road.

E: *Strawberries Romanoff, Meringue Glacé, Coupe aux Marrons, and homemade cheesecake. Need I say more.*

"The best landscape in the world
is improved by a good inn in the foreground."
—Dr. Samuel Johnson

The Inn on Lake Waramaug
New Preston, Connecticut
06777

Innkeepers: Dick and Bobbie Combs
Telephone: 203-868-0563, 212-724-8775
Rooms: 25, all with private bath, air conditioning, and television.
Rates: $61 to $89, per person, double occupancy, MAP. Package plans available.
Facilities: Open all year. Closed on Christmas. Breakfast, lunch, dinner, bar. Indoor pool, sauna, game room, cross-country skiing, ice skating, boating, lake swimming. Tennis, golf, horseback riding, and downhill skiing nearby. All major credit cards accepted.

The second largest natural lake in Connecticut fills part of the view you have from this old Colonial inn that dates back to 1795. There are enormous 100-year-old sugar maples and a magnificent Hawthorn tree.

There is so much to do here both inside and outside the inn. Winter is a fairyland. The innkeepers keep an ☞ area on the lake cleared for skating. Cross-country skiing starts just outside the door. Downhill skiing is but twenty minutes away. And how about a ☞ horse-drawn sleigh ride, compliments of the inn. Summer brings boating and swimming, or just enjoying the shaded lawns and sandy beach. The inn has a showboat that takes you around the lake. A nice way to see it all. Bicycles are also available. Nearby are golf, tennis, and horseback riding.

Inside the inn is year-round fun. A ☞ heated swimming pool with a whirlpool lagoon plus a sauna snuggle up to the Barefoot Bar. The game room has pool, Ping-Pong, electronic and other games, and even a juke box.

The Sand Bar on the patio at the beach is open in summer. During winter's blustery weather a glowing fireplace in the inn and drinks from Dudley's Tavern will keep you warm.

The dining rooms are large and well appointed, serving good food all year round. On one occasion I had Steak Diane, tender beef laced with brandy, mustard, and mushrooms, and oh, so good.

For antique lovers there is a gracious old fireplace made from the bricks that once were ballast on English sailing ships.

This is a wonderful place for the whole family or just one tired "inn creeper" like me. I arrived at a long day's end and spent about an hour in the pool. What a way to relax.

How to get there: From New York take I-84 to Route 7 in Danbury and follow it north to New Milford. Take a right onto Route 202 to New Preston. Take Route 45 West and follow signs to the inn. From Boston take the Massachusetts Turnpike to I-86. Follow it to I-84. Exit from I-84 onto Route 4 in Farmington. Continue on Route 4 to Route 118, and in Litchfield, pick up Route 202 and follow it to Route 45 West.

E: *Christmas is a fabulous festival, with lighted Christmas trees, reindeer ice sculptures in front of a sleigh, red and white tablecloths, soft music. It's truly a winter wonderland.*

— Olive Metcalf

Silvermine Tavern
Norwalk, Connecticut
06850

Innkeeper: Francis C. Whitman, Jr.
Telephone: 203-847-4558
Rooms: 10, all with private bath.
Rates: $46 to $52, single; $62 to $67, double; continental breakfast included.
Facilities: Open all year. Restaurant closed Tuesdays from September to May. Lunch, dinner, Sunday brunch, bar. Television in parlor. All major credit cards accepted.

Although the colonial crossroads village known as Silvermine has been swallowed up by the surrounding Fairfield County towns of Norwalk, Wilton, and New Canaan, the Silvermine Tavern still lies at the heart of a community of great Old World beauty. It has a remarkable way of sweeping you worlds back in time.

This is one of the most popular dining places in the area, ☛ known for delicious New England traditional food. Thursday night is set aside for a fantastic buffet supper featuring steaks, fried chicken, and many salads, all of which you top off with a great array of desserts. Sunday buffet brunch features twenty different dishes. Some of the inn specialties are Oysters Country Gentlemen, Scallops Nantucket, mussels steamed in wine, and roast duckling with an apple cider sauce. The food may be savored in one of the six dining rooms or ☞ on the riverside deck, which is open from June through September. On the old millpond below, the ducks and swans wait, hoping for some leftovers.

Silvermine Tavern is furnished with old oriental rugs, antiques, old portraits, and great comfortable chairs and sofas surrounding the six huge fireplaces. The main dining room is decorated with over 1,000 antiques, primarily old farm tools and household artifacts. Also in here is an 1887 Regina music box. The drop of a coin will turn a huge disk and the music will begin. This is a really fun antique.

The guest rooms are comfortably furnished, many of them with old-fashioned tester beds. One of my favorite rooms has its ☞ own deck overlooking the lovely millpond.

If you wish, you can stroll by the waterfall and feed the ducks and swans on the millpond. Across the road from the Tavern you will find the Country Store, run by Frank's wife. It has a back room that is a museum of antique tools and gadgets. It also has a fine collection of Currier & Ives prints. Do take a leisurely drive around the back roads near the inn, too. They are a delight. Also in this area you have the well-known Silvermine Guild of Artists.

How to get there: From the Merritt Parkway take Exit 39 onto Route 7 South. Go south to the first traffic light and turn right onto Perry Avenue. In 2½ miles you'll find the inn at the intersection of Perry and Silvermine Avenues.

🍷

E: *In the front parlor, in front of a cheery fire, you can enjoy sherry and petit-fours at the end of your day. This is the life.*

Norwich Inn
Norwich, Connecticut
06360

Innkeeper: Gene Bryant
Telephone: 203-886-2401
Rooms: 75, including suites, 69 with private bath.
Rates: $65 to $95, per room; $95 to $155, suites; EP.
Facilities: Open all year. Breakfast, lunch, dinner, Sunday
 brunch, bar, lounge. Putting green, tennis court, swim-
 ming pool, spa. Executive retreat and conference center.
 Cross-country skiing and 18-hole golf course adjacent to
 inn. All major credit cards accepted.

The Norwich Inn began as a hotel in 1929 and has a colorful past. For the present it has been totally refurbished and
it is truly elegant. The inn is a lovely red brick building on a
hill, surrounded by huge elms, maples, and oaks. The
grounds are beautifully manicured.

Everything you could possibly want is here. The magnificent restaurants are beautifully decorated. The Prince of
Wales Bar has a log-burning fireplace, and the Windsor

Room is set up for games. The Hunt Room, a meeting room, is done in English decor. There are other conference rooms on the lower floor. The Grand Ballroom is so nice for weddings, banquets, and meetings. The Sunroom is a tranquil place to have a cocktail, and the ☞ deck is so lovely. It overlooks the Norwich Golf Course. Lunch, dinner, and Sunday brunch are served here in warm weather months.

Best of all is the ☞ fabulous spa, due to open early in 1985, which will feature the most advanced exercise equipment. It will have a gravity alignment device, Dynavit bike, hydrotherapy equipment, herbal wraps, sauna, Jacuzzi, and much more. Heavenly! This is one inn where you can have a business conference, bring the family, and relax. Every member of the family will have a fine time.

I love chintz, and the huge lobby has chintz upholstered armchairs and sofas. An ☞ enormous bird cage in which two white Mexican fantail doves live is the focal point of the room. Their names are Pat and Mike.

The seventy-five rooms and suites are just so lovely. Many have raised four-poster beds, all new, of course, and very comfortable. You'll need to use the stepstool that is thoughtfully placed here to climb up into bed. What luxury.

This is a different type of inn, business and pleasure together.

How to get there: From the Boston area, take I-95 South. Take Exit 83 onto Route 32 North. The inn is in 1.2 miles on the left side. From New York, take I-95 North to Exit 76 onto I-395. Take Exit 79A onto Route 32 North. The inn is 1.5 miles north, on the left side.

E: *For a special party, there is a pit for a clambake. Lobster, clams, mussels, corn, and potatoes cook all day and are so good.*

Olive Metcalf

Bee and Thistle Inn
Old Lyme, Connecticut
06371

Innkeepers: Bob and Penny Nelson
Telephone: 203-434-1667
Rooms: 11, 9 with private bath.
Rates: $49 to $75, double occupancy, EP.
Facilities: Open all year. Closed Christmas Day. Breakfast. Lunch and dinner every day except Tuesday. Sunday brunch, bar, lounge, library. All major credit cards accepted.

This lovely old inn, built in 1756, sits on five and one-half acres bordering the Lieutenant River in historic Old Lyme, Connecticut. During summer the abundant flower gardens keep the inn filled to overflowing with color.

The guest rooms are all tastefully decorated. Your bed, maybe a four-poster or canopy, is covered with lovely old quilts or afghans. The bath towels are big and thirsty. How I love them.

There are six fireplaces in the inn. The one in the parlor

is most inviting, a nice place for a cocktail or just good conversation. On Saturdays there is ☞ a harp player in here, and she is excellent.

☞ Breakfast in bed is an especially nice feature of the inn. ☞ Freshly squeezed orange juice is a refreshing way to start any day. Muffins made fresh each day, buttery crepes folded with strawberry or raspberry preserves, and much more. Lunch is interesting and inventive. One item is cold sliced duck served with a basil and tomato mayonnaise and melon. Sunday brunch is really gourmet. ☞ Stir-fried duck and pheasant are glorious. I could eat the menu. And, of course, dinners here are magnificent. Candlelit dining rooms, ten appetizers, and entrees such as fresh tuna baked with shrimp and artichoke hearts and served with a sauce made of white wine, lemon, tarragon, and shallots. The list goes on and on. The menu changes seasonally, each time bringing new delights.

This is a fine inn in a most interesting part of New England. You are in the heart of art, antiques, gourmet restaurants, and endless activities. Plan to spend a few days when you come.

How to get there: Traveling north on I-95, take Exit 70 immediately on the west side of the Baldwin Bridge. At the bottom of the ramp, turn left. Take the first right at the traffic light, and turn left at the next light. The inn is the third house on your left. Traveling south on I-95, take Exit 70 and turn right at the bottom of the ramp. The inn is the third house on your left.

E: *You can walk down to the river with a book, or just sit and watch the water. It's beautiful down here.*

olive Metcalf

Old Lyme Inn
Old Lyme, Connecticut
06371

Innkeeper: Diana Field Atwood
Telephone: 203-434-2600
Rooms: 5, all with private bath.
Rates: $55 to $60, continental breakfast included.
Facilities: Open all year. Closed Mondays. Lunch, dinner, bar. All major credit cards accepted.

The food here is 🖝 excellent and unusual. From the fresh soup stocks to the 🖝 tender and flaky pastry shells, everything is homemade. The desserts are wonderful. The menu changes delightfully every three or four months. Some entrees I have tried and thoroughly enjoyed are Filet Mignon with a green peppercorn sauce, Quinelle of Halibut, and chicken served in cider with apples. They usually have a special of the day, and whatever it is, try it. You may gain a little weight, but you will enjoy yourself immensely.

Throughout the inn the chairs are blue velvet, luxuriously soft and comfortable. The large cocktail lounge has a bar that seats six, and a back bar the innkeeper found in Philadelphia that is over 100 years old. This back bar has a beveled mirror that most museums would covet.

In addition to the two-level, lovely main dining room, there is a private room off the lobby for eight to twelve people, a really nice way to entertain good friends.

There is much to do in this area, with antique shops all over, the beautiful Connecticut River two minutes away, historic Essex just across the river, and a small, interesting museum called The Florence Griswold House almost directly across the street. Here you will get a fascinating glimpse of the art colony that flourished in Old Lyme at the beginning of the century.

How to get there: Traveling north on I-95, take Exit 70 immediately on the west side of the bridge. At the bottom of the ramp turn left. Take the first right at the traffic light, and turn left at the next light. The inn is on the right. Traveling south on I-95, take Exit 70. At the bottom of the ramp turn right. The inn is on the right.

E: *The bar is a real favorite spot of mine, with a bartender who remembers what you drink.*

> *Where else, in all good conscience,*
> *could I stay but at a country inn.*

The Elms
Ridgefield, Connecticut
06877

Innkeepers: Robert and Violet Scala
Telephone: 203-438-2541
Rooms: 20, all with private bath, television, and telephone.
Rates: $75, single; $85 to $105, double occupancy; EPB.
Facilities: Open all year. Closed Wednesdays and Christmas
   Day. Lunch, dinner, Sunday brunch, bar. Piano enter-
   tainment on Fridays, Saturdays, and at Sunday brunch.
   All major credit cards accepted.

In 1760 a master cabinetmaker built this charming Colonial house that is now known as the Elms. It is on a historical site, for it was here that the Battle of Ridgefield was
fought during the Revolution. Since 1799, when the house
became an inn, the same loving care and artistry that marked
its beginning has been applied to every phase of its operation.
   There is a ☞ comfortable four-poster in one of the quiet
rooms upstairs. Another bedroom has maple spool twin beds,
and many of the rooms have their ☞ own fireplace.

The quiet charm here induces slumber and assures the weary traveler of a restful night.

The brochure says, "To partake of a meal is no mundane experience in eating, but rather an adventure in dining." And so it is, with quail fresh from the fields, escargots flown fresh from France, and on and on, all of it delicious. The list of hors d'oeuvres is very impressive, with herring in cream, Scampi Romani, and smoked salmon but a few of the selections. There are five delicious soups, with the Onion au Gratin a specialty. Entrees like ☛ broiled English lamb chops with kidney and bacon, curry of sliced capon with wild rice and chutney, veal, steak, and rack of lamb are all on the menu. The dessert list is as long as the hors d'oeuvres list, with pears burgundy, tortonis, spumoni, and an old favorite of mine, zabaglione.

Ridgefield is a lovely town off the major highways. There are concerts in the park, tons of good shops to wander into, and good summer theater nearby.

How to get there: The inn is located at 500 Main Street in Ridgefield. From Route 7 take Route 35 right into town.

E: *Any place that serves ☛ Coupe Elizabeth has to get my nod. It is bing cherries bathed in cherry herring, sprinkled with cinnamon, and poured over vanilla ice cream. Yum. Yum.*

olive Metcalf

Stonehenge
Ridgefield, Connecticut
06877

Innkeepers: David Davis and Douglas Seville
Telephone: 203-438-6511
Rooms: 11, plus 2 suites, all with private bath, color television
and telephone. Guest cottage, guest house.
Rates: $70 to $105; suites $170; double occupancy, EP.
Facilities: Open all year. Closed Tuesday and New Year's
Day. Breakfast, lunch, dinner, Sunday brunch, bar,
lounge. Swimming pool. All major credit cards accepted.

The setting for Stonehenge is serenely beautiful. The
old white farmhouse overlooks the pond, which is bedecked
with swans and aflutter with Canada geese and ducks stop-
ping in on their migratory journeys. The Stonehenge Room,
which once was a porch, faces the pond and has a great view.
This is where ☛ breakfast is served, a lovely way to start your
day.
　　The inn has a sumptuous new addition. There are two
suites and two glorious rooms that are almost suites. The

suites have facilities for light cooking. They all are color coordinated and oh, so comfortable. All of the rooms in the inn, the guest cottage, and guest house have been refurbished in an elegant fashion. Most of the rooms have queen- and king-sized beds. Two have working fireplaces.

The chef, ☞ Jean-Maurice Calmels, is French born and trained, and nonpareil. Address yourself seriously to the food. The appetizers are unusual. I had the Mushroom Crepe Mornay. Another in my party had the ☞ inn's own smoked sausage in a pastry crust with a mustard wine sauce. The soups are poetic. The ☞ trout is live. "How long ago?" I asked. "About five minutes," was the reply. "The time it takes to come from the 'trout house.' "

This is fine gourmet dining. The luncheon selections are superb. The inventive touch with vegetables, the care taken with the sauces, all reflect the dedication with which M. Calmels approaches his task.

The dining room is beautiful by day or night, but for a quiet dinner à deux, reserve a table in the bar. There ☞ Len Gendal plays wonderful piano. He is excellent.

If you are tired of the "same old thing," book yourself into Stonehenge for a long weekend and find out what "haute cuisine" is all about. It is expensive, but worth every centime.

How to get there: From the Merritt Parkway, take Exit 40. Go north on Route 7. The inn's sign is in 13 miles, on the left. From I-84, go south on Route 7. The inn's sign is in 4½ miles, on the right.

E: *My favorite room is the big one in the front of the main house. Any season, any weather, it is a home away from home with wine and cheese waiting and breakfast served on the spot.*

olive Metcalf

West Lane Inn
and
The Inn at Ridgefield
Ridgefield, Connecticut
06877

Innkeepers: Maureen Mayer and Henry Prieger
Telephone: West Lane 203-438-7323
    Ridgefield 203-438-8282
Rooms: 20, all with private bath, air conditioning, and television; some with fireplace.
Rates: $85 single; $90 to $100, double; EPB.
Facilities: West Lane Inn open all year. The Inn at Ridgefield closed Mondays. Lunch, dinner, Sunday brunch, bar, lounge, piano nightly. American Express, MasterCard, and Visa accepted.

Ridgefield is a lovely town, and we have a first here, two totally separate inns next door to each other. West Lane has the rooms, and the Inn at Ridgefield has the food.

40

West Lane's bedrooms are wonderfully spacious and lovely, with magnificent decor. They are furnished with comfortable chairs, either queen- or king-sized beds, deluxe blankets, and huge, thirsty towels. There is a carved wood screen on the second floor you must not miss. West Lane does have a small dining room for breakfasts, and when you are ready for lunch or dinner you go across the driveway to the Inn at Ridgefield.

Chef Raymond Peron has a rather prestigious background, having been executive chef of the Hay-Adams Hotel in Washington, D.C., and of the S.S. *France.* He cooks superbly. There are seven or eight hors d'oeuvres, among them ☛ cold mussels in mustard sauce. A cold and a hot soup are served, and the entrees make my mouth water as I write. The Duck à l'Orange is a favorite, as is the Dover Sole. The inn special is a seafood platter served deliciously cold. Desserts, as expected, are grand, and a final touch are the ☛ special coffees.

Both inns are just around the corner from the famous Cannon Ball House, which was struck by a British fieldpiece during the Revolution. There are several museums in town, in addition to fine shops. You are also close to three summer theaters, Candlewood, Darien, and Westport.

How to get there: Coming north from New York on Route 684, or Route 7 from the Merritt Parkway, get off on Route 35 and follow it to Ridgefield. The inns are on Route 35 at the south end of town.

ᗡ

E: *The ends of* ☛ *old, wooden wine and whiskey crates that line the porch of the Inn at Ridgefield let you know there are good things inside.*

Olive Metcalf

Old Riverton Inn
Riverton, Connecticut
06065

Innkeepers: Pauline and Mark Telford
Telephone: 203-379-8678
Rooms: 10, all with private bath.
Rates: $48 to $75, double occupancy, EPB.
Facilities: Open all year. Restaurant closed Mondays, Christmas Day, and first two weeks in January. Lunch, dinner, bar. Dining room has wheelchair accessibility. All major credit cards accepted.

The village of Riverton was once called "Hitchcocksville," after the famous Hitchcock chairs that are still being manufactured in the old factory on the banks of the Farmington River opposite the inn. The factory is open every day except Monday until 5 p.m., and guests are always welcome.

Old Riverton Inn was originally opened in 1796. It was on the post road between Hartford and Albany, and was known as Ives Tavern. The inn was restored in 1937, and again in 1954. The ☞ Grindstone Terrace was enclosed to

42

make it available for year-round use. The floor of this room is made of grindstones, which, according to 100-year-old records, were quarried in Nova Scotia, sent by ship to Long Island Sound, and then up the Connecticut River to Hartford. From there they were hauled by oxen to Collinsville, where they were used in the making of axes and machetes.

The Colonial dining room has low ceilings, Hitchcock chairs, excellent food, and ☞ home-baked breads and pastries. The Hobby Horse Bar has saddles for seats, and in charge of this charming room is a ☞ Philippine bartender who, like most of the help, has been here for many years.

☞ Mints on the pillows at night is a very special touch I love. All of the rooms are cheerful, comfortable, and assure you of a good night's sleep. There is a lovely library area on the second floor that is a nice spot to relax in after looking at all of the things this charming village has to offer.

Antiques, galleries, a general store, the Hitchcock Museum, the Seth Thomas factory outlet, the Tartan Shop, Kitchen Shop, not to mention the Cat Nip Mouse Tearoom, are all here.

How to get there: The inn is 3½ miles from Winsted. Take Route 8 or Route 44 to Winsted. Turn east on Route 20, and it is approximately 1½ miles to the inn.

☒

E: *The drive on Route 20 between the inn and East Hartland or Granby is one of the most scenic in the state.*

The register of a country inn
is a treasure of the names of good people.

The White Hart Inn
Salisbury, Connecticut
06068

Innkeeper: Susan Redmond
Telephone: 203-435-2511
Rooms: 26, 23 with private bath; one suite; all with air conditioning, television, and telephone.
Rates: $45 to $70, double occupancy, EP.
Facilities: Open all year. Breakfast, lunch, dinner, bar, lounge. Gift shop. Skiing nearby. American Express, MasterCard, and Visa accepted.

On the village green in Salisbury sits a classic, white clapboard country inn with ☛ spacious porches shaded by several of our few surviving, lovely wineglass elms.

The house became an inn in 1867 and was owned in the 1930s by Edsel Ford, son of Henry Ford. He loaned Admiral Richard Byrd the plane he used to go to the North Pole.

There once was a large country store in the inn. The present owners wisely turned this room into a ☛ delightful bar and lounge area. The comfortable couches, love seats, and chairs, and attractive fireplace really make you feel at home. A much smaller gift shop is still in the inn.

The inn's kitchen is open from early in the morning until midnight, and even later on the weekends, creating glorious food. All of the breads and pastries are baked here and it really does make a difference. Whatever you desire you will find in one of the four dining rooms. The Salisbury Room is the most formal. The menu has some unusual offerings. I love names for food, such as Poulet Sauté Forestière. This is filets of chicken, served in a sauce of red wine, mushrooms, diced truffles, and garnished with an artichoke bottom filled with a chestnut brandy puree. There are many more, equally tantalizing dishes.

The conservatory is a lovely setting for the very good lunch. It has hanging plants and lush floor plants. I know you can not eat the daisies, but ambience helps. Breakfast, well of course it's super.

How to get there: The inn is at the intersection of Routes 44 and 41 in Salisbury. You get to Salisbury by going north on Route 7 from the Merritt Parkway.

E: Complimentary newspapers in the morning; how nice.

Modern man has done wondrous things
in preserving the whooping cranes
and country inns.

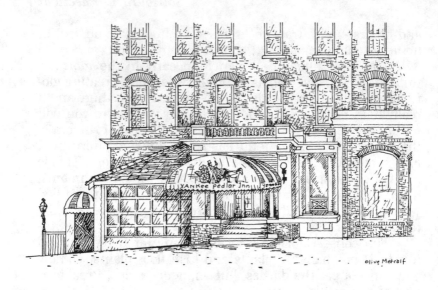

Olive Metcalf

Yankee Pedlar Inn
Torrington, Connecticut
06790

Innkeepers: Arthur and Gerald Rubens
Telephone: 203-489-9226
Rooms: 75, all have private bath, air conditioning, television, sprinkler system, and smoke alarm.
Rates: $45, single; $55, double; EP. Package plans available for off-season weekends.
Facilities: Open all year. Breakfast, lunch, dinner, bar, lounge. All major credit cards accepted.

The Yankee Pedlar is a bit different from the other inns in that it is an in-town inn. There were, at one time, many such inns, but now only a few survive. Nice that this inn was a survivor.

There is a wood sign in the dining room written by an English minister, "Fate cannot harm me—I have dined well to-day." And so will you as the food here is very good. One specialty of the house is ☞ Sauerbraten with Potato Pancakes, and, boy, do I love it. The veal is so tender you can cut

46

it with your fork. All breads and desserts are prepared right here. The inn has a beautiful ☞ silver serving cart now used to hold vintage wines. A nice way to present them.

All of the rooms are beautifully furnished with Hitch-cock colonial furniture. ☞ Dorothy Rubens decorated six of the newer rooms, and they are lovely with hand-stencilled walls and fine furniture. Dorothy really has done an out-standing job. And one of the rooms has a fireplace. A beauty.

The lobby-living room has a large fireplace over which is mounted a pair of 1935 skis. They belonged to J. Franklin Ellis, the first ski instructor in the Mohawk ski area. The skis are not much, but he made them work.

There is much to do while visiting this inn. The Corn-wall and Bull's covered bridges are nearby. You also have the Lime Rock races, but best of all is just driving around this beautiful section of country.

How to get there: From I-84 pick up Route 8 North at Water-bury. Take Route 8 to Exit 44 at Torrington. From Hartford, take Route 44 to Route 202 to Torrington. The inn is right in the center of town.

E: The staff really tries to satisfy your every wish.

Man has tendencies of many temperatures,
the warmest of which is hospitality.

The Captain Stannard House
Westbrook, Connecticut
06498

Innkeepers: Arlene and Ed Amatrudo
Telephone: 203-399-7565
Rooms: 6, all with private bath; suite.
Rates: $50, single; $60 to $70, double; EPB.
Facilities: Open all year. Breakfast only meal served. BYOB.
No pets, and no children under 6. Bicycles, lawn games.
Swimming, boating, golfing, tennis, and restaurants
nearby. All major credit cards accepted.

The inn dates back to 1850 and has been known by
many names. It's a beautiful old charmer of a house. ☛
Floor-to-ceiling windows and a magnificent staircase with an
interesting newel post are but a few of its fine features.

The rooms are very attractive. All have handmade afghans, color-coordinated sheets, and extra pillows and blankets. A lovely canopy bed is in one room. ☛ Plenty of towels

are available; this alone is a nice touch. A radio and a clock are in each room, and fresh flowers, fresh fruit, cheese and crackers, and mints are provided. Hand-drawn stencils decorate each bedroom. In the two-room suite, one room is a lovely bedroom, and the other room across a hall is the living room with a comfortable hideabed, so a family could stay here. The private bath for this suite has an old-fashioned ☛ clothes wringer for a towel rack, very quaint. There's a guest office on the second floor for your use—a very nice feature for the business traveler.

Breakfast of fresh juices, fresh fruits in season, homemade goodies, and hot and cold cereals is served in a charming room. Finger towels are the placemats and napkins. There's a refrigerator for guests to use and a set-up bar. Wicker baskets full of ice are in a freezer.

If you want, you can buy the antiques that are for sale in the inn.

How to get there: Take I-95 to Exit 65. Turn toward Westbrook Center. Go west on Route 1 for ⁴/₁₀ mile. The inn is on the left, on the corner of South Main and Kingfisher Lane.

E: *This is a nice area to walk in, and it's just a short walk to the beach.*

> *If all inns were alike*
> *they simply would not be inns.*

olive Metcalf

Cotswold Inn
Westport, Connecticut
06880

Innkeeper: Albert Peretti
Telephone: 203-226-3766
Rooms: 3, 1 suite, all with private bath, color cable television, and telephone.
Rates: $140 to $165, per room, EPB.
Facilities: Open all year. Breakfast only meal served. Many nearby restaurants. BYOB. Swimming, sauna, racquetball, and theaters nearby. American Express, MasterCard, and Visa accepted.

The Cotswold Inn is a rare gem quietly tucked among the historic homes of downtown Westport in beautiful Fairfield County. The ☞ innkeeper himself also is a rare gem. Albert is here to help you in any way he can, with suggestions where to dine and shop; passes to the attractive nearby YMCA for swimming, saunas, and racquetball; and information about how to obtain tickets to the Westport Country

Playhouse. And if you need a secretary, Albert will get one for you. All this and a charming French accent, too.

Furnishings in the inn are sumptuous. The area rug in the living room is pink, beige, and blue. The fireplace is white brick with niches built in for a book or vase. All of the furniture and appointments are accurate reproductions of the originals. The whole inn is color coordinated, squeaky clean, and just so lovely. An elegant country home is a good way to describe it.

The guest rooms have names. Bedford is done in smoke blue and cream with a queen-sized canopy bed. Jesup is moss green and white and Sherwood is china blue. Both have queen-sized four-poster beds. The Wheeler Suite is apricot and white with a canopy bed and a sleigh bed in the adjoining room. ☞ Fresh flowers and bedside mints, ☞ oversized fluffy towels, and imported scented soaps are lovely touches in all the rooms to make you feel pampered.

Breakfast is a full one and just delicious. Complimentary wine and cheese are served upon request in the early evening.

How to get there: From Route 1 in Westport turn right on Myrtle Avenue and look for the signs for the inn. It is at 76 Myrtle.

🌹

E: *Fresh-squeezed orange juice is a nice way to start your day.*

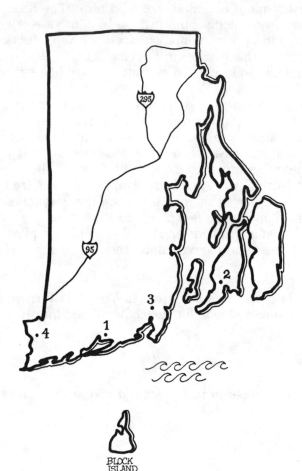

BLOCK
ISLAND

Numbers on map refer to towns numbered
on index on opposite page

Rhode Island

olive Metcalf

The General Stanton Inn
Charlestown, Rhode Island
02813

Innkeepers: Janice and Angelo Falcone
Telephone: 401-364-8888
Rooms: 15 14 with private bath.
Rates: $50 to $70, double occupancy, EP.
Facilities: Open all year. Breakfast, lunch, dinner, bar,
lounge. Flea market on premises April to October. Five
miles to ocean beach. American Express, MasterCard,
and Visa accepted.

One of the oldest, continuously run inns in America is
in the little state of Rhode Island, dating back to 1667. That's
old, folks. From the mid-1800s until well after the repeal of
Prohibition, the inn was a mecca for gamblers from all over
the country. Many nationally known names are in the guest
books, including future presidents, generals, and theater
people. This information came from their brochure. ☛ Janice, the historian, hostess, and chef, needs no encourage-
ment to talk about the Stantons. The General is buried in the

family cemetery on the grounds of the inn. There have been only five owners of this property since the Indians owned the land.

The five dining rooms are a bit different from each other. There is a collection of old hats in one and a lovely sleigh in another. Each one is homey and comfortable. The girls serving the meals wear long gowns from years gone by, and certainly have the perfect look for this old inn.

The food is so very good. I had a jumbo shrimp cocktail. The snails are nice and garlicky and the scallops are freshly harvested from nearby waters. One menu phrase I love is, "Mrs. Stanton's Old-Fashioned Baked Hickory Glazed Ham."

The inn's lounge area has entertainment on Friday and Saturday, and there's a television in here.

This is a charming, old, old, inn; come and enjoy the past.

How to get there: From I-95 take Exit 92 onto Route 2. Follow Route 2 south a short distance to Route 78 (Westerly By-pass), which leads directly to Route 1. The inn is located 12 miles north on Route 1.

☀

E: *The history of the area and the Indians is spectacular. So are the innkeepers.*

The cheers of millions are for politicians,
while the quiet appreciation of a well cooked chop
is but for a few.

Olive Metcalf

The Inn at Castle Hill
Newport, Rhode Island
02840

Innkeeper: Paul McEnroe; Jens Thillemann, general manager

Telephone: 401-849-3800

Rooms: 18, 14 with private bath.

Rates: Depending on the season, rates range from a low of $50 to a high of $125, double occupancy, continental breakfast included.

Facilities: Inn open all year. Restaurant closed December through March. Lunch and dinner served daily from May through October. In April and November, dinner served Thursday, Friday, and Saturday. Sunday brunch served from April through November. Bar. Entertainment. Live jazz on Sunday afternoons. Swimming from inn's private beach. All major credit cards accepted.

Newport is a fabulous place to visit any time of the year. And to be able to go to Newport and stay at the Inn at Castle Hill is a rare treat. I have always loved the warm atmosphere of this inn. It was built as a private home in 1874 and has been little changed over the years. Thirty-two acres of shoreline right on the entrance of Narragansett Bay offer a natural setting for almost anything a person could desire. The views from any place, in or about the inn, are breathtakingly beautiful. ☞ The Atlantic Ocean and the bay are at your feet.

As for things to do, there is everything. Newport is the home of America's Cup Races, the Tennis Hall of Fame, and is famous for its great "cottages" lining the waterfront.

The inn has four dining rooms. The small one with only six tables, each set with different serving plates, is very special. Another is a light and airy oval room which, like the others, looks over the water. The chef is very good and the food he creates is delicious. The menu changes seasonally. Veal, beef, lamb, fowl, and seafood are prepared many ways and are beautifully served. Every day there are three homemade soups, together with an endless variety of appetizers. The inn has always had a ☞ sumptuous ten-course New Year's Eve dinner, which is now held on November 30 with all their old fanfare of December 31.

The Tavern is a different room, with a beauty of a bar and a view unmatched, if you love the sea. There are Chinese teak and marble tables in the living areas, and the bannister on the staircase is its own delight.

Almost all the rooms are quite large and beautifully furnished. The paneling is magnificent, as are the oriental rugs that have been left here.

Innkeeper McEnroe has refurbished the entire inn with wallpapers that are color coordinated with spreads and drapes, plus thick towels. Here the view outside is not enough for our innkeeper. He cares about the interior look, too.

How to get there: From the north take Route 138 into Newport, and follow Thames Street about 4½ miles to Ocean Drive. Look for the inn's sign on your right. From the west come across the Newport Bridge and take the scenic Newport Exit that goes into Thames Street.

🍺

E: *The 10-mile ocean drive is among the most strikingly beautiful areas in New England. And do remember that Sunday brunch is very active with jazz.*

Olive Metcalf

Larchwood Inn
Wakefield, Rhode Island
02879

Innkeepers: Francis and Diann Browning
Telephone: 401-783-5454
Rooms: 19, 10 with private bath.
Rates: $30 to $60, EP.
Facilities: Open all year. Breakfast, lunch, dinner, bar, tavern. Swimming, fishing, and skiing nearby. All major credit cards accepted.

Over the fireplace in the homey bar is carved "Fast by an Ingle Bleezing Finely," a quotation from the Scots' Robert Burns. ☞ His birthday, January 25th, is celebrated here, and every year a couple of pipers come over from Connecticut to help the party along. The Scottish flavor is all over this homelike country inn.

The Tam O'Shanter Cocktail Lounge serves up a delectable lunch that includes huge sandwiches, good salads, hamburgers, and quiche. There are four other lovely rooms for dining or private entertaining. Dinner ideas are rack of lamb for one or two, lots of fresh fish, and a ☞ beefeater's special, a thick slice of Prime Rib Angus. Come summer the meals are served on the covered patio in the garden.

The Brownings have added more rooms to their inn with the Holly House across the street. It is the same age as the inn; both were built in the 1830s. It is so well done. ☞ Diann has a real touch. The wallpapers are glorious and one room is an especially lovely salmon color. All of the inn's guest rooms have been individually decorated and are beautifully furnished.

The inn is situated in the heart of Rhode Island's beautiful South County. Saltwater beaches for bathing, fishing, and sunning are close by. In the winter it is only a short drive to Pine Top and Yawgoo Valley for skiing.

Rhode Island isn't all that big, you know, so it's never very far from anywhere to the Larchwood Inn.

How to get there: Take I-95 to Route 1. Exit from Route 1 at Pond Street, follow it to the end, and the inn will be immediately in front of you.

☒

E: *Pipers and Haggis is a Scottish man's dream come true.*

When you have but one night to spend
which inn to choose is as difficult
as the choice you had years ago
at the penny candy counter,
and equally rewarding.

Olive Metcalf

Shelter Harbor Inn
Westerly, Rhode Island
02891

Innkeepers: Jim and Debbye Dey
Telephone: 401-322-8883
Rooms: 18, all with private bath; one with fireplace.
Rates: $47 to $57, single; $52 to $62, double occupancy; EPB.
Facilities: Open all year. Lunch, dinner, Sunday brunch,
    bar. Two paddle tennis courts with night lighting. Pri-
    vate beach. Summer theaters nearby. All major credit
    cards accepted.

If you would like a three-mile stretch of uncluttered
ocean beach located just a mile from a lovely, old country inn,
find your way to Rhode Island and the Shelter Harbor Inn.
Bring the children. When they're not playing in the ocean
surf, there's a salt pond near the inn for them to explore.

Eight of the guest rooms are in the restored farmhouse,
and ten more are located in the barn. There is a large central
living room here that opens onto a spacious deck, how ideal
for families. Or if your business group is small, have a meet-

ing right here. There is also a library with comfortable leather chairs where you can relax with a book.

The menu reflects the location of the inn, and at least half the items offered are from the sea. ☛ The Finnan Haddie is specially smoked in Narragansett. You can choose your place to eat, from the formal dining room, the new, small private dining room with a fireplace, or the new glassed-in terrace room. The sun porch has been turned into a pub bar. There is a delightful old wood stove to warm you, and Debbye's plants are everywhere. If weather permits, take a drink out to the secluded terrace.

If you can tear yourself from the beach, there is much to see around here. You are about halfway between Mystic and Newport. The ferry to Block Island leaves from Port Judith, takes an hour to cover the twelve miles, and when you arrive you will find it a super spot for bicycling. You can charter boats for fishing, or stand on the edge of the surf and cast your line into the sea. In the evenings there is Theater by the Sea in nearby Matunuck, or the Heritage Playhouse in Hopkinton.

How to get there: Take I-95 to Route 1. Follow Route 1 out of Westerly for about 5 miles. The inn is on the right side of the road when you're heading northeast.

E: *Authentic johnnycakes are served here. Delicious!*

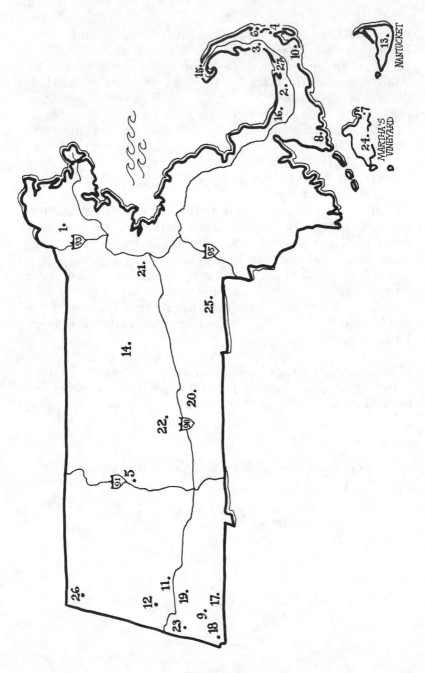

Numbers on map refer to towns numbered
on index on opposite page

Massachusetts

Olive Metcalf

Andover Inn
Andover, Massachusetts
01810

Innkeeper: Henry Broekhoff
Telephone: 617-475-5903
Rooms: 33, 23 with private bath, some with running water;
    all with air conditioning, television, and telephone. One
    suite.
Rates: $37 to $55, single; $47 to $65, double; $100, suite; EP.
Facilities: Closed last two weeks of August. Dining room
    closed on Christmas. Breakfast, lunch, dinner, Sunday
    brunch, bar. Accessible to wheelchairs. Elevator, barber-
    shop. All major credit cards accepted.

    The inn is on the campus of Phillips Academy. You ex-
pect ivy-covered buildings, and you get them in abundance.
When you walk through the gracious front door of the inn
you are greeted by a wonderful living room with fireplace.
    The bar in the right corner of the main entrance room is
one of the coziest I have seen. ☛ The stools are overstuffed,
and so comfortable you hate to leave.

Rooms here have every modern convenience, including color television, radio, direct dial telephone, air conditioning, and full baths, all with a view of either the delightful inn gardens, the neighboring pond, or Phillips Academy.

The dining room is elegant, with crisp napery and crystal chandeliers. The food is superb. Full breakfasts and ample lunches fit well with the broad dinner menus. And there is a special Sunday brunch from 11 to 2:45 p.m.

I am glad to say that the inn still has the unique Sunday special called ☛ Rijsttafel. It is an original Indonesian dish prepared the right way, and eaten in the proper manner. It consists of dry, steamed rice and an indefinite number of side dishes and sauces. The menu tells you how to eat this fabulous feast. It is served on Sundays only, from 4 to 8:45 p.m., and is by reservation.

How to get there: The inn is 25 miles north of Boston on Route 28, near the intersection of Routes 93 and 495.

E: ☛ *Monday through Saturday evenings guests enjoy light classical music on the grand piano.*

Olive Metcalf

Cobb's Cove
Barnstable Village, Massachusetts
02630

Innkeeper: Evelyn Chester
Telephone: 617-362-9356
Rooms: 6 suites, all with private bath.
Rates: $98 to $109, double occupancy, EPB.
Facilities: Closed mid-January to mid-February. Dinner available to house guests only. BYOB. No credit cards honored, but checks will be accepted.

The moment you walk in the door and are greeted by Evelyn and Henri-Jean, you know you have happened on a distinctive and delightful inn. You are taken to your suite, and what a marvelous view you have. ☞ The third-floor suite has the biggest skylight I have ever seen. It goes from almost the gable down to the eave. There is a couch in front of this skylight where you can sit and see all of Cape Cod Bay, Sandy Neck, and all the way to Provincetown Light. The other suites also have grand views, deliciously comfortable beds, and all the extras you expect at an extraordinary inn.

The baths all have ☞ whirlpools, so relaxing after a day of travel. The soaps and bubble bath are pear-scented, a nice touch. Plenty of big towels and good, soft pillows.

The inn is on a very secluded and scenic piece of property. The bay is right at hand. The inn was built of twelve-by-twelve-foot rough-cut timbers and many of the walls are done in rough burlap. The keeping room has a large Count Rumford shallow fireplace, comfortable chairs, and wonderful smells that come from Henri's kitchen. There is a terrace full of bird feeders made by Harry Holl of the Scargo Pottery. Harry also made many of the kitchen things Henri uses, including a huge salad bowl that is a rare beauty. In summer, breakfast is served on the terrace.

The dining room-library has a long hutch table that seats fourteen quite comfortably. Dinner is served in three or five courses. One night I was there it started with ☞ delicious mussels, then a special cauliflower dish done Henri's way. This was followed by a ☞ fish (cod, I believe, and you can only believe because Henri reveals no kitchen information at all) so white and so tasty you wonder why you had ever eaten meat. Next came a salad, and finally a crème caramel for dessert, topped off by a great cup of espresso coffee, a Henri specialty.

This is fine dining, and believe me, the innkeeper who joins you for every course is the reason this inn is such a success.

How to get there: Take Exit 6 off Route 6. Turn left on Route 132 North to Route 6A. Go about 3 miles and pass through the light in the middle of Barnstable Village. After you pass the church on your left, look for a sign saying "Cobbs Cove." Turn left and within 100 yards on your left you will see a driveway marked "Evelyn Chester." Take this drive to the inn.

E: *Vickey is the inn cat. He was given this name when he was very small and before anybody knew he was a male.*

Oliue Metcalf

Inn of the Golden Ox
Brewster, Massachusetts
02631

Innkeepers: David and Eileen Gibson
Telephone: 617-896-3111
Rooms: 7, all share bathroom facilities.
Rates: $35 to $48, double occupancy, continental breakfast
    included.
Facilities: Open all year, but may be closed first two weeks of
    February. In season, lunch Friday and Saturday, Sunday
    brunch, dinner every day. From December 1 to April 1,
    dinner served Thursday through Sunday. Bar, lounge.
    American Express accepted.

David and Eileen are both graduates of the ☞ Culinary
Institute of America and that, for starters, is a good indication of the food that is served here. There are three lovely
dining rooms, the Cranberry Room, the Bay Room, and the
Brewster Room. It really does not matter where you eat, for
the food is excellent.

Here's just a hint of the food to expect. For appetizers

there's Mousseline of Seafood with Sauce Americaine, chowder of the day, and the others are equally tantalizing. And for dinner, sauerbraten the way it should be served, roast duckling with orange and cranberries, and a variety of veal and fresh fish dishes prepared with a lot of imagination. All the desserts, of course, are homemade and delectable.

You are sure to enjoy the generous cocktails served in the lovely relaxed atmosphere of the Decoy Lounge. All the common rooms are quiet and tastefully decorated, as are the seven sleeping rooms.

The inn was originally a church, completed in 1828. In 1852 the growing congregation prompted the church's move to larger quarters, which have since become the Brewster General Store. The original church was converted to an inn, and the Golden Ox was born. The church steeple was removed and sold for one dollar and seventy-five cents. Things were surely different back then.

How to get there: Take the Sagamore Bridge across Cape Cod Canal and follow signs for Mid-Cape Highway (Route 6) to Brewster Exit 10. Take Route 124 North to Route 6A.

E: Okemo is a beauty of an English setter and Slinkey is a black cat.

The good morning greeting and the
good night good wish can only be found in a country
inn.

The Captain's House Inn of Chatham

Chatham, Massachusetts
02633

Innkeepers: Cathy and Dave Eakin
Telephone: 617-945-0127
Rooms: 9, all with private bath; one suite.
Rates: $60 to $99, per room, EPB.
Facilities: Closed last two weeks in January. Breakfast only meal served. BYOB. Restaurants, swimming, and sailing nearby. No children under 12. All major credit cards accepted.

Cathy and Dave were Pennsylvanians until they discovered the joys of the Cape. Now, with their beautiful inn and thirty-five-foot sloop, they feel right at home. And so will you.
If you like to sail, ☞ charter the Eakin's sloop for a day. Stay the night in the inn and sail to your heart's content all day. What a superb way to enjoy the Cape and her waters.
The ambience of the whole inn is terrific. The rooms are

named after ships that were sailed by Captain Hiram Harding who built the house in 1839. The rooms are clean and well appointed with beautiful furniture. The good reading chairs and new mattresses afford you a comfortable stay. A four-poster canopied bed and fireplace are in one room. Three of the rooms are in the Captain's Cottage. Here are another fireplace and lovely four-poster bed. The inn also has a Carriage House and a garden efficiency apartment, which are rented by the week.

A good breakfast is the only meal served, except by a whim of the innkeeper. They may surprise you by serving dinner once in a while. However, there are other inns and restaurants in the near vicinity to serve you.

This whole area offers many activities, fishing, swimming, boating, or just plain loafing. Whether you enjoy being relaxed or energetic, it's a nice place for it here.

How to get there: Take Route 6 (Mid-Cape Highway) to Route 137, Exit 11, and south to Route 28. Turn left to Chatham Center. Follow the rotary out of town on Route 28 toward Orleans. The inn is on the left in about one-half mile.

☀

E: *A beautiful miniature schnauzer, newspapers, and such peace. Only in a country inn.*

How good of you to have asked me in.

Olive Metcalf

The Queen Anne Inn
Chatham, Massachusetts
02633

Innkeeper: Guenther Weinkopf
Telephone: 617-945-0394
Rooms: 30, all with private bath.
Rates: $90 to $110, per room, continental breakfast included.
Facilities: Inn open all year. Dining room closed in January.
Dinner, Sunday brunch, Tuesday clambakes in summer. Game room. Swimming and boating nearby. Fishing tours can be arranged. MasterCard and Visa accepted, but personal checks preferred.

Guenther has a fine inn. The rooms are so very comfortable. On the garden side the rooms have ☞ private balconies, which are a nice addition to the inn. Rooms looking south have a good view of Oyster Pond Bay.

There is a very pleasant lounge to relax in, and then there is the Earl of Chatham, the dining room, serving the most unbelievable food you can imagine. The help is beautifully trained. The chef has a ☞ briefing with them each night, so they can explain each course.

I have never seen appetizers presented this way. There were four different mousses. I tried Sea Bass and Salmon Mousse with lobster sauce. I really wanted them all. And such different soups. I had cold leek and cream of carrot soup, thick and sumptuous. There is a very complete herb garden at the inn, and all the herbs are used in the kitchen.

Several different ☞ sorbets are served before the entree. Cantaloupe, grapefruit, and kiwi sorbets are but a few. I had lobster and medallions of veal, and oh, were they good. All this time you are looking at a magnificent dessert cart with an unbelievable array of sweets. I finally had to choose and had chocolate mousse topped with strawberries in Grand Marnier and real whipped cream. A snifter of Rémy Martin and I could hardly leave the table.

I needed a walk and there are nice places to go. The water is close at hand and every Friday night band concerts are held in nearby Kate Gould Park. ☞ On Tuesday nights clambakes are held at the inn. What a nice way to meet the other guests.

How to get there: From Route 6 take Exit 11, go south on Route 137 to its end, take a left on Route 28 to Chatham Center. At your first traffic light, in about three miles, go right on Queen Anne Road. The inn is on your right.

E: *Imagine receiving this lovely place for a wedding gift. True. It happened in 1840.*

The Town House Inn
Chatham, Massachusetts
02633

Innkeepers: Russell and Svea Peterson
Telephone: 617-945-2180
Rooms: 22, all with private bath, television, refrigerator, and
   telephone; two have water beds; one cottage with fire-
   place.
Rates: $75 to $105, double occupancy, EPB.
Facilities: Closed in January. Breakfast daily. Dinner May to
   September. Beer and wine license. Friday night band
   concerts, golf, tennis, and beaches nearby. All major
   credit cards accepted.

   The front porch that overlooks Main Street beckons me.
The 4th of July parade, one of the summer's biggest events,
goes right by the front door. Best seat in town is the porch of
this inn.
   The original structure dates back to the 1820s. Remains
of the foundation still can be seen in the cellar, and some of
the original woodwork is here. The carved moldings and

wood trim depict harpoon and oar motifs. The floors are made of hemlock, and the original walls, recently exposed, have hand-painted scrolling.

The ☞ rooms are immaculate; matter of fact, the whole inn is. If you have always wanted to try a water bed, here is your chance. I think they are neat. The rest of the beds are very comfortable, also. All of the linens and towels are laundered right here by Svea. She likes to hang them out, when weather permits, for that ☞ lovely smell of fresh air.

Breakfast is not a ho-hum thing here. Russ bakes the muffins and Svea does wonders with Scandinavian goodies. Favorites are Svea's ☞ Finnish pancakes with a fresh fruit melange on top and her French toast with apricots.

The restaurant is called Two Turtles. Using her mother's recipes, Svea prepares Swedish pickled herring and Swedish meatballs as well as desserts. The chef provides a nice array of appetizers and main courses. Some specialties have been deluxe-cut Western lamb chops, scampi cooked with Svea's homegrown dill, and, of course, fresh fish.

How to get there: Take Route 6 (mid-Cape highway) to Exit 11, Route 137 south to Route 28 and east to the center of downtown Chatham. Watch for the Eldredge Library on your left. The inn is next door at 11 Library Lane.

⧖

E: *The living room and library are very cozy and overlook the main street.*

Deerfield Inn
Deerfield, Massachusetts
01342

Innkeeper: Paul J. Burns
Telephone: 413-774-5587
Rooms: 23, all with private bath and air conditioning.
Rates: $70 to $75, single or double occupancy, EP.
Facilities: Open all year. Closed Christmas Day. Breakfast,
   lunch, dinner. Cocktail lounge, two bars. Elevator. Color
   television in lounge. Museum, Deerfield Academy, historic house tours nearby. All major credit cards accepted.

A few years back a serious fire did extensive damage to
this lovely old inn, but alumni of Deerfield and many others
banded together and rebuilt the inn. They did such an exquisite job the Federal government has designated the inn a
☞ National Historic Site.
   ☞ The rocking chairs on the front porch somehow let
you know how lovely things will be inside. The parlors are
beautifully furnished with mostly twentieth-century copies

or adaptations. The Beehive Parlor, done in shades of blue, is a restful place for a cocktail or two. The main dining room is spacious, serving the kind of food befitting the setting. The chef prepares a daily special, taking advantage of seasonal and local market offerings. He also does magic things with veal, chicken, and fish.

The luncheon menu has some interesting and quite different offerings, such as Lamb Brochette, marinated lamb with vegetables on a skewer, and very good. There is also Chicken Mandarin Salad that will light up your day. By the way, all the baking is done right here.

The bedrooms are joys, ☞ Beauty-Rest mattresses, matching bedspreads and drapes, comfortable chairs, ☞ and good lights for restful reading or needlework. The baths have been color coordinated with the rooms they serve. Little to nothing has been left to chance in this restoration.

There is a coffee shop on the lower level, which gives off onto an outdoor garden. Perfect spot for informal meals, and a place the children will love.

How to get there: From I-91 take Exit 24 northbound. Go 6 miles north on Route 5. At the sign for Old Deerfield Village take a left. The inn will be on your left just past the Academy.

E: *For an old "inn creeper" like me this inn is the icing on the cake.*

The Nauset House Inn
East Orleans, Massachusetts
02643

Innkeepers: Diane and Al Johnson
Telephone: 617-255-2195
Rooms: 14, 8 with private bath.
Rates: $35 to $65, double occupancy, EP.
Facilities: Open April 1 to November 20. Full or continental
breakfast only meal served. BYOB. Restaurants, antique
shops, bicycling, hiking, and ocean beach nearby. Mas-
terCard and Visa accepted.

Nauset Beach at East Orleans is the first of the great Atlantic beaches that rim Cape Cod; rolling dunes, dashing
surf, and wide swaths of sand run southward for more than
ten miles. There are quiet, out-of-the-way coves that offer the
beachgoer an ideal place to sun and picnic, or just to relax
and enjoy. If your tastes are for fresh water, there are dozens
of inland ponds at hand.

Breakfast is the only meal served here, but it is a real ☞
old-fashioned country one, and so good. One beautiful morn-

ing I had the best French toast that I had tasted in a long time.

A unique feature of the inn is its 1908 conservatory filled with plants and flowers and a dolphin fountain. The very comfortable wicker furniture makes this a great spot to while away a summer evening.

The guest rooms are nice and cozy. One has a balcony and some have a sitting area. It's great to come back to a lovely inn like this after a day on the beach or in a boat.

The Johnsons have two dogs, Roo and Wendy, who are fun dogs. They will pick up small stones and bring them in to the guests.

There's so much to do in this area. There is a multitude of good restaurants, antique stores, and shopping spots for your every need. It's a great area for biking, hiking, boating, and fishing, and, of course, for enjoying the beautiful beach. And if you want a less active day, drive out to Provincetown. It is not too many miles away and well worth the trip.

How to get there: From the Mid-Cape Highway (Route 6), go to Main Street in East Orleans. Turn right onto Beach Road, and the inn is on your right.

E: *The patio with a view of the sea is so tranquil.*

Snug in a country inn, I have finally found
the perfect topping to a windy Cape Cod day.

The Charlotte Inn
Edgartown, Massachusetts
02539

Innkeepers: Gery and Paula Conover
Telephone: 617-627-4751
Rooms: 24, 22 with private bath; some with fireplace.
Rates: In season, $98 to $185; off season, $38 to $185; suite
$250 in August and $195 rest of year; double occupancy,
EPB.
Facilities: Open all year. In season, lunch and dinner. Off
season, dinner on weekends. Sunday brunch year
round. Reservations a must. Gift shop and gallery. Sailing, swimming, fishing, golfing, and tennis nearby. MasterCard and Visa accepted.

The start of your vacation is a forty-five-minute ferry
ride to Martha's Vineyard. It's wise to make early reservations for your automobile on the ferry. There are also cabs if
you prefer not to take your car.
When you open the door to the inn you are in the ☛ Edgartown Art Gallery, with interesting artifacts and paintings,

both watercolor and oil. This is a well-appointed gallery featuring such artists as Ray Ellis who has a fine talent in both media. The inn also has an unusual gift shop.

Food here is French. The restaurant, called Chez Pierre, is small and intimate with many artifacts, plants, unusual windows, and oh, the food! The hors d'oeuvres are unlike any you have ever had, such as sliced smoked Nantucket pheasant, or fresh seafood marinated in a combination of lemon and lime juices. There are more of these goodies. The entrees change with the seasons. Just a few are ☞ Broiled Swordfish with Caviar, Poached Fillet of Whitefish with Spinach Cream Sauce, and the list goes on, one better than the next. Desserts I will let you discover, and I do not want to meet your diet doctor.

Sunday brunch is worth the trip alone, ☞ freshly squeezed orange juice, Salt-cured Salmon with Dill Sauce, freshly baked croissants. Heaven!

The rooms are authentic. There are early American four-poster beds, fireplaces, and the carriage house is sumptuous. The second-floor suite with fireplace I could live in. Paula has a touch with rooms, comfortable furniture, ☞ down pillows, down comforters, and all the amenities. As an example, the shower curtains are eyelet and so pretty. As a finishing touch, there are plenty of large towels.

Across the street is the Garden House, and it is Edgartown at its best. The living room is unique and beautifully furnished, and has a fireplace that is always set for you. The rooms over here are just so handsome. Paula, by the way, has green hands, and all about are gardens that just outdo each other.

How to get there: Reservations are a must if you take your car on the ferry from Woods Hole, Massachusetts. Forty-five minutes later you are in Vineyard Haven. After a 15-minute ride, you are in Edgartown, and on Summer Street is the inn.

E: *Gery and Paula are special innkeepers, but they do need the help of Kim, the dog, and Oscar and Cricket, the cats.*

Coonamessett Inn
Falmouth, Massachusetts
02541

Innkeeper: Joe Badot
Telephone: 617-548-2300
Rooms: 25 suites, all with private bath.
Rates: $50 to $100, per room, EP.
Facilities: Open all year. Breakfast, lunch, dinner, bar. Parking. All major credit cards accepted.

In 1796, in a rolling field that sloped gently down to a lovely pond, Thomas Jones constructed a house and barn that was to become Coonamessett Inn (Indian, for "the place of the large fish"). The framework of the house is finished with wooden peg joints, and much of the interior paneling is original. Many of the bricks in the old fireplaces are thought to be made of ballast brought from Europe in the holds of sailing ships. Hanging in the inn are many paintings by the primitive American artist, Ralph Cahoon. They represent much of the history of the Coonamessett.

The food is excellent, offered from a large, varied menu,

and served by friendly waitresses. Breakfasts are memorable. Lunch attracts a large group, for this place is really well known. And dinner is great, with lobster served four different ways. You can even have lobster sauce on your scrod. Meat eaters are not forgotten either; two favorites are featured, roast prime ribs and a lamb chop mixed grill. ☛ Desserts have a menu all their own. Fantastic.

There are no guest rooms in the inn itself. ☛ The cottage suites are very nice and large, consisting of bedroom, sitting room, and private bath.

I love the Cape off season, and it is good to know that no matter what day I decide to come, I will receive a cordial welcome here. The inn grounds are beautiful and are kept in mint condition year round. All around you will see the loveliest array of grass, trees, flowers, shrubs . . . and peace. Don't forget the peace.

How to get there: Take Route 28 at the bridge over the canal, and go into Falmouth. Turn left on Jones Road, and at the intersection of Gifford Street you will see the inn.

E: *I wish I lived closer, because I like the whole thing, starting with the flower arrangements, fresh every other day, that are done by a man who really knows how to arrange.*

The chill of a wood-stove-warmed bedroom evaporates in the crisp smell of bacon for breakfast.

Mostly Hall
Falmouth, Massachusetts
02540

Innkeepers: Jim and Ginny Austin
Telephone: 617-548-3786
Rooms: 7, 5 with private bath.
Rates: $45 to $65, per room, EPB.
Facilities: Closed three weeks in February. Breakfast only meal served. Menus available for nearby restaurants. BYOB. Children over 16 are welcome. Bicycles. Beaches, ferries to islands, four-mile ocean bike path, summer theaters nearby. No credit cards accepted.

Jim and Ginny perfectly complement each other. Jim is in charge of decoration and Ginny is the chef. Jim has covered the walls of the guest rooms with sheets. Each room is different and so unusual. In one room he had to use upholstery fabric in order to get a blue check. He has done well. The furniture is comfortable. ☛ Good mattresses are so important for a good night's sleep.

The inn is an authentic New Orleans home built in

1849 by Captain Albert Nye as a wedding present for his Southern bride. There are floor-to-ceiling windows and thirteen-foot ceilings. Slowly revolving Bombay fans make this handsome inn even better.

The large living room has two neat couches covered in a striped blue velvet fabric. I felt right at home. I have a big comfortable chair at home done in the same fabric. Breakfast is served in here at a large oval table. In summer it is served on the marvelous porches that surround the inn.

Ginny comes up with some real winners for breakfast. ☛ Ham and Mushroom Gratinée. Popovers and Creamed Eggs. Chicken Pie with Cornbread Topping. Homemade breads, fresh fruit and juice, coffee, tea, and milk. What a great way to start a day.

How to get there: Take Route 28 to Falmouth. Go left on Route 28 South. It is 500 yards to the inn. The address is 27 Main Street. The inn is on the right, set well back from the road.

E: *There is a lovely gazebo at the rear of the property, watched over by Tasha, the cat, and Solo, the Sheltie.*

> *"Enough," he cried*
> *and left with all speed*
> *for the neighborhood inn.*

olive Metcalf

Windflower Inn
Great Barrington, Massachusetts
01230

Innkeepers: Barbara and Gerald Liebert, Claudia and John
   Ryan
Telephone: 413-528-2720
Rooms: 13, all with private bath, many with fireplace.
Rates: $50 to $70, per person, double occupancy, MAP.
Facilities: Open all year. Breakfast, dinner, full license. Res-
   ervations a must. Swimming pool. Golf, tennis, downhill
   and cross-country skiing, music, and theater nearby. No
   credit cards honored, but personal checks accepted.

   Barbara and Claudia, mother and daughter, are the
chefs in this lovely inn. They give you a choice of three entrees each evening, and all are cooked fresh. The summer
vegetable garden is a seventy-by-ninety-foot spread of delights.
I am sure a lot of the produce is preserved for winter use. The
breads, pies, muffins, and cakes are all ☞ homemade. The
dining room features Currier & Ives snow scenes on the
walls and a ☞ coffeepot bubbling on the mantel all day. Late

afternoon you have your choice of tea or cocktail with a great assortment of hors d'oeuvres.

The rooms are spacious, and all the beds are new. All rooms have private baths, and many have fireplaces.

A game room offers choices of chess, cribbage, back-gammon, Scrabble, and jigsaw puzzles. The living room, full of good early American antiques, is comfortable. Barbara has a way with flowers and plants. The inn is full of beautiful specimens of her talent.

The inn animals are Tawny, a yellow Lab, Libby, a beautiful Springer spaniel, and Max and Perry, Libby's children.

There is so much to do in this area it is hard to recount it all. Golf is across the street. The inn's own pool is very relaxing, and in summer you have Tanglewood, Jacob's Pillow, and the Berkshire Theater nearby.

How to get there: The inn is on Route 23, 3 miles west of Great Barrington.

E: *Gerald moved his grandmother's kitchen table down here from the Tulip Tree Inn in Vermont that they owned. He kneads his good French bread on it.*

> *Our sympathy for the hardships*
> *of our forbears should be somewhat mitigated*
> *by the fact that they had the best*
> *of country inns.*

Country Inn
Harwichport, Massachusetts
02646

Innkeepers: David and Kathleen Van Gelder
Telephone: 617-432-2769
Rooms: 7, all with private bath.
Rates: $55 to 60, double occupancy, EPB.
Facilities: Open all year. Dinner by reservation. Lounge, bar, and private dining room for small parties. Tennis, swimming pool. Ocean beach privileges. American Express, MasterCard, and Visa accepted.

The Country Inn is what its name implies, a lovely old Cape home on six acres, covered with rambling roses. Centrally located on the Cape, it makes a great home base for exploring this wonderful part of the world, with its excellent shopping for just about everything.

The dining room is open to the public for dinner and offers a varied menu, from French and Italian dishes to the more traditional New England fare. All meals include absolutely delicious ☞ homemade cranberry, lemon, and pumpkin breads. Fish specials include escalloped oysters baked in heavy cream, and ocean-fresh haddock, baked, or baked and stuffed. From fish you can turn to Chicken Cape Cod with ☛ cranberry-spice glaze, Chicken Cordon Bleu, or Filet Mignon. The perfect ending is homemade Apple Crumb Pie with homemade Cinnamon Ice Cream. To make your meal complete they have a choice of five unusually spirited coffees.

Breakfasts are special fun. The normal eggs and omelets are all done differently, which, with the inn's homemade breads, make the whole meal a delight.

The inn has eleven fireplaces. Three are in use downstairs. The rest are in the bedrooms and are lovely to look at, but unfortunately cannot be used.

David has recently acquired a boat and his captain's license. For a modest fee, he will take house guests on day trips to Monomoy (part of the National Seashore) for birdwatching, picnicking, and swimming. The fee includes your picnic lunch.

The Van Gelders have another fine inn just one mile away called Captain's Quarters. It has five rooms, all with private baths, and all new queen-sized beds. It is Victorian in style.

How to get there: Take Route 6 to Exit 10. Go right on Route 124 and continue to a stop sign, about 2 miles away. Take a right on Route 39, and in one mile the inn will be on your right.

☒

E: *The inn was once the guest house on the estate of one of the founders of the Jordan Marsh Company.*

Olive Metcalf

The Morgan House
Lee, Massachusetts
01238

Innkeepers: Beth and Bill Orford
Telephone: 413-243-0181
Rooms: 12, one with private bath.
Rates: $25 to $75, double occupancy, EPB.
Facilities: Open all year. Lunch, dinner, bar, lounge. American Express, MasterCard, and Visa accepted.

The Morgan House is another of my few in-town inns. Very nice to have in any town. The inn has a long and interesting history dating back to 1826 when it was built as a private home. In 1853 it was converted into a stagecoach inn, and an inn it has remained.

The lobby is papered in ☞ old registration sheets, many of them showing the names of the noted visitors over the past 100 years, such as Ulysses S. Grant, Robert E. Lee, Buffalo "Bill" Cody, Horace Greeley, and George Bernard Shaw. Many of the pages are beautifully decorated in flowing script advertising the bill at the local opera house.

The guest rooms are furnished with early American pieces. The walls are stencilled, and everything is clean and crisp. There is a porch on the second floor looking over Main Street for the guests' use. Wicker chairs make an afternoon here extremely delightful.

Now for the best part, the food. The veal is butchered and pounded here in the inn's kitchen. You just know it will be good. The menu shows thirteen different appetizers to go with the entrees, every one of which is prepared here. One different entree you should try is the Yankee Pork Chops, two generously cut chops served with a dressing of apples and raisins. All breads and desserts are created in the kitchen. An example is Pear Helen, ice cream capped with half a pear, laced with chocolate sauce, and topped with a dab of sweet whipped cream.

You can host a small meeting or special occasion in the Coach Room on the second floor. The room can accommodate fifty people.

There is so much to do in this lovely part of the world I just may write a book on the subject.

How to get there: From the Massachusetts Turnpike, take Exit 2. Follow Route 20 West one mile to the center of Lee. The inn will be on your left.

E: *The inn is famous for its New England Duckling. The young duckling is brushed with imported mustard, topped with Provolone cheese, roasted to a delicate crispness, and finished with a special Triple Sec sauce. Yum yum.*

olive Metcalf

The Candle Light Inn
Lenox, Massachusetts
01240

Innkeepers: Lynne and James DeMayo
Telephone: 413-637-1555
Rooms: 4, all with private bath; 5 suites.
Rates: $45 to $110, double occupancy, EP.
Facilities: Open all year. Lunch, dinner, Sunday brunch,
   piano bar. Pub with entertainment on weekends. All
   major credit cards accepted.

Christmas is a time of royal splendor here at the inn.
They  decorate for each season, but Christmas is just something special and worth a trip from anywhere.

An old wagon and an old double sled are on the lawn,
Tiffany lamps are on the porch, and a lovely flower cart is in
the entrance hall. Straight ahead is the bar, and what a bar,
done pub-style with some of the ☞ greatest stemware I have
ever seen.

The dessert cart sits at the entrance of one of the dining
rooms with a beautiful array of all ☞ homemade desserts,

each one better than the next. There is a gracious fireplace in this dining room. Napery is bluest white. The chairs are comfortable, and the food divine. All the food is fresh and cooked to order; nothing frozen in this chef's kitchen except the ice cubes. The hors d'oeuvres list is more than ample, with four different kinds of clams, shrimp, and oysters, in addition to my favorite, garlicky escargots.

Entrees are interesting. At lunch do try the Chicken Pot Pie. It is deliciously different. Dinner entrees like Shrimp, Crabmeat and Scallops Mornay en Casserole are a delight. Stuffed crepes, or one of the chicken dishes, tempt me to try eating everything on the menu.

The chef-owner, Jim, cooks only with copper utensils, and the food is even served from copper. ☞ Fresh strawberries are served here almost every month of the year.

Flowers are all over the inn, with Boston ferns at the windows, and fuchsias in abundance, usually hanging together with impatiens. And the backyard in summer is a wealth of blooms.

How to get there: The inn is at 53 Walker Street. Turn into Lenox on Route 7-A, off Route 7.

E: The small bar with the gleaming stemware is just a great way to end a day.

Man has tendencies of many temperatures,
the warmest of which is hospitality.

The Gateways Inn
Lenox, Massachusettss
01240

Innkeepers: Lilliane and Gerhard Schmid
Telephone: 413-637-2532
Rooms: 8, all with private bath; one suite with fireplace.
Rates: $80 to $110, double; $200, suite; continental breakfast
included.
Facilities: Open all year. Restaurant closed Sundays and
Mondays in winter. In summer, dinner by reservation
only. Free guest privileges at Haus Andreas. MasterCard
and Visa accepted.

The Gateways began as a mansion built for Harley
Procter of Procter and Gamble, the Ivory soap magnate. It is
in the shape of his favorite product, a cake of soap. It is
square and flat on top.

Chef-owner Gerhard was the winner of both ☞ a silver
and a gold medal in the 1968 International Culinary Competition, and three Olympic gold medals in 1976. Gerhard also
had the honor of preparing Boston's royal luncheon for

Queen Elizabeth during her bicentennial visit in 1976. To add to the laurels, the Gateways rates ☞ four stars in the Mobil Guide. There is really not much more I can say about the food. It is just superb.

Two bedrooms, with their high ceilings, are perfect for the massive furniture with which they are furnished. The other bedrooms, equally lovely, have colonial-style furniture. Color-coordinated towels add just the right final touch. The suite is called the Fiedler Suite because Arthur Fiedler stayed in it so many times. ☞ It is lavish in its appointments, and worth all it costs to spend a night in.

The sister inn, Haus Andreas, is named for the Schmids' son, and is but five miles away. It is a lovely, old colonial mansion with a charming pastoral view. Here you will have complimentary guest privileges entitling you to swim, play tennis, and ride bicycles.

How to get there: Take Route 7 to Route 7A. The inn is on Route 7A, one block away from the intersection of Routes 183 and 7A.

E: *The oval windows beside the front door and the magnificent stairway alone are worth a visit here.*

The time between sunset and the completeness of night should be spent around a well laid board with assurances of a warm bed to follow.

The Village Inn
Lenox, Massachusetts
01240

Innkeepers: Clifford Rudisill and Ray Wilson
Telephone: 413-637-0020
Rooms: 27, 15 with private bath.
Rates: $40 to $105, double occupancy, EP.
Facilities: Open all year. Breakfast, afternoon tea, dinner Friday through Sunday, Sunday brunch. Dinner reservations required. In July and August, late after-concert suppers on Friday and Saturday. Village Tavern. Skiing, tennis, golfing, swimming, horseback riding, fishing, hiking, Tanglewood, and Jacob's Pillow nearby. MasterCard and Visa accepted.

There is a saying here at the inn, "If you can't be a house guest in the Berkshires, be ours." This surely would be a fine choice. The rooms are so clean and cheerful. The inn's walls are covered with stencilled wallpapers, the maple floors have oriental rugs, and antiques are found throughout the inn.

The Village Tavern was built in the old cellars of this 1771 house, and is furnished with seats made from church pews. On those blustery winter days there is a cheery fire to go with your drink. The living room, called the Common Room, is a delightful place to sit and listen to the grand piano being played. There is a nice television and reading room for your comfort.

A real first is an authentic English tea served from 3:30 to 5:00 every day with homemade scones, pastries, and small tea sandwiches. To make it perfect, you are provided with ☛ Devonshire-style clotted cream.

Breakfast is a thing of joy. Any inn that serves eggs Benedict with ☛ a glass of champagne gets my hearty applause. Another clap of the hands goes for their Irish coffee. There are many other good things to eat here. The dinner menu begins with such specialties as snails sautéed in brandy and white wine on toasted crusts with a shallot and garlic cream, and smoked Maine trout with horseradish cream. The summer menu offers your choice of cold fresh fruit soup (blueberry, raspberry, or strawberry), followed by fresh Columbia River poached salmon with a gingered hollandaise sauce, or ☛ Fresh Vegetable Plate, steamed and lightly sautéed vegetables. This dish is not seen often enough on a menu.

The inn is near many activities, churches, shops, the library, and the bus stop.

How to get there: Take Route 7A off Route 7 and turn on Church Street in Lenox. The inn is on the right.

E: *Once a month on Sunday afternoons the inn features chamber music concerts. All this and English tea. Oh my.*

olive Metcalf

Wheatleigh
Lenox, Massachusetts
01240

Innkeepers: Susan and Linfield Simon
Telephone: 413-637-0610
Rooms: 17, all with private bath.
Rates: $95 to $300, double occupancy, continental breakfast
   included.
Facilities: Open all year. Dinner served Tuesday through
   Sunday, bar, lounge. Children over 8 are welcome; pets
   are not. Swimming, tennis, cross-country skiing. All
   major credit cards accepted.

   In the heart of the beautiful Berkshires, overlooking a
lake, amid lawns and gardens on twenty-two self-contained
acres stands the estate of Wheatleigh, former home of the
Countess de Heredia. The centerpiece of this property is an
elegant private palace fashioned after an Italian palazzo. The
cream-colored manse recreates the architecture of sixteenth-
century Florence. You must read the brochure of Wheatleigh, for it says it all so well.

Patios, pergolas, porticos, and terraces surround this lovely old mansion. The carvings over the fireplaces, ☞ cupids entwined in garlands, are exquisite. In charming contrast, the inn also has the ☞ largest collection of contemporary ceramics in the New England area. There are many lovely porcelain pieces on the walls.

The bar-lounge, with bookcases lining the walls, a piano, and a great collection of records, makes a drink rather special.

And imagine a ☞ great hall with a grand staircase right out of a castle in Europe. There are also exquisite stained glass windows in pale pastels, plus gorgeous, comfortable furniture. From the great hall you can hear the tinkle of the fountain out in the garden.

The rooms are ☞ smashing with lots of white dotted swiss and eyelet material for the canopy beds. Do you long for your own balcony overlooking a lovely lake? No problem. Reserve one here.

One dines by candlelight in the Victorian dining room on such things as Shrimp Mario, sautéed jumbo shrimp served with their own special wine sauce. Lamb chops ☞ one and one-half-inches thick are perfection. A wonderfully complete wine list caps any meal here.

How to get there: From Stockbridge at the Red Lion Inn where Route 7 turns right, go straight on Prospect Hill Road, bearing left. Go past the Stockbridge Bowl and up a hill to Wheatleigh. From the Massachusetts Turnpike, take Exit 2, and follow signs to Lenox. In the center of Lenox, take Route 183, pass the main gate of Tanglewood, and then take the first left on West Hawthorne. Go one mile to Wheatleigh.

E: *An intimate private dining room with fine china, silver, and crystal is a wonderful way to have a party.*

Olive Metcalf

The Four Chimneys Inn
Nantucket, Massachusetts
02554

Innkeeper: Betty Gaeta
Telephone: 617-228-1912
Rooms: 10, all with private bath.
Rates: $85 to $150, double occupancy, continental breakfast included.
Facilities: Closed mid-November to Daffodil Festival. Continental breakfast only meal served. BYOB. American Express, MasterCard, and Visa accepted.

The inn is on famous Orange Street where 126 sea captains built their mansions. It was constructed circa 1835 by Captain Frederick Gardner. In 1856 Freeman Adams purchased this home and converted it into "The Bay View House." The house had a motto by Mr. Adams: "No pains will be spared to insure the comforts of its patrons." This feeling is being carried out by the present owner who has done an excellent restoration job.

All the rooms have been decorated with unbelievable period furnishings. One of the bedrooms has a four-poster, canopy bed and a ☞ huge armoire that beggars description. Many other rooms have canopy beds, and one room has its ☞ own porch. The third floor of the inn has marvelous views of the sea and the quaint rooftops of Nantucket town.

There is a grand staircase to the second floor. It does not take much imagination to envision beautifully gowned ladies floating down to join you.

The sitting rooms have fireplaces, and you have the use of the game table, cable television, and piano.

Continental breakfast, the only meal served here, always includes some unusual muffins which are excellent. In the late afternoon ☞ hors d'oeuvres are served to go along with your drinks. The inn has an extensive collection of menus from area restaurants to help you choose a spot for your lunch or dinner.

How to get there: Go up Main Street to the bookstore on your left. This is Orange Street where you turn left. The inn will be on your left.

☷

E: *The antique Chinese rugs are what you dream the old ship captains brought back with them.*

Olive Metcalf

Jared Coffin House
Nantucket, Massachusetts
02554

Innkeepers: Philip and Margaret Read
Telephone: 617-228-2400
Rooms: 58; 9 in main house; 16 simpler rooms in Eben Allen
Wing; 3 rooms in Swain house, connected to the Eben
Allen Wing; 12 rooms in Daniel Webster house across
the patio; 18 rooms in two houses across the street.
Rates: $50, single; $80 to $125, double; EP.
Facilities: Open all year. Breakfast, lunch, dinner, taproom.
Eben Allen Room for private parties. Near swimming
and tennis. All major credit cards accepted.

It is well worth the thirty-mile trip by ferry, or the plane
trip from Boston or New York, to end up at the Jared Coffin
House. Built as a private home in 1845, the three-story brick
house with slate roof became an inn only twelve years later.
The inn passed through many hands before it came to the extremely ☞ capable ones of Philip and Margaret Read.
The public rooms at the inn reflect charm and warmth.

102

The furnishings are Chippendale and Sheraton, and showing the results of the world-wide voyaging by the Nantucket whalemen are Chinese and Japanese objets d'art and furniture.

To add to the charm are many fabrics and some furniture that have been made right here on the island. In addition to the main house, there are several other close-by houses that go with the inn. All are done beautifully for your every comfort.

☛ The taproom, located on the lowest level, is a warm, happy, fun place. Here you meet the local people and spin yarns with all. Old pine walls and hand-hewn beams reflect a warm atmosphere. Luncheon is served down here with good burgers and great, hearty soups. During the winter this is a nice spot for informal dinners.

The main dining room, ☛ papered with authentic wallpapers, is quiet and elegant. Wedgewood china and pistol-handled silverware make dining a special pleasure, and reflect the good life demanded by the nineteenth-century owners of the great Nantucket whaling ships.

The inn is located in the heart of Nantucket's Historic District, about one-eighth mile from a public beach, and one mile from the island's largest public beach and tennis courts. It's a pleasant three-mile bicycle ride to superb surf swimming on the South Shore.

How to get there: To get to Nantucket, take a ferry from Hyannis (April through January) or Woods Hole (January through March and summer months). First call 617-540-2022 for reservations. Or take a plane from Boston, Hyannis, or New York. The House is located 2 blocks north of Main Street, and 2 blocks west of Steamboat Wharf.

♒

E: *The size and the quantity of the luxurious bath towels pleased me greatly. The housekeeping staff does a wonderful job, and the exquisite antiques reflect their loving care.*

olive Metcalf

Country Inn at Princeton
Princeton, Massachusetts
01541

Innkeepers: Don and Maxine Plumridge
Telephone: 617-464-2030
Rooms: 6 suites, all with private bath.
Rates: $95 and $115, double occupancy, continental break-
fast included.
Facilities: Inn open all year. Dining rooms closed Mondays
and Tuesdays. Dinner served Wednesday through Sun-
day. Sunday brunch. No children under 12. American
Express, MasterCard, and Visa accepted.

"The year 1890 had a certain charm and way about it,"
says the inn's brochure, and it is so right. The inn is a ☞ Victorian delight. It was built with meticulous attention to every
detail by Charles G. Washburn, an industrialist and outspo-
ken senator, and a close friend of Theodore Roosevelt.
The parlour-living room is exquisite with swirling Casa
Blanca ceiling fans with chandeliers, Victorian chairs and
couches that are beautifully upholstered, and oriental rugs.

The fireplace is massive and so cozy on a chilly night. All through the inn you will find greenery and fine art crafts displayed with taste.

During the warmer months, guests can enjoy cocktails on the expansive wraparound veranda or garden terrace. There are three elegant dining rooms. The Library Den, striking in its Chinese-Ming Red wallcoverings, is available for private dining or small parties up to twelve guests. There is the Garden Room; there's also the more formal Washburn Room. There is so much to look at and enjoy. From the dining room windows you have a distinct view of Boston's twinkling lights.

Country French Cuisine, both creatively and lovingly prepared, is presented by five-star chef, Frank McClelland. The menu changes seasonally. One of the entrees I enjoyed was roasted farm-raised Pheasant with Cabbage and Currant Moussette. A Pineau Charentes and Peeled Grape Sauce perfected this elegant dish. Other menu options may be Baby Quail, Baby Salmon Trout with Littleneck Clams, Pork Tenderloin Pistachio, and Grilled Veal Loin Chop with Pesto Raviolis and Eggplant.

I keep returning to sample the new magic created by the chef.

How to get there: From just north of Worcester on Route 290 take Route 140 north to Route 62 and turn left to Princeton. From Route 2 take Route 31 south to Princeton. In both cases, when you read the blinker by the post office turn right, and the inn is on your right just up the hill.

E: *The accommodations are six extremely* *spacious parlor suites. They are sumptuous. Each one is different, and I could live forever in any one of them.*

Oceans Inn
Provincetown, Massachusetts
02657

Innkeepers: Mark Cross and Horace Stowman
Telephone: 617-487-0358
Rooms: 16, 10 with private bath, the rest with running water.
Rates: $45 to $70, double occupancy, EP.
Facilities: Inn closed late November to April 1. Bar and restaurant open all year. Brunch, dinner. American Express, MasterCard, and Visa accepted.

The bar and lounge are the inn's answer to Sardi's. The walls are covered with autographed photographs of Provincetown's wide family of performing artists. The bar itself is fun, and interesting drinks are served. Brandy snifters of either twelve- or twenty-two-ounce capacity are used for an array of about thirty-five to forty different frozen fruit drinks. All the glassware used is in excellent taste. Someone has taken the time to do it right. I think it makes a drink taste much better to be in exactly the right glass.

The dining room is decorated with original etchings by

☛ Al Hirschfeld, the *New York Times* theater section illustrator. The menu covers are also done by him, and they are creative and excellent. He does not do the food, however, but a great chef does. Whether it is brunch or dinner, it is delicious.

Brunch and dinner, weather permitting, are served on the garden patio and on the deck overlooking famous, old Provincetown Harbor. In summer every ☛ Friday afternoon different artists display their work in the patio garden. Rain date is Sunday.The art and the food combine to make a wonderful experience.

The inn is old and comfortably furnished with wicker chairs and either king-sized or double beds. On the third floor are two rooms with expansive views of the harbor.

It is hard to list all there is to do out here in Provincetown, theater, arts, shops, but just walk out of the inn and turn right. You will find more than enough.

How to get there: Take Route 6 (Mid-Cape Highway) all the way out to Provincetown. The inn is at 386A Commercial Street (the main street of town).

E: *Over the bar is this sign: "May the roof above us never fall in, and we friends gathered below never fall out." Liked it.*

> *"Enough," he cried*
> *and left with all speed*
> *for the neighborhood inn.*

The Dan'l Webster Inn
Sandwich, Massachusetts
02563

Innkeeper: Steve Catania
Telephone: 617-888-3622
Rooms: 42, all with private bath.
Rates: $45 to $105, per person, MAP. $39 to $150, double occupancy, EP.
Facilities: Closed Christmas Day only. Breakfast, lunch, dinner, Sunday brunch, bar, lounge. Swimming pool, gift shop. Doll museum, glass museum, Heritage Plantation, and beaches nearby. All major credit cards accepted.

A 250-year-old linden tree, complete with bird feeders, stands outside the Conservatory, one of the inn's three lovely dining rooms. This is a glassed-in room, overlooking a beautifully landscaped courtyard and swimming pool. The Webster Room has china cabinets to display ☞ old Sandwich glass on loan from the museum. There's a portrait of Daniel Webster's second wife in here. The Heritage Room has a huge open fireplace and a grand piano on the stage for your entertainment. A ☞ dance band is here on weekends, and they surely sounded good to me.

These dining rooms provide the perfect atmosphere for the excellent food. Breakfasts are hearty, with eggs, six different omelettes, sausage, croissants, fruit, and much more. The lunch menu lists salads, sandwiches, and quite a few hot choices. Dinner is an adventure. The hors d'oeuvres list is extensive. I had clams casino and also tasted the escargots, which were served en croute with mushrooms, garlic, and herb butter. There are four veal offerings, chicken, ten different seafood specials, and, of course, beef. I had Châteaubriand, very nice because it was served for one. It was very good. Desserts are sinful, and there are special coffees.

The Devil 'n Dan Tavern is a cozy spot, with stained glass windows and very nice wooden bar stools. There are tables and chairs here for those who are not barflies.

All the guest rooms are a little different. Most have Hitchcock furniture. Some have canopy beds. All of the beds are comfortable. The new Webster Suite on the third floor of the inn has two bedrooms and two bathrooms. One bath has a Jacuzzi, and the other has a steam tub.

In the lovely Fessenden House next door are four suites. I was in the Captain Ezra Nye suite. A ☞ whirlool tub is in each of these suites as is a marble fireplace. They are beautifully furnished with classic antiques. I had to go up two steps to get into bed. Oh my, I do like it here.

How to get there: Go over the Bourne Bridge to a rotary; go ¾ of the way around it, taking the Route 6A exit that parallels the canal. Stay on this road until you come to the third set of lights. This is Jarves Street. Go right, then right again onto Main Street. The inn is on the right, close to the corner.

E: *A split of wine is waiting in each guest room. How nice.*

Stagecoach Hill Inn
Sheffield, Massachusetts
01257

Innkeepers: Ann and John Pedretti
Telephone: 413-229-8585
Rooms: 15, all with private bath; one 2-bedroom apartment.
Rates: $35 to $50, per room, double occupancy, EP.
Facilities: Open all year. No breakfast, but there are coffee
makers in each room. Lunch May to October, dinner,
bar, lounge. Swimming pool. All major credit cards ac-
cepted.

The inn is located on a winding country road at the foot
of Mount Race. This was a real stagecoach stop all those
years ago.

John and Ann are ☞ both chefs and, needless to say, the
food is meticulously prepared. There is a very distinct feeling
of England here. Ann is from Lancashire County, and some
of the food reflects this in a most delightful way. ☞ Steak and
kidney pie is here as is steak and mushroom pie, and, on Saturdays, roast beef and Yorkshire pudding. The inn also

serves a delicious ☞ New England oyster pie, and a carpet-bagger steak that is stuffed with oysters. At lunch one day I had the thickest Quiche Lorraine I had ever seen, and a salad with a white French house dressing that was delicious. The rolls that came with my meal were fresh, hot, crisp, and yummy.

The dining rooms, done in red and white, are charming. Portraits of the royal family plus a lovely one of Prince Charles and Lady Diana make dining here a very cozy experience.

The pub-lounge with a roaring fire in winter beckons me. The warm, dark paneling, comfortable bar, and a piano complete the picture. English beer on tap is here, of course.

As a special plus for your visit, do see the chalet at the rear of the property. It has hand-stencilled walls and draperies.

There is so much to do in this area it would take a book to tell it all. Come and discover for yourself.

How to get there: Take Exit 2 from the Massachusetts Turnpike. Follow Route 102 west to Stockbridge. Take Route 7 south to Great Barrington and follow Route 41 south to the inn.

E: *Two chef-owners! How can you miss.*

*I love all good inns, but secretly I have
a rather special fondness if the boniface is fat.*

The Weathervane Inn
South Egremont, Massachusetts
01258

Innkeepers: Anne and Vincent Murphy
Telephone: 413-528-9580
Rooms: 8, 6 with private bath.
Rates: $55, per person, MAP.
Facilities: Open all year. Breakfast, dinner, Sunday brunch,
    bar, lounge. Swimming pool, outside games. MasterCard
    and Visa accepted.

The sign over the bar says, "Kiss the cook." Anne is the
chef and pretty enough for a kiss. Chicken soup was bubbling on her stove one time I was here, and what an aroma. It
tasted even better. Some of Anne's specialties are ☛ Chicken
Cordon Bleu, Stuffed Filet of Sole with Shrimp Sauce, and
delicious baked ham. I would love to be here for Sunday
brunch to try her blueberry pancakes with Canadian bacon.
    The dining room is very cheery and bright. Anne
changes the table decor with the seasons.
    The inn is so fresh and clean in every corner that you

know you have good innkeepers at hand. One of the rooms is named the Norman Rockwell Room because Anne has three of his works on the wall. The first has two youngsters looking at the moon. The second has the youngsters, now a bit older, at the soda fountain, and in the last they are even older, at the registrar's desk getting a license to marry. Anne has some other Rockwell paintings at various places in the inn.

There is one room that needs special mention. It is over the kitchen and has a tiny bathtub with a hand-held shower, really neat.

All the public rooms are comfortable, and there is so much to do in this area year round that you could stay a month.

Bear is the inn dog and is perfect for the part. He is an English cocker spaniel.

How to get there: Follow Route 7 to Route 23 West. You are now 3 miles from South Egremont. The inn will be on your left.

☀

E: *A porch with rockers. Makes an inn.*

Man's cruelty to man knows almost no horizons.
His continued existence, however, is justified
when he says to a stranger, "Come in."

Olive Metcalf

The Inn at Stockbridge
Stockbridge, Massachusetts
01262

Innkeepers: Lee and Don Weitz
Telephone: 413-298-3337
Rooms: 7, 5 with private bath.
Rates: $75 to $140, double occupancy, EPB.
Facilities: Open all year. Dinner by reservation. BYOB.
Swimming pool. No credit cards honored, but personal
checks accepted.

There is a small red and gold sign by the side of the road
directing you into the lane to this lovely inn with stately
white columns. Wonderful spot.

The living room-library has soft sofas and chairs, and is
done in an intriguing blue print. Plenty of books and a fireplace are at hand. A room as cozy as this makes me want to
curl up with a book or needlework.

Lee's dining room is beautiful, from the gleaming ☞
mahogany table to the sideboards groaning under the weight
of her silver services. It is just grand. There is a real country

kitchen, spacious and clean. What a wonderful place to cook.

And cooking is something Lee knows a lot about. Her breakfast is a real treat. Eggs Benedict, Breakfast Souffle (a ham, cheese, and egg souffle), and French Toast with Grand Marnier whipped butter are a few of the treats Lee makes to start your day. These are accompanied by home-baked goodies and fresh fruit and served on bone china. Mimosas are served on Sunday. The patio is a good place to savor breakfast in the summer.

The rooms are colorful and pleasant. They have king-sized or twin beds, double pillows, and ☞ heavy, thirsty, color-coordinated towels. You'll be pampered by such nice touches as turned-down beds and a mint on your pillow. Sheer comfort and joy.

There are twelve acres to roam about in and a large swimming pool to relax in. The trees that surround the whole scene are beautiful.

Lee sometimes can be coaxed to play her piano. This is quite a treat.

How to get there: From the Massachusetts Turnpike, take Exit 2 onto Route 102 to Stockbridge. At the intersection of Routes 102 and 7, take Route 7 north 1.2 miles to the inn's driveway. (Look for the small red and gold sign on your right after you pass under the turnpike.)

E: *Cheese and wine in the afternoon. Lovely.*

"The best landscape in the world is improved by a good inn in the foreground."
—Dr. Samuel Johnson

olive Metcalf

The Red Lion Inn
Stockbridge, Massachusetts
01262

Innkeeper: Betsy Holtzinger; Church Davis, Director of Lodging
Telephone: 413-298-5545
Rooms: 110, 80 with private bath; 6 suites in summer, 2 in winter.
Rates: $42 to $110, winter; $50 to $150, summer; double occupancy; EP.
Facilities: Open all year. Breakfast, lunch, dinner, bar. Heated swimming pool. Elevator. Accessible to wheelchairs. Pink Kitty Gift Shop. All major credit cards accepted.

The Red Lion Inn is a four-season inn. In summer you have the Berkshire Music Festival at Tanglewood and the Jacob's Pillow Dance Festival, both world renowned. The inn's own ☛ heated swimming pool is a nice attraction. Fall's foliage is perhaps the most spectacular in New England; in winter there are snow-covered hills; in spring come the lovely green and flowers. All go together to make this a great spot anytime of year.

The inn is full of lovely old antiques. The halls are lined with antique couches, each one prettier than the next. From a four-poster, canopy bed to beds with great brass head-boards, all the rooms are marvelously furnished and comfortable as sin. Whether in the inn itself or in one of the inn's three adjacent houses, Stafford House, Blantyre, and Ma Bucks, you will love the accommodations. ☛ The wallpaper in Ma Bucks is a delight. All rooms have ☛ extra pillows, which I love.

Excellent food is served in the lovely dining room, or if you prefer, in the Widow Bingham's Tavern. There is an almost hidden booth designed for lovers in here. Blantyre is a grand place for an elegant party.

The Lion's Den is downstairs with entertainment nightly, and it has its own small menu. In warm weather the flower-laden courtyard with its Back of the Bank Bar is a delightful place for food and grog.

Be sure you find an opportunity to visit the Red Lion Inn.

How to get there: Take Exit 2 from the Massachusetts Turnpike and follow Route 102 west to the inn.

🍺

E: Norman Rockwell lived in Stockbridge. The Corner House is a step down the street, so do not miss this great museum of this wonderful artist's works.

olive Metcalf

Colonel Ebenezer Crafts Inn
Fiske Hill, Sturbridge, Massachusetts
01566

Innkeeper: Pat Bibeau
Telephone: 617-347-3313
Rooms: 6, all with private bath; 2 suites.
Rates: $69 to $72, off-season; $75 to $78, in season; suites higher; double occupancy, continental breakfast included.
Facilities: Open all year. Afternoon tea. Publick House nearby for other meals. Small swimming pool. Near Old Sturbridge Village. All major credit cards accepted.

In Colonial times the finest homes were usually found on the highest points of land. Such a location afforded the owners commanding views of their farmland and cattle. It also set them above their contemporaries. So David Fiske, Esquire, a builder, built this house in 1786 high above Sturbridge. The house was magnificently restored by the management of the Publick House and named after the inn's founder, Colonel Ebenezer Crafts.

Patricia Bibeau, the innkeeper, will greet you when you arrive and give you a tour of the house. Do ask to see a bit of the ☞ Underground Railroad of Civil War days. The slave hole is still here. These old homes certainly do take you back in time.

The bedrooms are large, full of good antiques and period reproductions, and offer sweeping views of the surrounding Massachusetts hills. Fruits and cookies are on your night table, and terrycloth robes are provided for the rooms and swimming pool. To make things just right, you will find your ☞ covers neatly folded back at night.

Your breakfast of freshly baked muffins, fresh fruit, juice, and coffee comes with a copy of the morning paper. In the afternoon, tea, sherry, and sweets are served. For lunch and dinner just go two miles down the road to the famous Publick House in Sturbridge. There you will find some of the best food this side of heaven, including those always-present ☞ sticky buns.

How to get there: Take Exit 3 from I-86, and bear right along the service road into Sturbridge. Continue to Route 131 where you turn right. Turn left at Hall Road and then right on Whittemore Road, which becomes Fiske Hill Road.

☖

E: *Buddy Adler, the innkeeper at Publick House, is justifiably proud of this beautiful old house.*

There is no definition of a proper inn.
Like night and day it either is or is not.

119

olive Metcalf

Publick House
Sturbridge, Massachusetts
01566

Innkeeper: Buddy Adler
Telephone: 617-347-3313
Rooms: 18 plus 6 suites, all with private bath, air conditioning, and telephone.
Rates: January 2 through June 30, $59 to $92, double occupancy, EP. July 1 through January 1, $64 to $100, double occupancy, EP.
Facilities: Open all year. Breakfast, lunch, dinner, bar. Ramp
to restaurant. Television in lounge. Gift shop. Near Colonel Ebenezer Crafts Inn and Old Sturbridge Village. All
major credit cards accepted.

It's a real pleasure to me to keep coming back to the
Publick House and finding it always the same, always excellent. As a matter of fact, very little has changed here in the
last 200 years. The green still stretches along in front of it,
and the trees still cast their welcome shade. The Publick
House is still taking care of the wayfarer, feeding him well,

providing a comfortable bed, and supplying robust drink.

The Publick House calendar is fun to read. Throughout the year there are special celebrations for holidays. They *do* keep Christmas here! All twelve days of it. The Boar's Head Procession is truly unique, complete with a roast young suckling pig, a roast goose, and plum pudding. Wow!

Winter weekends are times for special treats, with chestnuts roasting by an open fire, and sleigh rides through nearby Old Sturbridge Village, a happy step backward in time.

The guest rooms are decorated with period furniture, while the penthouse suite has the modern conveniences of a television and king-sized bed. The wide floorboards and beamed ceilings have been here since Colonel Ebenezer Crafts founded the inn in 1771.

The barn, connected to the main house with a ramp, has been transformed into a restaurant. Double doors, topped by a glorious sunburst window, lead into a restaurant that serves hearty Yankee cooking such as delicious Lobster Pie. There is a little musician's gallery, still divided into stalls, that overlooks the main dining room. Beneath this is an attractive taproom, where a pianist holds forth, tinkling out nice noises.

A blueberry patch and a garden which covers more than an acre of land provide the inn with fresh fruit and vegetables during the summer.

I found my way by following my nose around behind the inn to the Bake Shoppe, where every day fresh banana bread, sticky buns, deep-dish apple pies, corn bread, and muffins come out of the ovens to tempt me from my diet! Take some along for hunger pangs along the road.

How to get there: Take the Massachusetts Turnpike to Exit 9. The Publick House is located on the Common in Sturbridge, on Route 131. From Hartford, take I-84 to I-86, Exit 3, which brings you right into Sturbridge.

E: *The inn's good jams, mustards, relishes, chowders, and more can now be enjoyed at home. They are beautifully packaged and mailed to you wherever you wish.*

Longfellow's Wayside Inn
Sudbury, Massachusetts
01776

Innkeeper: Francis J. Koppeis
Telephone: 617-443-8846
Rooms: 10, all with private bath, air conditioning, and telephone.
Rates: $40, single; $45, double, EP.
Facilities: Open all year. Closed Christmas Day. Breakfast for house guests only, lunch, dinner, bar. No room service or television. Pets limited, horses boarded. Gift shop, museum. All major credit cards accepted.

☛ Since 1959 Francis Koppeis has been the innkeeper here, and what a wonderful job he does. Once you meet him you will understand why this famous old inn functions so well and so happily.

Eight generations of travelers have found food and lodging for "man and beast" at the Wayside Inn. Route 20 is the old stagecoach road to Boston, now well off the beaten track. The inn looks much as it did 280 years ago, and still supplies the traveler with hearty food and drink and a comfortable bed.

As with many old buildings, "improvements" were made to the inn in the nineteenth century, but a complete restoration in the 1950s afforded the opportunity to put many things back the way they were in the beginning. Now part of the inn serves as a museum with priceless antiques displayed in their original settings.

There is a large dining room, and several smaller ones, a bar, a gift shop, and a lovely walled garden. At the end of the garden path is a bust of Henry Wadsworth Longfellow, who was inspired by the inn to link together a group of poems known to all schoolchildren as "Tales of a Wayside Inn."

Henry Ford bought 5,000 acres surrounding the inn in 1925, and since then this historic area has been preserved. A little way up the road stand a lovely chapel, the little red schoolhouse that gained fame in "Mary Had a Little Lamb," and a stone gristmill that still grinds grain for the rolls and muffins baked at the inn. I bought some of their cornmeal because ☞ the muffins I ate at the inn were exquisite. This is a most interesting building to visit as all of the equipment in the mill is water-powered.

As a final touch, the inn boasts of the oldest mixed drink in America. It is called ☞ "Coow Woow." You must taste it to discover how well our forefathers lived.

How to get there: From Boston, take the Massachusetts Turnpike to Route 128 north. Take Exit 49 west onto Route 20. Wayside Inn Road is 11 miles west, just off Route 20. From New York, take the Massachusetts Turnpike to Route 495, and go north to Route 20 east. It is approximately 8 miles to Wayside Inn Road.

E: *Only in my country inns do you normally find the innkeeper. And here, when you find Francis, you find a real winner.*

The Wildwood Inn
Ware, Massachusetts
01082

Innkeepers: Margaret and Geoffrey Lobenstine
Telephone: 413-967-7798
Rooms: 5, all share 3 baths.
Rates: $27 to $49, double occupancy, continental breakfast
   included.
Facilities: Open all year. Breakfast only meal served. For a
   small extra charge there are "country yummies" available. BYOB. Swimming, canoeing. MasterCard and Visa
   accepted.

The Wildwood is a modest, small inn in the town of
Ware. Ware, in turn, is a particularly well-preserved old New
England factory town undergoing a well-modulated renova-
tion.
   There is a wraparound porch with rockers, which is my
idea of how to while away a summer afternoon. Inside, the
living room is inviting. It is a family room with puzzles,
games, books, an old spinning wheel, an old cradle, and even

☛ *Life* magazine from 1937. This was really fun to page through.

The rooms are each named for the antique quilts on the beds. They are beautiful. For a modern touch, there are dual-controlled electric blankets on each bed.

While they serve breakfast only, they make this meal rather special with very good homemade breads, popovers, peach butter, and much more. The menus of area restaurants are posted for your use. Also, for your drinks they provide ice and pewter goblets.

The Ware River flows by at the back of the inn property, and you will find a canoe for your use to see more of the river. ☛ There is even an old swimming hole at hand. Such fun. The grounds are spacious. There is a hammock in a tree, a grill if you wish to cook, and just lots of room with beautiful trees for idling about.

How to get there: From the Massachusetts Turnkpike take Exit 8. Go left on Route 32 about 8 miles until it becomes Ware's Main Street. At second set of working traffic lights, turn left onto Church Street. (South Street is to your right.) The inn is on your right, ¾ mile up where the sidewalk ends.

E: *The hammock in the trees. So restful.*

*Cats, birds, flowers and dogs
in companionate confusion are to be found
where hospitality has bested the world of commerce.*

Olive Metcalf

The Williamsville Inn
West Stockbridge, Massachusetts
01266

Innkeepers: Carl and Elizabeth Atkinson
Telephone: 413-274-6580
Rooms: 8 rooms and one suite in winter; 6 additional rooms
    in summer; all with private bath.
Rates: $69 to $115, double occupancy, EP.
Facilities: Closed last three weeks in April and first three
    weeks in November. Breakfast, afternoon tea, dinner.
    Sunday brunch from December to June. Tavern. Swim-
    ming pool, clay tennis court. No pets or small children.
    MasterCard and Visa accepted, but personal checks pre-
    ferred.

    Built in 1797 as a farmhouse, this inn is the second old-
est house in the hamlet of Williamsville. It is a charmer.
    You will find ☞ fireplaces all over the inn; so important
in this part of the world where there is so much winter. The
fireplaces in the dining rooms are raised hearth and espe-

cially warming. There also are fireplaces in two bedrooms, the sitting rooms, and the tavern.

The garden room is a lovely sitting room with a ☛ puzzle going most of the time, books, television, and a music center with stereo and tapes. The comfortable chairs and couches make this such a cozy room for afternoon tea. Tom Ball's Tavern, which is a delight, has nice stencils on the walls.

The guest rooms and suite are so attractively styled and furnished with a sense for old-fashioned grace and comfort.

There are three candlelit dining rooms for your pleasure. Service is unhurried and the food is outstanding. There are seven appetizers. Salmon mousse with green mayonnaise was yummy, and the onion soup is baked to perfection with Swiss and Gruyère cheese and croutons. Here are just a few ideas of the entrees. Boneless chicken stuffed with artichokes, mushrooms, and Gruyère cheese, or scallops baked in a delicately flavored cream sauce with stoneground wheat crumbs. And this is a real winner. ☛ Boneless shell steak coated with crushed peppercorns and served with a brandy cream sauce.

Desserts, of course, are freshly made. Lemon angel pie is so good, and nice liqueur parfaits are always in order. Eating my way through New England is so much fun.

So much to do in this area, from skiing, theater, and antiques, to just loafing at this lovely inn.

How to get there: Take the Massachusetts Turnpike to Exit 1 which puts you on Route 41. Turn left toward Great Barrington. The inn is 4 miles south of the turnpike on your right. From the New York Thruway, follow directions for Berkshires Spur, Exit 33. Go south on Route 22 to Route 102, east on Route 102 to Route 41, south on Route 41 toward Great Barrington.

E: *Fresh flowers all around the inn. How nice.*

Lambert's Cove Country Inn
West Tisbury, Massachusetts
02575

Innkeepers: Banning (Repp) and Libby Repplier
Telephone: 617-693-2298 (Mailing address: Box 422, RFD, Vineyard Haven, MA 02568)
Rooms: 15, all with private bath.
Rates: In season, $80 to $95; off season, $55 to $85; double occupancy, continental breakfast included.
Facilities: Open all year. Dinner daily in season, Thursday through Sunday off season. Sunday brunch. BYOB. Tennis court. Swimming, cross-country skiing, and pond ice skating nearby. Weekly booking preferred in summer, but will take two-day bookings. All major credit cards accepted.

At the end of a tree-shaded country road you will find this gem of an inn. The original house was built in 1790 and over the years it was enlarged and a carriage house and barn added. Today the carriage house and barn have been beautifully renovated for guest use, and half of the rooms are here.

One of the rooms in the carriage house has a ☞ green-house sitting room at one end. Nice to have your cocktails in here and look up at the stars. All of the rooms in the inn are done with imagination. Libby has chosen her wallpapers well. The mattresses are new, and there are plenty of ☞ pillows and lush color-coordinated towels.

When you enter the inn you are in an elegant center hall done in soft beige. Up a magnificent staircase and you are in a restful sitting area with wicker furniture and bookcases full of books. There also is a delightful library, a huge room with walls lined with volumes of books, and furnished with tables for games and really comfortable furniture. On a cold day a fire in the fireplace here feels great.

A big deck opens from the library and dining room and looks out on an apple orchard. There are five decks in all at this inn.

The food is ☞ glorious. Just a hint: shrimp and scallops flamed in cognac and served in a cream herb sauce. Fish, duck, it's all here. At Sunday brunch I had some shrimp salad. It was all shrimp and so good. They have their own ☞ vegetable and herb gardens; a nice touch. Continental breakfast, which is included in the room rate, is delicious, or you may order a full country breakfast.

This is real country. Walk to the Lambert's Cove beach, or just walk anywhere. It's just a beautiful part of the world.

How to get there: After driving off the ferry, take a left, then a right at the next stop-sign intersection. Stay on this road for 1½ miles to Lambert's Cove Road, on your right. Three miles from this point look for the inn sign, on the left.

E: *The jolly innkeeper and Libby have the help of two cats, Poodie and White Feet.*

Olive Metcalf

The Victorian Inn
Whitinsville, Massachusetts
01588

Innkeeper: Martha Flint
Telephone: 617-234-2500
Rooms: 8, all with private bath.
Rates: $79 to $98, double occupancy, Continental breakfast
included.
Facilities: Open all year. Dinner every day except Monday,
Sunday brunch. American Express, MasterCard, and
Visa accepted.

This wonderful Victorian house, built in 1871, has been
treated kindly through the years. One owner (there have
been only three) moved in, decided to go to Paris for a vacation, and was so sick on the boat going over that he never
came home. Fortunately, he had left a caretaker in his house,
so it survived. Several years later when Martha Flint began
searching for a country inn to buy, she came here.

☛ Food is the name of the game here. Beautifully
served and deliciously different, there are twelve dinner en-

trees, some purely classic and others wonderfully unique. Desserts are mind-boggling, and there are exotic coffees, too. Our Victorian forebears should have had it so good.

The rooms are delightful, huge, and furnished in a style to match the house. There are three dining rooms, a library, and an elegant drawing room. The hand-tooled leather wainscoting in one room is a marvel, and one of the bedrooms has its original wallpaper. Martha not only has a flair for food, she also is an exceptionally gifted decorator. The picture wall in the little dining room is fair testimony.

How to get there: From the Massachusetts Turnpike take Exit 11 and drive 14 miles south on Route 122 toward Uxbridge. Turn right onto Linwood Avenue where a sign says, "Entering Uxbridge." The inn is 200 yards around that corner, on the right.

E: *The menu cards, circa 1924, bring a charming touch of Art Deco into this lovely inn.*

olive Metcalf

Le Jardin
Williamstown, Massachusetts
01267

Innkeeper: Walter Hayn
Telephone: 413-458-8032
Rooms: 6, all with private bath.
Rates: Moderate, EP.
Facilities: Closed November 1 to April 1. Lunch, dinner,
    Sunday brunch, bar. MasterCard and Visa accepted.

Hemlock Brook burbles past the sugar maples from
which Walter makes ☞ his own maple syrup. In early spring
each tree is festooned with old-fashioned sap pots, and in the
kitchen there is a huge pot boiling it all down.

The old-fashioned rooms have been renovated to make
your stay more than comfortable. One of the rooms, the one
where I always want to stay, has a whirlpool tub. What
heaven it is to relax in after a long, tiring day.

The menu is excellent. There are ☞ four different salad
choices at lunch, and this to me is ideal. Of course there are
sandwiches and hot selections, also. The dinner menu is

132

more than a little French, though nicely translated into the language of the country. The essence of good food is time, but even the hasty diner is taken care of here with good steaks and chops. The hors d'oeuvres are sinful. The quiche is a Gruyère cheese custard pie. I adore garlic, and ☛ the escargots are a garlic lover's dream come true. The entrees are deliciously different, including ☛ filet of sole topped with spinach and glazed with a classic, delicate white cream sauce, or chicken with mushrooms in light wine cream sauce inside a pastry shell that is light as a feather. The steak tartare, I learned from a reliable source, is the best ever. Desserts are something else. I well remember sitting at the bar talking with Walter while he plied me with three different calorie-laden desserts he had just made.

The bar is delightful, with comfortable bar stools, tables, an old piano, and most important, a red setter who really runs the inn. His name is Strider.

How to get there: The inn is right on Route 7, just 2 miles south of Williamstown, on the right.

♍

E: Terry Perry is manager of the dining room. She does a superb job.

Who can refuse the beckoning
of a cozy country inn?

Olive Metcalf

The Colonial House Inn
Yarmouth Port, Massachusetts
02675

Innkeeper: Malcolm J. Perna
Telephone: 617-362-4348
Rooms: 12, all with private bath.
Rates: $50 to $65, double occupancy, MAP.
Facilities: Open all year. Lunch, dinner, bar. All major credit
    cards accepted.

This was a lovely old sea captain's home, and now is a
lovely old country inn serving some very fine food. At lunch,
one time that I was here, the Quiche du Jour was eggplant
and the Crepe du Jour was chicken. I had to have a taste of
both and they were excellent. I also had ☞ lobster salad that
was superb, not all overdressed with dressing, but done just
right. The chef also whips up daily a different cheese dip for
your crackers.

The dinner menu with beautiful treats from the sea,
Tournedos Rossini, steaks, and chicken, is a joy. Meals are
beautifully served in one of three intimate dining rooms. The

Oak Room is so named because there are ten different kinds of oak in here. The Colonial Room has hand-stencilled walls, and the Common Room is a glass-enclosed veranda with a view of the garden and 🖝 a lovely waterfall and fountain.

The rooms are furnished with antiques, comfortable beds, and tons of charm. All have private baths.

This is a very comfortable place to be, shady old oaks and spacious lawns, a rocker on the porch, and good food, plus all the delights of the Cape right at your doorstep. What more can one ask for.

How to get there: Leave Route 6 (the Mid-Cape highway) at Exit 7 and go north to Route 6-A. Turn right and in about 1¼ miles, midway between Willow and Union streets, on your right is the inn.

E: *Malcolm, the innkeeper, just makes you feel so at home.*

Well cooked, well served, and well eaten,
a meal at a good country inn.

Old Yarmouth Inn
Yarmouth Port, Massachusetts
02675

Innkeeper: Shane E. Peros

Telephone: 617-362-3191

Rooms: 22; 8 in inn, 4 with private bath; in manor house next door, 14, all with private bath, air conditioning, and television.

Rates: $55 to $75, double occupancy, continental breakfast included. Off-season package plans available.

Facilities: Open all year. Lunch, dinner, bar. Theater and beaches nearby. All major credit cards accepted.

Whenever I get the feeling that I want to step back in time, I go to the Old Yarmouth Inn. It is the oldest inn on Cape Cod. Built in 1696 as a wayside staging inn, it has had many owners, but it maintains its charm. The building sags a bit, and when you come in it is like savoring a bit of yesterday, with old leather suitcases, quaint, papered hat boxes, dusty coats, hobnail boots, and ancient horse brasses, all combining to carry you back to the olden days.

There is salt air here, flowers, sunshine, some days a little fog. You can dine indoors or out at the Old Yarmouth Inn, and seafood is, of course, a specialty of the house.

I love eating here because their salad bar is so good. All their salad ingredients, vegetables, and herbs come fresh from the garden; flaky pastries, rich cakes, and hot breads burst from the ovens.

You are only four miles from the famous Cape Playhouse at Dennis, one of the original "straw hat" theaters. There are several fine beaches nearby, and fishing, boating, and day trips to Nantucket and Martha's Vineyard can be arranged.

How to get there: Leave Route 6 (Mid-Cape Highway) at the Yarmouth Port Exit to Route 6A. Turn right, and one mile will bring you to the Old Yarmouth Inn.

E: *The antique bug is gonna bite me, sure's I live, if I keep coming back to Yarmouth Port.*

*The aroma of freshly baking bread told me surely
I was awakening in a good country inn.*

The Wedgewood Inn
Yarmouth Port, Massachusetts
02675

Innkeepers: Jill and Jeff Jackson
Telephone: 617-362-5157
Rooms: 5, all with private bath; one suite.
Rates: $85 to $115, double occupancy, continental breakfast
   included.
Facilities: Open all year. Breakfast is only meal served.
   Menus from area restaurants available. BYOB. Gift shop,
   gallery. No children under 10. MasterCard and Visa ac-
   cepted.

The Wedgewood Inn is a large and beautifully restored
colonial home. Peacefully set among towering trees, back
from one of Cape Cod's busy main streets, the inn was built
in 1812.

It is so attractively furnished. In the entry hall is a built-
in cabinet clock. I've never seen one quite like this. Much of
the inn's furniture is handmade by a local craftsman. He is
wonderfully talented.

Four guest rooms have working fireplaces, and two of the rooms have their ☞ own private screened porch. Most of the beds have either cannonball or pencil posts. They are so very handsome. I was in the one suite, which has a small sitting area with a beautiful bow window. The sunlight is streaming in while I write about this inn.

The breakfast room is elegant. Jill has chosen her dishes ☞ well; they perfectly complement the delicious continental breakfast. Juice is served in a stem glass. I was served fresh fruit, melons, grapes, banana, and strawberries, followed by a basket of delicious blueberry muffins and croissants. They were piping hot. There is another bow window in here full of plants and sunlight. This very relaxed room becomes a common room for guests after breakfast. It is such a nice room to sit in and visit with other guests.

Jill is a talented artist. Her work is in a gallery and unique gift shop behind the inn. You will find works by other artists here too.

If you wish, a picnic lunch is available in the summer. ☞ In a basket are a split of wine, French bread, cheese, and cold cuts. A nice touch.

The inn is on two beautifully groomed acres. What a nice place to take a walk or to sit under a tree and savor the surroundings.

How to get there: From Route 6 (Mid-Cape Highway) take the Willow Street (Exit 7) exit. Turn right toward Yarmouth Port and turn right on Route 6A. The inn is at 83 Main Street.

E: *Take Simon and Schuster for a walk with you. They are two English Labrador retrievers.*

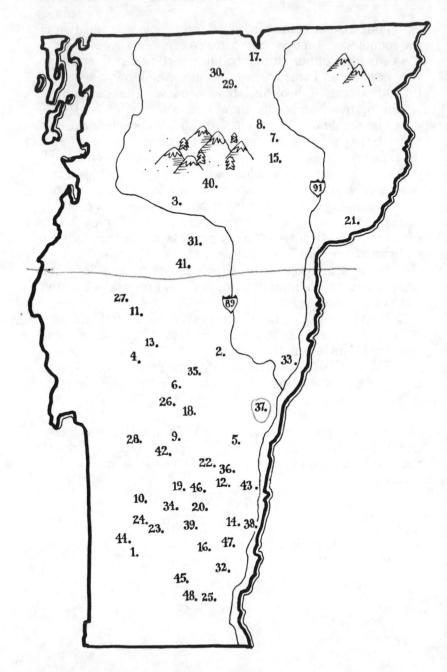

Numbers on map refer to towns numbered
on index on opposite page

Vermont

Olive Metcalf

The Arlington Inn
Arlington, Vermont
05250

Innkeeper: Ron Brunk
Telephone: 802-375-6532
Rooms: 8, all with private bath.
Rates: $48 to $85, double occupancy, EPB.
Facilities: Open all year. Lunch, dinner, Sunday brunch, bar and lounge. Fishing in the famous Battenkill. Master-Card and Visa accepted.

If you want to go back in time, this is the inn to do it in. You can recapture the gracious living of the Victorian period in this historic Greek Revival mansion. It was built in 1848 by Martin Chester Deming. The lovely rooms in the inn are named after Deming family members. There are Sylvester's study, Pamela's suite, Martin Chester's room, Sophie's room, Mary's room, and (I love this name) Chloe's room. The rooms are beautifully furnished and very comfortable.

The parlor or sitting room has a wonderful red oriental

rug on the floor and, in the winter, a fire roaring in the fire-place. The whole inn is magnificent.

The dining rooms are well appointed. There is a new solarium for dining that's perfectly lovely. Plants, fountains, and beautifully landscaped outside. The best part, of course, is the food. There are eight appetizers. I love garlic and the escargots are divine. So is the Fettucine à la Parma. The soups and salads are very special. They have a house dressing I would love to steal, it is so good. The main courses vary from day to day. Salmon, baked with tomato and spinach butter cream sauce, or stuffed with shrimp and topped with a creamy dill sauce. Get the idea? It's great. Sunday brunch is inventive, with a really super menu. Spinach and mushroom salad with a lemon and Pomery mustard dressing is just one selection. You really must go.

How to get there: The inn is located on Route 7 in the middle of Arlington.

☀

E: *The tavern has live entertainment on Friday and Saturday nights. If you get tired, there's a huge oversized rocking chair out on the porch.*

In the autumn, especially as one ages,
a firelit tavern in an excellent inn cannot be bettered
by the smallest mansions in Christendom.

Olive Metcalf

West Mountain Inn
Arlington, Vermont
05250

Innkeepers: Mary Ann and Wes Carlson
Telephone: 802-375-6516
Rooms: 12, 7 with private bath; one suite; one apartment
with housekeeping facilities.
Rates: $40 to $65, double occupancy, EP.
Facilities: Open all year. Breakfast, dinner, Sunday brunch,
bar. James Walker Stoneware Studio in the stable-barn.
Hiking, cross-country skiing, fishing, swimming. All
major credit cards accepted.

Wes and Mary Ann are really the ideal innkeepers.
From the minute you arrive until you leave you feel at home.
The inn is always being updated. There is a new lovely
suite of rooms with a fireplace. There also is a new room and
bath with ☛ complete facilities for the handicapped. The
nicest touch is the thought. There are too few people who
care enough to spend a bit more for other people's comfort.
Wes loves ☛ exotic goldfish. They are in the ponds

around the inn and in a huge aquarium inside that is so nice to watch. Wes also raises African violets. He puts one in each room and invites you to take it home with you. The ☞ bowl of fruit, chocolate bar, and trail map are also for your pleasure.

The rooms, all named for famous people, are quite different. I have stayed in the Norman Rockwell Room, which is up in the treetops. Icelandic comforters and wool blankets are provided to keep you toasty warm.

The inn prepares a great Sunday brunch. Eggs Benedict, omelets, souffles, and many other tempting dishes. And for dinner, well you just know it's going to be good up here. Wes has some excellent wines in an extensive wine cellar. They are the perfect complement to the dinner.

This inn is truly in the country, with 150 acres of trees, trails, pastures, and ponds, all on the mountainside overlooking the village of Arlington. Cross the trout-filled Battenkill River, wind your way over the bridge, which is flower-laden in summer, go by the millhouse, up past the main cottage and spring-fed rock quarry, to the seven-gabled inn. ☞ The grounds around the inn are reputed to have more species of evergreens than any other place in New England. There are lovely trails for hiking, jogging, or cross-country skiing, depending on the season.

How to get there: Midway between Bennington and Manchester, the inn is one-half mile west of Arlington on Route 313. Turn onto River Road, cross the river, and go up the hill until you come to the inn.

Ö

E: *Jim's stoneware studio in the barn displays his work and his wife's. I was fascinated watching him throwing pots on the wheel.*

olive metcalf

Greenhurst Inn
Bethel, Vermont
05032

Innkeepers: Lyle and Barbara Wolf
Telephone: 802-234-9474
Rooms: 12, 4 with private bath.
Rates: $40 to $60, double occupancy, EPB.
Facilities: Closed last two weeks in November. Dinner only
by advance reservations. Other restaurants nearby.
BYOB. Tennis courts. Downhill and cross-country ski-
ing, fishing, hiking, and golfing nearby. American
Express, MasterCard, and Visa accepted.

The Greenhurst Inn was built in 1891. The Wolfs have
restored it so beautifully that it is now listed on the National
Register of Historic Places. There are eight unusually beautiful fireplaces throughout the inn.

As you enter the inn, you are in a huge foyer with one of
the fireplaces and a very interesting staircase. Photographs
that are for sale hang on the walls up the staircase. Lyle does

the framing himself, and very well I might add. He gave me a beautifully mounted shell.

The inn's library has three thousand volumes; ☞ each guest room has a selection. The rooms are decorated with antiques and loving care. Every effort is made to ensure your comfort. ☞ Perrier in every room, mints on the pillows, thick and thirsty towels, electric blankets, and Martha Washington bedspreads. A game cupboard in the north parlor is at your disposal and you are invited to make use of the television and piano in the south parlor. This was said so well in the Wolfs' brochure that I just stole it.

However, the brochure does not say that after dinner Lyle plays the piano while everyone sings. This is a nice touch. The south parlor is a wonderful room to sit in and watch a football game; it is so cozy and comfortable.

A unique touch are the Wolfs' well-done ☞ walking and driving tours. They have little brochures that are fun to read and very informative.

This inn is beautifully furnished, clean as a whistle, and well run. Go and enjoy.

How to get there: From I-89 take Exit 3. Go west on Route 107. The inn is in 3 miles on your left. From Rutland, go east on Route 4, north on Route 100, and east on Route 107.

☙

E: A really interesting zebra finch, called Edwin, and two dachsunds, Muffin and Mopsie, are at the inn.

*A country inn piled high with snow
is a cheery fortress against the cold.*

The Black Bear Inn
Bolton Valley, Vermont
05477

Innkeepers: Sue and Phil McKinnis
Telephone: 802-434-2126
Rooms: 20, all with private bath and color television.
Rates: $39 to $69, double occupancy, EP.
Facilities: Closed mid-April to mid-May and November to
    mid-December. Breakfast, dinner, bar, lounge. Heated
    swimming pool, cross-country skiing, hiking. Tennis,
    fishing, downhill skiing, and golfing nearby. MasterCard
    and Visa accepted.

Four miles up twisting, curving Bolton Valley Road you
come across this contemporary country inn, nestled in the
mountainside as if it has been here forever. Once inside, you
are greeted by the warmth of a woodburning stove and the
aroma of ☛ freshly baked breads and muffins that fills the
air.

Sue is the chef, and she does wonderful things with all
foods. Everything is homemade. ☛ You could stay here for

two weeks and not be served the same thing twice, and that even includes Sue's breads and muffins. A single entree is served each night; however, Sue has something in reserve if a dietary problem arises. I had delicious veal one night. Sue prepared it with great care; believe me, it was perfect. Another night's entree sounds scrumptious: layered fresh salmon and white fish, filled with a julienne of carrots and leeks, and served with a flavorful red wine sauce.

The rooms are well appointed, with color televisions, good beds, and lovely balconies where in summer you may sit and smell the good clean air and enjoy the views. They are spectacular this far up in the mountains.

In summer the grounds are covered with wildflowers. The heated pool beckons you, comfortable lawn furniture is all around, and the beautiful high blue skies are yours to enjoy. The inn's 54 miles of cross-country ski trails make good paths for a hike and you may also borrow a canoe. Tennis is a short stroll away.

☛ Phil, an avid fly fisherman, conducts guided tours of the mountain streams. He knows where to find that trout.

How to get there: Coming west on I-89, take Exit 10 at Stowe-Waterbury. Turn left, then turn right onto Route 2 and follow it 7 miles. Turn right onto Bolton Valley Road in Bolton where I-89 passes over Route 2. The inn is in 4 miles.

E: *My kind of innkeepers who take in stray cats. They have Bruin, Be Scotch, and Charlie. They must be good people.*

The Brandon Inn
Brandon, Vermont
05733

Innkeepers: Jim and Judy O'Connell
Telephone: 802-247-5766
Rooms: 52, 32 with private bath; 8 suites.
Rates: $36 to $56, per room, EP.
Facilities: Open all year. Breakfast, lunch, dinner, bar,
  lounge. Gift shop. Swimming pool, theater, trout fishing.
  Skiing, golfing, tennis, hiking, and antiquing nearby. All
  major credit cards accepted.

Facing the village green in lovely Brandon, Vermont, is
this Queen Anne-style brick inn that is listed in the National
Register of Historic Places. The inn has been here since
1786.

Newly restored, the inn is just beautiful. The living
room with its fireplace and good chairs and couches beckons
you to curl up with knitting or a good book. There are three
dining rooms. One is named after the famous Dr. Seeley Es-
tabrook. The Neshobe Tavern is a friendly spot for lunch.

There is a lovely gift shop right in the inn and nice wicker furniture on the porch.

The guest rooms are large and airy. They all are decorated with colonial wallpapers and period furniture. The rooms without private baths are smaller in size. Take your choice of twin, double, king, or queen beds. ☛ The whole inn is sprinklered for your safety.

The New England-style cooking is very good. Each day the chef prepares different, tasty specials. The wine list is very complete.

The inn's lower barn is the home of Brandon's summer theater and symphony orchestra. The Neshobe River on the inn's grounds provides ☛ excellent trout fishing. There is a crystal clear pool for you to relax in and nearby is plenty of skiing, golfing, tennis, hiking, and antiquing. Come on up and enjoy.

How to get there: The inn is on Route 7 in Brandon.

E: *A stroll down the tree-covered walks after dinner is a nice way to relax.*

The glowing carriage lamp beside the door
of a country inn when viewed through a cold rain
erases the rigors of the day
and promises a fine, fine evening.

olive Metcalf

The Inn at Mount Ascutney
Brownsville, Vermont
05037

Innkeepers: Eric and Margaret Rothchild
Telephone: 802-484-7725
Rooms: 9, 5 with private bath.
Rates: $38 to $65, double occupancy, continental breakfast
   included.
Facilities: Closed mid-March to May 1 and November. Din-
   ner Thursday through Monday, bar. Ice skating, swim-
   ming. Hang gliding and skiing nearby. MasterCard and
   Visa accepted.

   A country inn that serves ☞ tea at four in the afternoon
reminds me of jolly old England. Margaret is a ☞ Cordon
Bleu chef, and the inn features country cooking with a continental flair. The kitchen where Margaret cooks is part of the
dining room, so you watch this fine chef at work.
   The dining room and lounge were converted from an old
carriage house, and they still have the original beams and an
open hearth. There is a small dining room for small con-

ferences or special parties. A small room overlooking the meadow is reserved for breakfasts.

You know how I love inn animals. Here are two Samoyeds, Ebb and Flo, and one cat, Sherlock.

The inn is located directly across the valley from the Mount Ascutney ski area. In winter you can sit in the inn and watch the skiers, ☛ quite a sight at night when the lights are on. Most fantastic of all is to watch the hang gliders leaping into space from Brownsville Rock atop Mount Ascutney. The inn's pond is perfect for ice skating in the winter and swimming in the summer.

As the Rothchilds say, the amount of rest, relaxation, or action you'd like is up to you. This inn is a great spot to rub off the trials of everyday life.

How to get there: Take Exit 8 from I-91 northbound, or Exit 9 southbound. Then take Route 5 to Windsor, and proceed west on Route 44. Look for the inn's sign on your right just as you approach Brownsville.

E: *I am a chocoholic, and Margaret's own creation is called ☛ Chocolate Mount Ascutney. Need I say more. Delicious.*

The snow could pile as deep as a mountain
with no worry for me, for I was in the tavern
of a friendly country inn.

Olive Metcalf

Mountain Top Inn
Chittenden, Vermont
05737

Innkeeper: Bill Wolfe
Telephone: 802-483-2311
Rooms: 36, all with private bath.
Rates: $105 to $156, single; $145 to $196, double occupancy;
　　MAP.
Facilities: Open all year. Breakfast, lunch, dinner, bar,
　　lounge. Heated pool, lake recreation, tennis, lawn
　　games, pitch 'n putt with full-size greens, game room,
　　horseback riding, sauna, whirlpool, exercise room,
　　cross-country skiing, sleigh rides. Downhill skiing
　　nearby. American Express, MasterCard, and Visa ac-
　　cepted.

　　This is one of the most beautiful inns in New England.
The views are breathtaking. At a 2,000-foot elevation the inn
overlooks Mountain Top Lake, which is surrounded by fantastic mountains.
　　Everything is here, including crackling fireplaces,
sauna, whirlpool, and the great-and-only ☛ "Charlie James"

Cocktail Lounge, presided over by a regal fox. There is a spectacular ☞ two-story stairway of glass with natural cherry wood leading down to the lower level, where you will find the dining room and cocktail lounge. Food served here is truly gourmet, with Seafood à l'Indienne, a blend of seafood in a tangy curry sauce with chutney; or braised, boneless chicken breast in honey, rum, and pineapple; or crisp duck, lamb chops, and much more. And all so very good.

The rooms, most overlooking the lake and mountains, are large and luxuriously furnished, with ☞ king, double or twin beds, and all have spacious baths. A nice touch is your bed turned down at night with a maple sugar candy on your pillow.

Here at the inn they have an excellent ski touring program. To go with it is the old horse barn, where you can relax around antique stoves, sip hot apple cider, and discuss cross-country skiing.

There is ample room for all, with the inn's more than 1000 acres. This, with the adjacent National Forest land, gives you sixty-five miles of scenic trails meandering through mountains that are as beautiful to walk as they are to ski.

The inn has ski-sleds, toboggans, and an ice-skating area, and you alpine skiers are but twenty minutes or less from the Pico and Killington slopes.

How to get there: From Rutland, head north on Route 7. Pass the power station, turn right on Chittenden Road, and follow it into Chittenden. Follow the signs up to the inn.

E: ☞ *Sleighs drawn by draft horses are a wonderful yester-year experience.*

olive Metcalf

The Craftsbury Inn
Craftsbury, Vermont
05826

Innkeepers: John and Susan McCarthy
Telephone: 802-586-2848
Rooms: 10, 5 with private bath.
Rates: $85 to $110, double occupancy, MAP. EP rates available.
Facilities: Open all year. Breakfast, dinner, bar. Cross-country skiing. Canoeing, swimming, fishing, horseback riding, tennis, and golfing nearby. MasterCard and Visa accepted.

The inn is a lovingly restored Greek Revival house that was built circa 1850. The little town of Craftsbury, said by *The Boston Globe* to be Vermont's most remarkable hill-town, was founded in 1788 by Colonel Ebenezer Crafts and lies in what is called the Northeast Kingdom. The population today is something less than 700, and that includes Craftsbury, East Craftsbury, and Craftsbury Common.

One year I arrived here on a chilly day in the middle of

June and was greeted by a lovely ☞ fire in the television room. Boy, did it feel good! Speaking of fireplaces, the one in the living room is the original fireplace that warmed the first post office in Montpelier, Vermont's capital.

The rooms here are filled with antique wicker, and the beds have handsome ☞ heirloom quilts. Fresh paint and paper have made this lovely old inn even nicer.

☞ All ice creams, breads, and pastries are prepared here. They also make their own stocks, and this does make a difference in the taste of food.

Country French cooking is how they describe their menu. Cornish game hen with green pepper sauce is but one of the luscious items served. John is the breakfast chef, and he is a whiz at blueberry pancakes, eggs Benedict, and more. The McCarthys raise bees and sell Craftsbury honey, which is a very distinctive honey. They also have their own vegetable garden to ensure freshness.

There is much to do in this area. The McCarthys have just put in a cross-country ski trail that is connected to the Craftsbury Sports Center. In the summer, you can rent a canoe, swim in nearby lakes, fish, horseback ride, play tennis, or play golf at Vermont's oldest course in Greensboro where the greens are fenced to prevent intrusion of the grazing cattle. Throughout July and August the Craftsbury Chamber Players perform every Thursday evening. Come and enjoy.

How to get there: Take I-91 to St. Johnsbury, pick up Route 2 west, and at West Danville take Route 15 to Hardwick. Follow Route 14 north to Craftsbury. The inn is on the right, across from the general store.

E: *John hails from Allentown, Pennsylvania, where I was raised. Small world.*

The Inn on the Common
Craftsbury Common, Vermont
05827

Innkeepers: Penny and Michael Schmitt
Telephone: 802-586-9619
Rooms: 17, 13 with private bath; 5 with a fireplace or wood
    stove; all located in three buildings.
Rates: $50 to $75, double occupancy, MAP.
Facilities: Open all year. Food and drinks for house guests
    only. Heated swimming pool, clay tennis court, English
    croquet. Boating and cross-country skiing nearby. Ski
    touring and ski packages available. MasterCard and Visa
    accepted.

It is a long way up here, but it's worth every mile you
travel to be a guest of the Schmitts.

There are three buildings that make up the inn. The
north annex is on the common with a lovely picket fence
around it. All of its rooms are beautifully appointed. The wallpapers are ☛ Scalamandre reproduction from a South Carolina historic collection. The sheets throughout the inn are

brand new and Marimekko. There's a very unusual sofa, an English knoll; try and figure how the arms go down. Two of the bedrooms in the north annex have a fireplace. One of the bathrooms has such a cute, tiny bathtub. There's a lovely canopy bed in one room and, as Penny says, all the rooms in the inn are either large, medium, or small.

Across the street is the south annex. The guest lounge has a fireplace, comfy sofas, a large television, and ☞ Betamax. There's a library of over seventy-five films on tape so even in bad weather there is something to do. You can fix lunch, make tea, or whatever you wish in the guest kitchen. Two Jotul woodburning stoves keep the rooms warm and cozy.

In the main house is the dining room with a ☞ glass wall overlooking the rose gardens. All the gardens are lovely. Penny has green hands as well as a faithful gardener. The dining room has the perfect atmosphere to savor the sumptuous food. Roast native lamb with sorrel sauce is one entree; veal stew in an orange-lemon sauce is another. Salads are so good. I never had red pepper mousse before and it is delicious. If you are a ☞ vegetarian they are ready to serve you. Cocktail hour in the library is a fun, social time. Michael is bartender. He also selects the dinner wines to complement the meal.

A staff of naturalists run a sports complex near the inn. One hundred and forty acres include lake swimming, sculling, canoeing, cross-country skiing, nature walks, and bird watching. Come on up. There is something for everyone.

How to get there: Follow I-91 to St. Johnsbury, take Route 2 west, and at West Danville take Route 15 to Hardwick. Take Route 14 north to Craftsbury, and continue north into the common. The inn is on the left as you enter the village.

🍺

E: *The solar-heated swimming pool has a little waterfall to let the water in. It disturbs nothing in its peaceful location behind the south annex.*

Olive Metcalf

Shrewsbury Inn
Cuttingsville, Vermont
05738

Innkeepers: Lois and Don Butler, Laurie and Kerry Dillon
Telephone: 802-492-3355
Rooms: 7, all with assigned bath.
Rates: $35, per person, MAP, in fall and winter; $25, per person, EPB, in summer.
Facilities: Closed mid-April to mid-May and November. Breakfast, dinner in fall and winter. Pub lounge. Skiing nearby. MasterCard and Visa accepted.

Lois Butler should have been an interior decorator. She has done such a fantastic job with this marvelous country inn. ☞ All in the family is the theme here. Son, Kerry, is the pub keeper and all-around builder and fixer. Daughter, Pat, is a creative soft sculpture maker. She just finished making Abigail and Aloysius. They live in the upstairs hall.

Kerry's pub is delightful. In one permanent seat sits ☞ Agnes Cornpepper, another lifesize soft sculpture by Pat. No need to ever drink alone here. Agnes is at hand, and so is her friend, Angus. Wine labels cover the bar and are also on the ceiling above the chandelier. Don takes a real pride in his wine list.

The living room is just as inviting. Lois has done a superb job. One dining room is small and formal, and the other is a grand medieval one with a large table that seats six. Each bedroom is done better than the next. They are all large, airy, and beautiful.

Besides being a wonderful decorator, Lois is also a medieval buff. Everyone in son Gil's wedding was dressed in beautiful medieval costumes, all created right here. The costumes hang about the inn.

This truly is an "inn creeper's" delight.

How to get there: Go north on I-91 to Exit 6, then north on Route 103 to Cuttingsville. You may also go north on Route 7, right on Route 140 in Wallingford, and left on Route 103. The inn is on your left just short of the village.

Ⴃ

E: *Mr. Finnegan is the inn cat who looks and acts like one I once had. He has his own* ☞ *needlepoint sign on the front door telling whether he is in or out. Some class!*

olive Metcalf

Dorset Inn
Dorset, Vermont
05251

Innkeepers: Alex and Hanneke Koks, Sissy Hicks
Telephone: 802-867-5500
Rooms: 31, all with private bath.
Rates: $65, single; $90 to $100, double occupancy; MAP.
Facilities: Open all year. Breakfast, lunch in summer and
    fall, dinner, bar. Wheelchair accessibility to dining room.
    Swimming pool. Golf and theater nearby. MasterCard
    and Visa accepted.

Built in 1796, this is the oldest inn in Vermont, and it
has been continuously operated as an inn. Today, the inn has
been ☞ completely restored and recently has been listed in
the National Register of Historic Places. There are wideboard
floors, and beautiful Vermont pine is around the fireplace in
the living room.

While the inn has retained the feeling of the eighteenth
century, it is modern in its conveniences. It has been completely insulated. The bathrooms are new, some of the rooms

162

have been air conditioned, and new, firm mattresses have been purchased. The whole inn is clean and neat.

The breakfast and luncheon room has a lovely old ☛ lion fountain. I love the sound of the water. The bar-lounge is spacious. There is no crowding in this large and rambling inn.

☛ Sissy Hicks presides over the kitchen and is a very well known lady. Some of the luncheon items are curried mussels and noodles on spinach, beef, and scallions with rice, and biscuit-crust apple and turkey pie. Sounds great! At dinner the appetizers are numerous. One is New England cheese chowder. Sissy's entrees are really different. Breast of chicken with pear and cider cream. Or veal medallions with a lime-ginger sauce. The breakfast menu is pure ambrosia. I like it here. I think you can tell.

The Dorset Field Club, sporting one of Vermont's oldest nine-hole golf courses, ☛ extends golf privileges to guests of the inn. If culture turns you on, the Southern Vermont Arts Center and the Dorset Playhouse will provide the comedy and drama of good theater.

How to get there: Leave I-91 at Brattleboro and go left on Route 30 to Dorset. Or take Route 7 to Manchester Center, and go north on Route 30.

E: *A few years ago, before I ever thought I would be involved in this book, I stayed here on a ski trip. The inn is as lovely now as it was then.*

*When you have but one night to spend
which inn to choose is as difficult as
the choice you had years ago at the
penny candy counter, and equally rewarding.*

olive Metcalf

Village Auberge
Dorset, Vermont
05251

Innkeepers: Alex and Hanneke Koks
Telephone: 802-867-5715
Rooms: 4, all with private bath; 2 suites.
Rates: $50 to $85, EP.
Facilities: Closed April 15 to May 15, and November 15 to
    December 15. In summer closed Mondays, and in winter
    closed Mondays and Tuesdays. Breakfast, dinner, bar.
    Cornucopia Antique Shop. Tennis, golfing, swimming,
    and skiing nearby. MasterCard and Visa accepted.

Stained-glass windows are always lovely, and the one
that separates the bar from the dining room is especially well
done. Hanneke is an interior decorator and fashion designer
by profession. ☛ The inn reflects her talents.

The dining room is just beautiful. It seats only forty-five
people and is done in shades of warm green. The stunning
place plates are a floral pattern from Villeroy and Boch, and
Botanica made in Luxembourg. Needless to say, the food

164

served here is extravagant, with hors d'oeuvres and potages such as Prosciutto and Stewed Prune Relish, Cream of Mustard Soup, and my love, Escargots in Garlic Butter. A special of the day and many more entrees, from veal, steak, sweetbreads, and lamb to fish of the season are always available. Ready for dessert? You must come and taste for yourself and leave your calorie counter in your desk.

The bar is done in rich, warm wood, and is a beauty. There is a fireplace in the lounge. The bedrooms are lovely and the suites are marvelously spacious.

The innkeepers are extremely experienced. Alex attended hotel management school in The Hague, and he has owned and operated restaurants in Haarlem, Holland and Marlboro, Vermont. Hanneke, along with her other talents, operates a unique antique shop right on the inn property.

There is much to do in this area. Three downhill ski areas, cross-country skiing, and the Dorset Playhouse are less than a walk around the block from the inn. Nearby are tennis, golf, and swimming.

How to get there: Take I-91 north to Brattleboro, then take Route 30 to Manchester. At blinking lights take a right and an immediate left, which brings you back on Route 30 north. Go about 5½ miles north of Manchester. Look for the inn on your right.

E: *I have a special fondness for bay windows, and the dining room has a beauty.*

Olive Metcalf

The Waybury Inn
East Middlebury, Vermont
05740

Innkeepers: Betty and Jim Riley
Telephone: 802-388-4015
Rooms: 12, 8 with private bath.
Rates: $35, single; $55 to $79, double occupancy, EPB.
Facilities: Open all year. Dinner, Sunday brunch, bar, lounge. Swimming, fishing, hiking, and skiing nearby. MasterCard and Visa accepted.

The Waybury Inn was built in 1810 as a stagecoach stop at the base of the Green Mountains. Known as the Glen House, the inn provided rooms for women workers at the local glass factory for many years.

Guest accommodations today have very comfortable doubles, twins, or king-sized beds. The have 🖝 lovely Bombay fans on the ceilings, and all are carpeted, except one room that has the original stencils on the wood floor. There are nice 🖝 fluffy towels. The whole inn is spotlessly clean.

Throughout the inn are hand-hewn beams pine wide-board floors, and friendly fireplaces. The Waybury Pub is a fun place that is available for small parties. There are two fireplaces down here. The pub is used by the Middlebury Artists Association for the display of their art works. This is a nice touch.

Table napery is lovely, and so is the way the wine is displayed. The menu is very extensive and different. On the cover it reads: "The Waybury Inn stands as a symbol of tradition in country inns. Recognized as a National Historic Place, the Waybury Inn has delivered comfortable lodging and fine meals to travelers since 1810." Nine appetizers are listed. A real favorite seldom seen on a menu is ☞ Seviche. This is fresh bay scallops in citrus juices. I like a restaurant that offers roast leg of lamb, sliced thick or thin, your choice. Curried lamb is also offered. Vegetable crepe is another dish I have not seen elsewhere. The desserts are homemade and the wine list is very impressive.

How to get there: The inn is located 29 miles north of Rutland, Vermont, on Route 125 in East Middlebury.

E: *Take a swim in the local swimming hole, a natural gorge in the rocky river that splashes nearby.*

If I ever find an inn that bakes fresh macaroons daily, I shall rent a room for a hundred years.

Old Town Farm Lodge
Gassetts, Vermont
05144

Innkeepers: Fred and Jan Baldwin
Telephone: 802-875-2346
Rooms: 10, 3 with private bath.
Rates: $35 to $45, per person, double occupancy, MAP. EP
and EPB rates available on request.
Facilities: Open all year. Closed Thanksgiving and Christmas. Breakfast, dinner. BYOB. Parking. Horseback riding, cross-country skiing. Downhill skiing, swimming, golfing, and fishing nearby. American Express, MasterCard, and Visa accepted.

If you like to ski, throw everything in the car and head for the Old Town Farm Lodge. It is located ☞ in the heart of eleven ski areas, both downhill and cross-country, and the Baldwins can direct you to where the skiing is best. They also have their own limited cross-country trails right at the lodge.

Winter isn't the only fun time of year to be here. Hunting, fishing, hiking, golfing, and swimming are close at hand.

168

The Baldwins have it all, and without the swinging nightlife enjoyed by the singles crowd. The lodge is busiest during the foliage season, so be sure to reserve ahead if you are going leaf-peeping.

☛ Cycle Inn Vermont is a bicycle touring service put together by a few Vermont inns, Old Town being one of them. This is a wonderful way to see New England, and also to stay at a different inn each night. Your luggage is transported by car for you.

The Baldwins are busy all year, restoring and rebuilding the farmhouse that is over 100 years old. It was once known as the Town Farm, because the indigent of the neighborhood were given food and lodging here, in return for a hard day's work. The lodge is heated almost entirely by wood. There is a huge stone fireplace in the common room where the roaring fire is almost hypnotizing to watch.

One main course is offered each night at dinner. Some examples are baked boneless chicken breast with spinach souffle, and Pork Royale. These are preceded by homemade soups, such as carrot or cream of zucchini, and accompanied by homemade anadama bread. Desserts are delicious, featuring homemade pies or peaches and cream cheesecake. And Vermont Maple Syrup is served exclusively, of course.

How to get there: Gassetts is 5 miles north of Chester Depot on route 10.

E: *The handmade spiral staircase that curves to the second floor is beautiful, and it has been painstakingly restored to its original condition.*

Olive Metcalf

Blueberry Hill
Goshen, Vermont
05733

Innkeeper: Tony Clark
Telephone: 802-247-6735 or 802-247-6535
Rooms: 8, all with private bath.
Rates: In summer, $56; in winter, $72; double occupancy, MAP.
Facilities: Closed April to May 15 and November. Breakfast, packed lunch is available, dinner. BYOB. Cross-country skiing, swimming, fishing. MasterCard and Visa accepted.

The inn is a cross-country skier's dream come true. It is nestled at the foot of Romance Mountain in the Green Mountain National Forest and is surrounded by good clean air and well-groomed snowy trails. From the inn brochure I quote: "The Blueberry Hill Ski Touring Center, across from the inn, devotes itself to cross-country skiers of all ☞ ages and abilities. Inside the fully equipped Ski Center are retail and rental departments, a waxing area, repair shop, and an expert staff to see that you are skiing better with less effort. Upstairs you can relax, make friends, and share the day's events in our lounge with its large windows, comfortable seating, and old wood stove. Surrounding the Ski Center are seventy-five kilometers of both challenging and moderate terrain. A loop around Hogback, a race to Silver Lake, or just making tracks in a snow world all your own . . . the activities never cease—from seminars, waxing clinics, night and guided tours, to the 🖝 sixty-kilometer American Ski Marathon."

In the summer the ski trails are used for hiking, walking, or running. There is a pond for swimming and streams and lakes for fishing.

The inn is a restored 1813 farmhouse. Dinner is served family style in a lovely, candlelit dining room. There are four courses served in an unhurried, comfortable way. While I was here dinner included such delicious things as cold cantaloupe soup, scallion bread, broiled lamb chops with mint butter, stir-fried asparagus, lemon meringue tarts, and 🖝 homemade ice creams. Tony's son made strawberry ice cream, and it was so good. Breakfasts are served in the greenhouse just off the kitchen. It is full of glorious plants. Three of the guest rooms are out here, just beyond the greenhouse.

There are plenty of books to read, and the rooms are comfortable with many antiques, quilts, and 🖝 hot water bottles on the backs of the doors. Honest, they are there.

How to get there: From Rutland take Route 7 north to Brandon, then Route 73 east for 6 miles. Turn left at the inn's sign, and follow the signs up the mountain on a dirt road to the inn.

E: *Their upside-down gardens hanging from the ceiling beams are a colorful and imaginative use of straw flowers.*

olive Metcalf

The Old Tavern
Grafton, Vermont
05146

Innkeeper: Lois M. Copping
Telephone: 802-843-2231
Rooms: 35, all with private bath, in 6 houses.
Rates: $45 to $85, single or double occupancy, EP.
Facilities: Closed in April, and on Christmas Eve and Christmas Day. Breakfast, lunch, dinner, bar, television in lounge, parking, elevator. Swimming, tennis, nature walks. No credit cards accepted.

If you're looking for perfection in a country inn, go to a charming Vermont village called Grafton and you'll find the Old Tavern. It has been operated as an inn since 1801. Since 1965, when the inn was purchased by the Windham Foundation, it has been restored and is now one of those superb New England inns we are all seeking.

When you turn your car off pounding interstate highways to the tree-shaded route that winds to this quaint village, you step back in time. The loveliest of the old, combined

172

with the comfort of the new, makes this an unbeatable inn. No grinding motors can disturb your slumber when you are in ☞ the best beds in all New England. The sheets and towels are the finest money can buy, and there are extra pillows and blankets in each room. The spacious rooms are filled with antiques, all in mint condition.

There is no "organized activity" at the Old Tavern. ☞ The swimming pool is a natural pond, cool and refreshing. There are tennis courts nearby, and marked trails in the woods for walkers. This is the place to calm your spirits and recharge your batteries.

The cocktail barn is charming, connected to the inn by a covered walk. There are flowers everywhere, hanging in baskets, in flower boxes, and on various tables in the gracious public rooms. The food is excellent, with unusual soups, varied entrees, all cooked well, and served by pleasant waitresses.

☞ Up the street a bit there is a six box stall stable that will accommodate guest horses, plus a four-bay carriage shed, if you care to bring your own carriage. All this for the exclusive use of Old Tavern guests.

How to get there: From I-91 take Exit 5 at Bellows Falls. As you come down the exit ramp, watch for Route 121, which you'll take to the inn.

☒

E: *The houses across the street that are also part of the inn are enchanting.*

Highland Lodge
Greensboro, Vermont
05841

Innkeepers: Willie and David Smith
Telephone: 802-533-2647
Rooms: 11, all with private bath; 11 cottages.
Rates: $75 to $100, double occupancy, MAP.
Facilities: Closed April 1 to May 25, and after foliage season
    to mid-December. Breakfast, lunch, dinner. Beer and
    wine license only, setups are available. Parking. Swim-
    ming, boating, tennis. Golfing and horseback riding
    nearby. MasterCard and Visa accepted.

    I've been saying for years that the Highland Lodge is
the place to get away from it all, and I still feel that way. With
peace and quiet, delicious home-cooked meals, and the delightful Smith family, you can recharge your batteries for life
easily. ☛ Caspian Lake, with the lodge's own beach house, is
just across the road, with swimming, canoeing, sailing,

and fishing. Tennis, golf, and riding are available for those inclined.

People come back year after year to this friendly place. There are book-lined walls, puzzles to while away a long afternoon, but mostly, a good mix of genuine, down-home folksiness. It comes over you as soon as you walk through the door. There is a recreation house with supervised play for the youngsters, so a stay here can be a real vacation for parents.

In the fall this is one of the great spots for foliage, and it isn't far to the White Mountains or the Green Mountains. And cross-country skiing in winter is a delight in this unspoiled country. This area is personally recommended by my publisher, who used to summer in Greensboro. The rooms are decorated beautifully and are very comfortable.

How to get there: Greensboro is 35 miles northeast of Montpelier. Take I-91 to St. Johnsbury and follow U.S. 2 west to West Danville. Continue west on Vermont 15, to intersection with Vermont 16 about two miles east of Hardwick. Turn north on 16 to East Hardwick and follow signs west to Greensboro, at the south end of Caspian Lake. Highland Lodge is at the north end of lake on the road to East Craftsbury.

♆

E: The food served here is outstanding.

> "Drink wine, and live here blitheful while ye may;
> The morrow's life too late is, live to-day."
> —Herrick

olive Metcalf

Three Mountain Inn
Jamaica, Vermont
05343

Innkeepers: Charles and Elaine Murray
Telephone: 802-874-4140
Rooms: 9, 8 with private bath; 2 housekeeping cottages available by the week.
Rates: $60 to $70, per person, MAP.
Facilities: Closed April to June 15, except for special fishing weekends. Breakfast, dinner, pub, lounge. Swimming pool, cross-country skiing. Downhill skiing, tennis, golfing, fishing, and horseback riding nearby. No credit cards accepted.

The inn is well named, since it is within a few minutes of Stratton, Bromley, and Magic Mountains. Mount Snow is also within easy range. Skiers should love this location. Cross-country buffs will find a multitude of trails beginning at the inn's doorstep, including a ☞ dramatic trail along the long defunct West River Railroad bed.

This small, authentic country inn was built in the

1780s. The living room has a large, roaring fireplace, complete with an original Dutch oven. The floors and walls are of wide, planked pine, and there are plenty of comfortable chairs. A picture window offers views of the Green Mountains to complete the scene.

A cozy lounge and bar area make you feel very comfortable for sitting back to enjoy good conversation and a before or after dinner drink. ☞ A good wine selection is at hand.

The rooms are tastefully decorated. One room has a four-poster, king-sized bed in it. Another has a private balcony overlooking the swimming pool and garden.

Dinners are a special treat. The menu changes frequently, and you always can be assured of the freshest meats, fish, and vegetables available. Breads, soups, and desserts are all homemade. There are three dining rooms, one with a library, and dinner is always a candlelight affair.

How to get there: Follow I-91 to Brattleboro and take the second exit to Route 30, to Jamaica.

E: *There are guided tours for fly fishermen on the West and Battenkill rivers. Write for these package deals, and remember you will eat what you catch.*

> *If you have never been drawn shivering*
> *from the warmth of a good bed*
> *by the sizzling lure of bacon on the grill,*
> *you have never been in a country inn.*

olive Metcalf

Jay Village Inn
Jay, Vermont
05859

Innkeepers: Bob and Jane Angliss and family
Telephone: 802-988-2643
Rooms: 14, 10 with private bath.
Rates: In winter, $62, per person, double occupancy, MAP,
    includes gratuities. Rest of year, $22, per person, double
    occupancy, EPB.
Facilities: Closed last two weeks of April. Breakfast, dinner,
    Sunday brunch, bar. Television in lounge. Trout brook,
    swimming pool. Golf and tennis nearby. Cross-country
    and downhill skiing 3 miles away. MasterCard and Visa
    accepted.

When you get to Jay you are nearly in Canada, so this
makes the Jay Village Inn my most northern Vermont inn.
Nestled at the foot of Jay Peak, this is a delightful country
inn. Come any time of the year and enjoy the fireplace lounge
and bar. It is noted for its après-ski especially, but it's equally
pleasurable any season. Sip ☛ a hot buttered rum and enjoy

178

the flaming fire. They have a player piano and some great old songs. Do any of you remember "The Teddy Bear's Picnic"? It is here.

Bob is the breakfast chef, and he certainly turns out a good meal. He makes a full breakfast, and the choices are varied and hearty. In addition, Bob does a good deal of cooking for other meals. He makes homemade bread every day, and you must go and taste his sauces and soups. Crème Crecy is a traditional carrot-based potage with seasonings and a dollop of fresh cream. He also is the originator of the Chef's Pâté, minced veal and pork laced with brandy and spices. The inn still serves the best rack of lamb I have had in many a country mile.

Sunday brunch begins with a glass of chilled champagne or a mimosa. This is a nice touch. Strawberry soup is a real winner. Wild blueberry pancakes or apple pancakes are also served. It may be a long way up here, but boy, will you have a happy tummy.

If you are a skier you must know that Jay Peak has one of the longest, most dependable ski seasons in the east. The aerial tramway is a "trip," and there are exciting trails for every level of skiing, beginner to expert.

For other seasons there are two golf courses in the vicinity, and if you are a hiker you are close to the Long Trail. A relaxing summer day can be spent by the inn's pool that has a nice carpet-covered deck.

The dining room has been redecorated with crisp beige linens and nice new curtains. The guest rooms all have new mattresses so you will sleep well.

How to get there: Take I-91 to Exit 26. Take Route 5 north to Route 14 north to Route 100, a total of 8 miles. Go left here for 6 miles to Route 101, then right for 3 miles to Route 242. Go left on Route 242 for one mile to the inn.

E: *An independent spirit and a loveable dog is Barney, the Saint Bernard.*

Mountain Meadows Lodge
Killington, Vermont
05751

Innkeepers: Bill and Joanne Stevens
Telephone: 802-775-1010
Rooms: 15, 12 with private bath.
Rates: In winter, $31 to $42, per person, MAP. Lower rates in summer.
Facilities: Closed in May. Breakfast and dinner for house guests. BYOB. Television, game room. Hiking, swimming, boating, fishing. Cross-country and downhill skiing nearby. MasterCard and Visa accepted.

It was here that I met Bear, a mostly red setter, who had just come off the Appalachian Trail carrying his own backpack. True, I swear. If you are hiking inn-to-inn this is the sourthernmost inn and a good place to start.

The inn is very casual and relaxed and overlooks 110 acres of lovely Kent Lake. The lake is stocked with ☛ rainbow trout and largemouth bass. There are boats and canoes for your pleasure. You can swim either in the lake or in the inn's pool.

Vermont home-style cooking at its very best is featured. The inn has a BYOB bar and a game room.

The rooms are fully carpeted and comfortable as sin, but the place to really relax is the large living room, which has a big fireplace and lots of windows overlooking the lake. The view is lovely.

The inn has ☞ the largest ski touring center in the area, and for you more daring types, Killington and Pico Peak alpine areas are but minutes away.

How to get there: The inn is 10 miles east of Rutland, just off Route 4. Follow Route 4 from Rutland for 12 miles, and at Thundering Brook Road you will come to the inn sign. Turn left. The inn is ¼-mile beyond.

E: *Susqua is the gentle inn dog with only three paws.*

If all inns were alike they simply would not be inns.

181

The Vermont Inn
Killington, Vermont
05751

Innkeepers: Alan and Judy Carmasin
Telephone: 802-773-9847
Rooms: 14, 8 with private bath.
Rates: In summer, $30 to $42, per room, EPB; in winter, $35
   to $48, per person, MAP.
Facilities: Closed in May. Restaurant closed Mondays. Din-
   ner, bar. Television, game room, sauna, pool, tennis, law
   games. Gondola ride, summer theater, Norman Rock-
   well Museum, farmers' market, and skiing nearby.
   American Express, MasterCard, and Visa accepted.

You may be greeted at the door of this friendly red house
by a companionable Labrador named Tammy. Judy and Alan
are always here, and a nicer young couple you'll have to
travel a long way to find.
   The Vermont Inn is well known locally for the fine food
served in the lovely dining room. As a matter of fact, the restaurant has been ☞ awarded the silver spoon award for the

second consecutive year. Just a sample of the food is tender-loin of pork, so different, sautéed with fresh mushrooms and flavored in sherry wine with cream. Steak teriyaki is excellent, as is their good selection of fish dishes. There is also a children's menu, a true help for the traveling family.

The inn guests are a mixed bag. You'll run into young professional people from Boston or New York, a grandparent or two, families, anyone from honeymooners to golden oldies. Alan has cultivated a fine wine cellar to enhance the good food.

When the Carmasins took over the inn they redecorated all the rooms. Floors were recarpeted or painstakingly restored to the original wood. What a labor of love! This old house has sturdy underpinnings. Some of the original beams still have the bark on them, and how the rocks of the foundation were ever put in place I cannot imagine. Everything was changed around, the old dining room became a lounge to make the inn cosier, so take advantage of the beautiful view of Killington, Pico, and Little Killington, straight ahead across the valley.

Tammy's "Instructions to Guests" on how she is to be treated should be on the *must* list for every inn dog. They are tacked up at the desk. Drop in and read them, then stay awhile.

How to get there: The inn is 6 miles east of Rutland, via Route 4. It is also 4 miles west of the intersection of Route 4 and Route 100 north (Killington Access Road).

E: *There is a secluded stream, so quiet, just right for meditating, or, if you are brave, to put a foot in.*

The style is the inn itself.

Nordic Inn
Landgrove, Vermont
05148

Innkeepers: Tom and Judy Acton
Telephone: 802-824-6444
Rooms: 5, 3 with private bath.
Rates: $53 to $70, per person, MAP.
Facilities: Closed end of March to Memorial Day weekend.
Breakfast, lunch, dinner, Sunday brunch, bar, lounge.
Cross-country skiing, ski shop, hiking. Golf, tennis,
horseback riding, and downhill skiing nearby. All major
credit cards accepted.

    I think it's nice to be able to go to an inn and have almost everything you want right there, so you do not have to go running around in your car.

    This inn has ☛ twenty kilometers of groomed and marked trails through the Green Mountain National Forest. The varied terrain takes you through a winter wonderland, from stands of towering red pine, over beaver ponds, through meadows, and even past an old colonial cemetery on a hilltop.

There are guided backpack tours from the inn, and, of course, downhill skiing is nearby at Bromley, Magic, and my personal favorite, Stratton. To make it even nicer for you there is a ski shop right here and plenty of instructors, so come on up.

At other times of the year you can hike the trails or go fishing. Nearby is horseback riding, golf, and tennis. Summer theater is handy in Dorset and Weston.

The bar and lounge area has a large stone fireplace; very cozy on a snowy day. There are tables and chairs as well as a nice bar in here. The solarium is lovely. Imagine having some of their delicious food and watching the snow fall or the ski school in action. A very, very relaxing place to be.

The food is glorious, dinner or brunch. They serve dishes like a superb seafood salad, Mussels Provençale, veal and chicken done in special ways, and broiled loin lamb chops served with a Dijon mustard, ginger, and rosemary sauce.

The bar has a special drink, Hot Glögg containing vodka, cognac, red wine, slivered almonds, raisins, and cinnamon. Wow!

How to get there: The inn is between Bromley and Londonderry on Route 11, 14 miles east of Manchester.

☀

E: *Sissy, the inn cat, has the most unusual amber-cinnamon eyes I have ever seen on a cat. She shares the inn with Red, a golden retriever.*

> *Having had an excellent meal and*
> *a lovely evening, I tucked myself in bed knowing I*
> *had sinned but it did not seem to matter.*

185

The Village Inn
Landgrove, Vermont
05148

Innkeepers: Jay and Kathy Snyder
Telephone: 802-824-6673
Rooms: 20, 16 with private bath.
Rates: In winter, $30 to $54, per person, double occupancy,
   MAP; in summer, $35 to $55, per room, EPB.
Facilities: Closed April 1 to June 15, and October 20 to mid-
   December. Dinner, except on Wednesdays in summer.
   Pool, tennis, pitch-and-putt, bumper pool, Ping-Pong,
   volleyball, cross-country skiing. Downhill skiing nearby.
   All major credit cards accepted.

The Snyders, cordial, welcoming folks, have a friendly
relaxed inn way out in the country and not, despite the
name, anywhere near a village. I've always wondered how
this inn came to be named Village Inn.

The architecture is peculiar to Vermont, with one building built onto another building, onto another. It turns out to
be charming. There are some old rooms, and some new ones,

186

all spick-and-span and comfortable. The first part of the inn was built in 1810, and the last additions were made in 1976.

The snows lie heavy around here, and cross-country skiing on miles and miles of marked trails is wonderful. You are only a short hop by car to Bromley, Stratton, Snow Valley, Magic Mountain, or Okemo. Try your luck at ☞ snowshoeing or ice skating, and after a long day revive yourself in ☞ the whirlpool spa, and then enjoy the fireside warmth in the Rafter Room lounge. There is ☞ a couch in here that needs to be seen!

Summer brings other delights, a neat heated swimming pool, two plexipave tennis courts, hiking through the National Forest, and four-hole pitch-and-putt golf. Summer theater is nearby and riding and hunting are available in season.

How to get there: Via I-91, use Exit 6 at Rockingham. Take Route 103 to Chester, then Route 11 to Londonderry. Continue past the shopping center for approximately a half mile, and turn right on Landgrove Road. Go 4 miles to the Village of Landgrove. Bear left after crossing the bridge and continue one mile to the inn, on your right.

From Manchester, take Route 11 past Bromley Ski Area, and turn left into Peru Village. At the fork in Peru bear left and continue 4 miles through the National Forest to the crossroads in Landgrove. Turn left toward Weston, and the inn will be on your right.

ᕲ

E: *Lead me to the bumper pool. I must keep in practice; it's my favorite sport.*

Olive Metcalf

The Highland House
Londonderry, Vermont
05148

Innkeepers: Chris and Tim Hill
Telephone: 802-824-3019
Rooms: 7, with shared baths.
Rates: $45 to $51, double occupancy, EPB.
Facilities: Closed mid-April to mid-May. Dinner Wednesday
    to Sunday. Beer and wine license. Skiing, hiking, fish-
    ing, and hunting nearby. MasterCard and Visa accepted.

The Highland House dates back to 1840, and the wide
pine floorboards are good proof of its age. The rooms are
comfortable and neat. And the innkeepers are young and energetic. Here is another inn that will improve a bit each year
because of its fine innkeepers.

There is a wood stove in the dining room, and lovely
plants are in abundance. Fresh food is the order of the chef.
All ☞ the sauces, salad dressings, breads, and desserts are
made right here under her watchful eye. Roast New England
duckling, a favorite of mine, is slow-roasted until crisp, and

then is served with the chef's sauce du jour. To give you just another touch of her cooking, Veal Milanaise is served with Spaghetti Marinara. ☞ This is fine food served in a lovely small dining room.

Magic Mountain and Stratton Mountain are nearby ski areas. The Green Mountain National Forest is close at hand for hiking, fishing, hunting, or cross-country skiing in season.

This is a wonderful part of New England right on famed Route 100 which runs up the spine of Vermont. Plenty of antique shops and other shops to keep you busy.

How to get there: Take Exit 2 from I-91 at Brattleboro. Take Route 30 north to Route 100, and the inn is just north of town on Route 100.

🍷

E: *The inn sits back from this fine old road in the midst of a lovely, expansive lawn.*

> *Insomnia is almost a blessing if you are in an inn within easy earshot of a country church bell.*

Olive Metcalf

Rabbit Hill Inn
Lower Waterford, Vermont
05848

Innkeepers: Eric and Beryl Charlton and son Paul
Telephone: 802-748-5168
Rooms: 20, all with private bath.
Rates: $35 to $70, double occupancy, EP.
Facilities: Closed four weeks in early spring and after foliage
   season to mid-December. Breakfast, dinner, bar. Cross-
   country skiing, trout fishing. MasterCard and Visa ac-
   cepted.

There is a sign in the dining room in Gaelic. It means
100,000 welcomes, and these warm, friendly innkeepers
mean just that.

The dining room has wide floorboards, a Franklin-type
wood stove, and pewter and brass from the Charltons' own
collection. It is bright, airy, and the setting for fine food. The
innkeeper's selection is a nightly dinner special chosen from
the best the kitchen can conjure up, which is always a good
choice. There are, of course, many other entrees including

steak, lamb, veal, fish, and chicken. Do try ☞ Steak Farci, pan broiled fillet of beef stuffed with mushrooms and shallots, and served with a red wine sauce. Delicious!

Bedrooms are large and comfortable. Some have fireplaces, ☞ canopy beds, love seats, and all face east with a view of the Presidential Range. The porch on the second floor is a special spot for me to just sit, rock, and look.

There also is a library on the second floor full of good books. Please, when you take a book from this inn, or indeed any inn, send it back when you are finished.

The Briar Patch is the ski shop. It has instructions and rentals. Trails are beautiful, winter and summer, winding along Mad Brook down to the Connecticut River, or up into the woods by an active beaver colony. The old mill dam across the street from the inn has recently been repaired, ☞ offering trout fishing on the premises, and for the hardy an invigorating swim in a pond fed by clear mountain streams.

There is a lot of history up here, and this lovely village is on the most photographed list in Vermont.

How to get there: Take Route 2 east from St. Johnsbury and turn right onto Route 18. Or coming from Route 5, take Route 135 east to Lower Waterford.

E: *Many interesting musicians live nearby, and they wander into the inn to entertain. How nice.*

> *"Venite ad me ownes qui stomacho laboratoratis*
> *et ego restaurabus vos."*
> *"Come to me all whose stomachs cry out in anguish*
> *and I shall restore you."*

The Governor's Inn
Ludlow, Vermont
05149

Innkeepers: Charlie and Deedy Marble
Telephone: 802-228-8830
Rooms: 8, 6 with private bath.
Rates: $60, per person, double occupancy, MAP.
Facilities: Closed in April. Breakfast, dinner. Picnic hampers available for lunch. Bar. Skiing, boating, fishing, and numerous historical attractions nearby. All major credit cards accepted.

Deedy is the chef and she really does justice to the title. All the ☞ food is prepared each day for that day. She does not buy any pre-packaged portion-control type foods and there is no microwave oven. Breakfast may feature the Governor's Special Breakfast Puff or Charlie's nearly world famous ☞ Rum Raisin French Toast. In the picnic hamper for lunch you may find the Governor's Braised Quail, or cucumber and dill butter sandwiches with Pacific smoked salmon. Sounds so nice and tastes so great by the side of a bubbling brook or any other spot in this marvelous countryside.

Dinner is a grand six-course affair. I do not care for bluefish, but if I did, I'd surely have it here. It's flambéed with gin! Salads are different. One I like is Strawberry Chardonnay with Champagne. The after-dinner coffees and Victorian tea are also special.

I think you get the message. The food is excellent.

The dining room where you enjoy this good food has restful blue tablecloths and a beautiful collection of ornate tea cups, added to quite often by contented guests. The parlor has a magnificent 1895 marbleized slate corner fireplace, a real work of art. The Governor of Vermont who lived here surely had a beautiful home.

The bedrooms are so attractive, with lovely wallpapers. The beds have all new linen and a ☛ flannel top sheet to boot. There's one brass bed over 100 years old.

How to get there: Take Exit 6 north from I-91 and follow Route 103 west to Ludlow. The inn is at 86 Main Street.

🍇

E: Miniature cordials in your room are a nice touch.

The Okemo Inn
Ludlow, Vermont
05149

Innkeepers: Rhinard and Toni Parry
Telephone: 802-228-8834
Rooms: 12, 10 with private bath, some with brass beds.
Rates: $45 per person, double occupancy, MAP. Five-day ski and golf packages available.
Facilities: Open all year. Breakfast, dinner, liquor license. Fireplaces in public rooms. Swimming pool, sauna, cross-country ski trails. Downhill skiing and golfing nearby. All major credit cards accepted.

Two little brown dogs named Chevas and Barney welcome you when you arrive at Okemo Inn. Fast on their heels come the Rhinard Parrys, a hard-working young couple. Their house has been here since 1810, but there's nothing old-fashioned about the swimming pool. And ☞ the spacious sauna is the very thing to take the ache away from the first day of skiing.

Meals are served family style, and are hearty, home-cooked, featuring roast beef, ham, turkey, chicken, and if that fare seems a little plain, how about a little Stroganoff just for variety?

The inn is practically at the foot of Okemo Mountain, a fast-growing, popular place to ski. Both downhill and cross-country skiing are enjoyable in this area. This seems an ideal spot for a couple, or young family, who love skiing.

The inn has a liquor license, and there is a working fireplace and color television in the lounge.

A collection of "necessary china" for bedroom use in times bygone is displayed on the bookshelf in the second floor hall. It's a wonder.

How to get there: Take Exit 6 north from I-91, and follow Route 103 to Ludlow. The inn is located one mile from Okemo Mountain public transportation, which includes Vermont Transit buses and Amtrak trains to Bellows Falls, and 25 miles from Springfield or Rutland Airports.

E: The Parrys have an 1896 Edison gramophone that works.

A night at an inn adds a tinge to the coming day that cannot be described, only enjoyed.

195

Ollie Metcalf

1811 House
Manchester, Vermont
05254

Innkeepers: Mary and Jack Hirst
Telephone: 802-362-1811
Rooms: 9, all with private bath; one suite.
Rates: $60 to $120, double occupancy, EPB.
Facilities: Open all year. Breakfast only meal served. Other
   restaurants nearby. Bar. No pets. Children over 16 welcome. Biking, hiking, trout fishing, canoeing, golfing,
   tennis, music, theater, and cross-country and downhill
   skiing nearby. All major credit cards accepted.

This is a beauty. Built in 1770, the inn has been carefully and authentically restored to the Federal period of the
early nineteenth century.
   There are fireplaces throughout the inn. What a cozy
feeling they give. You can relax in front of the sitting room
fireplace on one of the comfortable chairs or couches. The library also has a fireplace and a beautiful love seat and couch.
A ☛ chess game is set up ready for players in here. The bar is

a delight. It has seven chairs. The bar rail was made from a staircase that was removed and, you guessed it, there's another fireplace in here.

The bedrooms are lovely. The suite, which has a fireplace, has its own sitting room with a delightful many-pillowed love seat. Two other rooms have their own fireplaces. Canopied beds, oriental rugs, and fine paintings add to the tasteful decor of the rooms. ☛ Extra feather pillows, so important to a traveler, are in each room. All rooms are color coordinated for eye appeal. One of the baths is different. The tub and shower are enclosed in marble.

Over three acres of grounds have been transformed into an English garden abounding with rock, herb, rose, and other flower gardens. This is truly a beautifully restored inn.

A ☛ full English breakfast is included with the room rate. Fresh fruits, juices, and much, much more.

How to get there: Traveling north on Route 7, the inn is on the right as you approach Manchester.

E: *Animals, I was in heaven. The dogs, all mutts, are Dickens, Dinah, and Dorset. The cat is Tuffy.*

Olive Metcalf

The Inn at Manchester
Manchester, Vermont
05254

Innkeepers: Harriet and Stan Rosenberg
Telephone: 802-362-1793
Rooms: 15, 7 with private bath.
Rates: In winter, $35 to $45 per person, double occupancy, MAP; rest of year, $45 to $70, per room, EPB.
Facilities: Open all year. Breakfast, dinner, beer and wine license. Swimming pool. Skiing, golf, tennis, and theater nearby. American Express, MasterCard, and Visa accepted.

Lush greenery in the bay window of the living room is the sight that greets you when you walk in the front door of this inn. The many fireplaces surrounded by restful sitting areas, the numerous good antiques, and the dining room with ☛ Tiffany lamps add up to a warm country inn atmosphere. The antique Champion oak stove is the focal point in the game room, which is an ideal spot to unwind after a day on the ski slopes. Here you can watch television, or play games or cards at a card table. A good library is in here also.

The guest rooms are spotless and so very nice.
Sheets, comforters, dust ruffles, and towels are color coordinated, and the good beds all are new.

The food is homemade, even the breads. Apple pancakes with local maple syrup can start anyone's day right. Fragrant soups, creamy desserts, and vegetables from their organic gardens are just some of the many good things you can expect to find here. Meals are served family style. The menu changes daily and beer and wine are available.

The inn is conveniently located in the heart of just about everything, with skiing, downhill and cross-country, only minutes away. Summer brings great antiquing, summer theater, specialty craft shops, and boutiques. Golf and tennis are within walking distance of the front door.

How to get there: The inn is approximately 22 miles north of Bennington, Vermont, on Route 7. It is on the left.

☀

E: *The in-ground swimming pool is in a lovely meadow between the barn and the creek.*

Olive Metcalf

The Reluctant Panther
Manchester Village, Vermont
05254

Innkeepers: Edward and Loretta Friihauf
Telephone: 802-362-2568
Rooms: 11, all with private bath and television; 6 with fireplace.
Rates: $50 to $90, double occupancy, EP.
Facilities: Closed mid-April to Memorial Day, and November to mid-December. Breakfast, dinner, bar, lounge. Elevator. No pets. No children. Golf, tennis, hiking, and skiing nearby. American Express, MasterCard, and Visa accepted.

The inn is mauve on the outside and a good bit of lavendar and wine colors are inside. These are colors I love and, believe me, the inn is hard to miss with its yellow shutters. There are marble sidewalks and beautifully manicured gardens and lawns.

The rooms are unique. In some rooms the carpets ☞ go right up the walls. In others there are mad wallpapers. One has loving owls, and the newer lavendar room has the wildest paper ever, and in extremely good taste. ☞ Six of these delightful bedrooms have a fireplace. There is nothing more restful than a crackling fire in your own room.

A very nice touch is a ☞ tiny elevator for those who have problems with stairs.

The greenhouse for dining makes a perfect atmosphere for the fine food served here. The menu is a five-course prix-fixe dinner. There are four selections for the first course. Peach Sparkle is divine; half of an Elberta peach under Brut champagne. The salmon mousse is also different. The second course is soup. Two cold and two hot. The third course is salad with a choice of homemade dressing. The entree is the fourth course. Some are brace of quail, baked in a special wine sauce, or smoked pork, and, of course, Loretta has daily specials. The fifth course is the dessert course. All are made right here. The coffee is also special and super fresh. They grind their own coffee beans, a small amount at a time.

The bar-lounge area is nice and comfortable and watched over by a large bear. He's "lit" at night. How about that.

How to get there: As you approach Manchester from the south on Route 7 keep an eye on the left and soon the Reluctant Panther will pop into view.

ⴲ

E: *I'm a lavendar lover, so, of course, I love it here.*

To eat merely to live
is a crime against man
for which the gibbet is
inadequate punishment.

The Worthy Inn
Manchester Village, Vermont
05254

Innkeeper: Barbie Mouat
Telephone: 802-362-1792
Rooms: 25, all with private bath.
Rates: $35 to $39, double occupancy, EP. Special package
    rates available.
Facilities: Open all year. Breakfast, lunch in July and Au-
    gust, dinner. Bar, lounge, pool, tennis. Golfing and ski-
    ing nearby. American Express, MasterCard, and Visa
    accepted.

    Many moons ago when I was still skiing we would stay
here at this inn. In those days we called it the Worthless Inn,
but you surely could use that name no more. Things have
changed, and Barbi has a very nice inn. Built in 1889, it has
some delightful Victorian touches.
    The upstairs halls have been ☞ hand stencilled. Rather
nice to see. The rooms have been done over in antiques and

ruffled curtains. This inn has become better and better over the years.

There is a large fieldstone fireplace in the living room with comfortable couches and chairs around it. The taproom is neat with a lovely bar and tables and chairs. Nice any time of the year.

Food served here is excellent. The breakfasts are really ☞ hearty; eggs in any style including Benedict, blueberry or plain pancakes, muffins, and more and more. The dinners are also expansive, ☞ veal served six different ways, beef five ways, topped by the chef's Drunken Chicken, a real winner. Here is a chef who is not only very, very good, but also is one who thoroughly enjoys his work.

The swimming pool and patio area are very pretty, surrounded by well-trimmed lawns and old birch trees. This would be a good spot for a summer wedding.

There is so much to do in this area, golfing, skiing, alpine slides, Equinox Skyline Drive, antique shops, and just walking and enjoying.

How to get there: Coming north on historic Route 7A you will find the inn on your left right in Manchester Village.

ᛘ

E: *The rockers on the front porch make it summer for me.*

The Four in Hand
Marlboro, Vermont
05344

Innkeepers: Peter and Sheila Kane
Telephone: 802-254-2894
Rooms: 6, all with private bath.
Rates: $40 to $50, double occupancy, continental breakfast
   included.
Facilities: Closed in April. Lunch in season, dinner, pub. En-
   tertainment. Near skiing. MasterCard and Visa ac-
   cepted.

Traveling west on Route 9 you come around a corner
and on the right-hand side, set back from the road, you'll find
the Four in Hand. Peter and Sheila, such energetic people,
have done a wonderful job of remodeling this inn.

The rooms, all doubles, are fresh and comfortable. The
owners have developed a delightful common room where you
can have coffee, read a paper, or just chat with other guests.

Richard Caplin is the chef and a good one. He has been
the chef here for a number of years. I feel sure when you

sample one of Richard's Four in Hand dinners you will agree that he is a lucky find for inn lovers. Try his special. It is always good.

The food is country French, and this young man really knows what it is all about. The desserts are sinful, and the wind cellar is a beauty.

 The Backdoor Pub is a treat, great for relaxing after skiing in front of a roaring fire. All is here from a good hot toddy or just about anything else you wish to drink, to burgers, chili, and hot dogs. Local entertainment is on Fridays, and during the school year there are films on Thursday evenings.

This is a nice family venture.

How to get there: From I-91 take Exit 2 at Brattleboro, then Route 9 west to Marlboro. The inn is on the right.

E: *The cat is named Jiggs, an orange cat. Orange cats are always good inn cats.*

olive Metcalf

Longwood Inn
Marlboro, Vermont
05344

Innkeepers: Tom and Janet Durkin
Telephone: 802-257-1545
Rooms: 13, 11 with private bath.
Rates: $75 to $110, double occupancy, EPB. $115 to $150, double occupancy, MAP.
Facilities: Open all year. Closed Christmas Eve and Christmas Day. Breakfast, lunch during music festival and foliage season, Sunday brunch. Dinner daily in season and Thursday through Sunday out of season. Bar. Music and skiing nearby. MasterCard and Visa accepted.

The copper lanterns at the door of this more than 200-year-old inn are magnificent. The inn has served many uses over its life, a dairy farm known as Five Maples when milk was eight cents a quart, a halfway house, a college dormitory, the site of a local theater, and now a lovely country inn. In the summer there is still live theater in the old red barn a

206

step across the yard from the house. In nearby Marlboro is the 🐄 world-renowned music festival each summer.

Any time of year is a good time to come to the Longwood. In winter you can ski downhill or cross-country close by. Bring your bicycle in the other seasons, or rent a horse and see this pretty area from the ease of a saddle.

The most important ingredient to good living found at Longwood's restaurant is the restful 🐄 luxury of dining at leisure. The menu invites you to partake of homemade soups, fresh vegetables, or a Caesar salad made at your table. Fish is a specialty of the house prepared in an almost endless variety of ways. Good garlicky shrimp is a favorite of mine. Desserts are delectable, coupes aux marrons, Kahlua cheesecake, or mousse au chocolat. Breakfasts are pure New England with homemade muffins and Wilhelmina blueberry pancakes with pure maple syrup. Sound good? Come on up and try it.

How to get there: From I-91 take Exit 2 at Brattleboro. Take Route 9 west to Marlboro. The inn is on the right.

E: *Barnaby, the inn cat, really runs the inn with an iron paw.*

> *The groaning breakfast board*
> *of a good inn always makes it difficult*
> *to remember the word "diet."*

olive Metcalf

Red Clover Inn
Mendon, Vermont
05701

Innkeepers: Dennis and Bonnie Tallagnon
Telephone: 802-775-2290
Rooms: 15, 11 with private bath.
Rates: $40 to $52, per person, double occupancy, MAP.
Facilities: Closed mid-April to mid-June, and mid-October to
    Thanksgiving. Breakfast, dinner, bar. Television, swim-
    ming pool. Downhill and cross-country skiing nearby.
    American Express, MasterCard, and Visa accepted.

In the center of Vermont, just five miles east of Rutland,
is a flower of a country inn. The red clover is the state flower
of Vermont. The inn is the former summer home of General
John Woodward, and was built around 1840.

This is beautiful, peaceful country, and nor far away
there are antique shops, outlet stores, and areas for cross-
country and downhill skiing. From June to October a ☛
Farmers Market is open every Wednesday and Saturday with
produce and preserves, local crafts, and musical talent. A

bike ride on some of the back roads around here is lots of fun.

The inn is very comfortable. The living room has cozy chairs and couches. Curl up in front of a fire with a good book or a friend! The pub is adjacent to the living room and will provide you with your favorite drink. The rooms are beautifully appointed and restful, just what you expect in a good inn.

There are three dining rooms and the food that comes out of the kitchen is divine. Dennis was tutored by his father and apprenticed in his kitchen in Switzerland. Some of his creations are chilled curried zucchini soup, smoked rainbow trout, and entrees such as Poached Sockeye Salmon with Béarnaise Sauce, veal scallopini, and broiled loin lamb chops served with a special hollandaise and seasoned with Dijon mustard, dry white wine, fresh ground pepper, and herbs. Desserts are glorious. Try ☞ Rhubarb Crisp. Breakfasts are not ho-hum either. Do come up here and enjoy. Dinner is by candlelight, of course.

How to get there: Take Route 4 east from Rutland, and the inn is on the right, down narrow Woodward Road.

❦

E: *The converted carriage house is the Plum Tree House, surrounded by plum trees, so Dennis serves his duckling with brandied plum sauce. Oh my.*

Middlebury Inn
Middlebury, Vermont
05753

Innkeepers: Frank and Jane Emanuel
Telephone: 802-388-4961
Rooms: 77, 65 with private bath, air conditioning, color cable
  television, and telephone.
Rates: $58 to $80, EP.
Facilities: Open all year. Breakfast, lunch, dinner, bar. Park-
  ing. Elevator, gift shop. Skiing, swimming, golfing, fish-
  ing, boating, and museums nearby.

There has been an inn standing at this same location
since 1788. There have been some changes, due to fire and
the inroads of time, but the present brick building, known as
the Addison House, was constructed in 1827. One hundred
years later, when the Middlebury Hotel Company took over,
extensive repairs were made, and in 1977 Frank and Jane
Emanuel became the innkeepers. Their efforts to restore the
inn to its former elegance are being aided by a grant from
the Vermont Historic Preservation Division.

The inn has an excellent central location in the delightful town where Middlebury College is situated. There are many historic buildings, museums, and shops to visit in the town, and all around is an abundance of outdoor activities.

In the Addison House there is a delightful veranda and a really large lobby. ☛ The dining room is beautiful, and the food that is served here is delicious. The elegant candlelight buffets shouldn't be missed, from the served appetizer and sherbet courses to the finishing touch of a fingerbowl. The Morgan Room Tavern and Terrace offers excellent liquid refreshment, including the inn's own ☛ "Candied Apple." Upstairs the wide halls wander and dip, up one step and down three, wide enough for those ladies of long ago to have maneuvered their hoopskirts with grace.

Additional rooms are in adjacent buildings, or wings off the original building. The Jonathan Carver Wing was constructed in 1897, and the Thomas Hagar House, which was built in 1816, is now attached to the Addison House. The Porter Mansion, built in 1825, has ☛ five handsome guest rooms, several fireplaces of rare black marble, and a lovely curving staircase in the front parlor. More contemporary-style rooms are found in the Governor Weeks House and the Emma Willard House.

Whatever type of room you need, you'll find a wide variety of good choices here.

How to get there: Go up Route 7, and you run right into Middlebury. The inn is in the middle of town.

E: I could stay forever, mooning over the jigsaw puzzles in the lobby or eating their nightly popovers.

Olive Metcalf

The Middletown Springs Inn
Middletown Springs, Vermont
05757

Innkeepers: Dee and Nancy Schnitzler
Telephone: 802-235-2198
Rooms: 10, 5 with private bath.
Rates: $65, double occupancy, EPB.
Facilities: Open all year, but check in April. Dinner by reservation. Beer and wine license. Skiing, hiking, biking, golfing, fishing, swimming, and canoeing nearby. MasterCard and Visa accepted.

The approach to this lovely old Victorian inn on the village green is quiet and peaceful. The white wicker on the front porch adds just the perfect accent to this stately building.

The windows throughout the inn are almost floor to ceiling. A beautiful ☞ curved staircase takes you upstairs to the spacious bedrooms, which are filled with antiques. I slept in a lovely sleigh bed in the honeymoon suite. The inn provides 🖝 robes for the rooms that share baths. This is a nice touch if you have forgotten to bring yours.

There are two high-ceilinged dining rooms. The rug in one of them is as old as the inn (1880) and really in great shape. Some of the furniture is massive and could be used only in a large home such as this. The library is unique, with a wood-burning stove and a revolving fan hanging from the ceiling. The music room has an old grand piano. Please go and play—the innkeepers would love you to.

One entree is served each evening. Seafood and chicken are specials. So is Beef Burgundy. All the soups, breads, and salad dressings are homemade. Do remember to make reservations for your dinner.

Behind the inn is the carriage house, built in 1840. It has three guest rooms with a shared bath. Nice for a large party of friends.

How to get there: From Manchester, Vermont, take Route 30 north to Pawlet to Route 133 north to Middletown Springs. The inn is at the junction of Routes 133 and 140.

E: *Patches is the inn dog, a nice friendly fellow.*

Olive Metcalf

Zack's on the Rocks
Montgomery Center, Vermont
05471

Innkeepers: "Zack" and Gussie Zachadnyk
Telephone: 802-326-4500
Rooms: One cottage, sleeps two.
Rates: $60 per night, EP.
Facilities: Open all year. Closed Mondays and Christmas
   Day. Dinner by reservations only, bar. MasterCard and
   Visa accepted.

After you finally find Zack's you really will not believe
what you see. His cottage home and restaurant are literally
hanging on the rocks over an incredible valley.

This is my smallest inn. A cottage that sleeps two has a
living room, dining ell, kitchen, two fireplaces, a bedroom,
and a *wow* of a bathroom with a sunken tub. Even if you
cannot stay here, stay in town and come up here to eat Zack's
food. It is ☞ fantastic, and so are he and Gussie, his wife.

Zack's is so unique that it is almost impossible to describe. When you approach the door of his restaurant you

will find it is locked. Ring the sleigh bells, and the door will be opened by Zack. He will be in a wondrous costume and the ☞ performance begins. I will tell you no more except about the food. The menu is printed on a brown paper bag which is in beautiful contrast to his restaurant and Gussie's bar. Zack does all of the cooking. He is the most ☞ inventive chef and innkeeper I have had the pleasure to meet. The dining room has to be seen to be believed.

And Gussie's bar is something special. It has an organ with a full grand piano top built over it. This is my first ☞ organ bar. The room has a stone fireplace and is done pub style but with a flair. The bar has five stools, but to go with it is the best stocked back-bar in Vermont. To top it all the inn plays music from the forties. What a pleasant sound.

The inn dog is Gypsy, the largest German shepherd north of the Mason-Dixon line, and probably below as well. Pyewacket is a noisy Siamese cat who runs the inn and Zack.

Reservations here are an absolute must.

How to get there: Going north from Stowe on Route 100, turn left on Route 118 at Eden. When you reach Montgomery Center, turn right on Route 58. The inn is up the hill on the left, after the road becomes dirt.

ᛐ

E: *Zack's cottage is called Fore-the-Rocks. The private home is called Off-the-Rocks, and the inn is called On-the-Rocks. Gussie's bar is After-the-Rocks. Lots of rocks up here.*

olive Metcalf

Black Lantern Inn
Montgomery Village, Vermont
05470

Innkeepers: Rita and Allan Kalsmith
Telephone: 802-326-4507
Rooms: 11, 10 with private bath; one suite.
Rates: In winter, $38 to $55, per person, double occupancy,
   MAP; in summer, $35 to $55, double occupancy, EP.
Facilities: Closed first two weeks in May. Breakfast, dinner,
   bar. Parking. Television in lounge, fireplace in sitting
   room. Cross-country skiing. Downhill skiing, fishing,
   swimming, golfing, and tennis nearby. MasterCard and
   Visa accepted.

When you get to Montgomery Village you are nearly in
Canada, perhaps six or seven miles from the border. This is a
quiet Vermont village, and the Black Lantern has been nicely
restored by its hard-working owners. Whether you come in
the snow for a skiing vacation, or on a green summer day,
there is a warm welcome at this friendly inn. It is also sur-

prising to encounter a rather ☞ sophisticated menu in this out-of-the-way corner of the world.

You can ski at Jay Peak, where there are fifty miles of trails for every kind of skier, outright novice to expert. Not too far away, over the border, there are four Canadian mountains, and ski-week tickets are available. Cross-country skiing starts at the inn door, and is undoubtedly the best way to see beautiful Vermont in the winter.

Summer brings the joy of outdoor life. Fishing, swimming, golfing, tennis, and hiking are all very near. You've heard about those country auctions, haven't you? Or would you rather spend the day browsing through antique shops? Whatever you choose to do, there will be a superbly quiet night to catch up on your sleep. The inn's guest accommodations are very comfortable, and the new three-room suite is a ☞ joy. It has a fireplace and a Jacuzzi. This is heaven.

The double-peaked roof on this nice, old, 1803 farmhouse covers a typical north-country inn. Small, friendly, and just a little bit different.

How to get there: Go north from Stowe on Route 100, and turn left on route 118 at Eden. This will take you into Montgomery Center. Continue down the main street and out of town, and before too long you will reach Montgomery Village and the inn. From I-89 in Burlington, turn right at St. Albans onto Route 105, toward Enosburg Falls. Pick up Route 118 at East Berkshire, and follow it to Montgomery Village and the inn.

Ⴤ

E: *What is there that is so special about yellow cats? The youngster that greets you at the door is a charming feline.*

Olive Metcalf

Camel's Hump View Farm
Moretown, Vermont
05660

Innkeepers: Jerry and Wilma Maynard
Telephone: 802-496-3614
Rooms: 8, one with private bath.
Rates: $18 to $21, per person, EPB. $30 to $33, per person, MAP.
Facilities: Open all year. Breakfast, dinner by reservation. BYOB. Game room. Fishing in Mad River. Skiing nearby. No credit cards accepted.

The inn is an 1831 farmhouse, complete with lots of animals. A herd of ☛ white-faced Hereford cows wanders along the banks of the Mad River out back of the inn. They are so friendly, they will come when you call them. There are also a pig and Missy, a Sheltie dog.

Wilma has a large garden; Jerry was busy working in it when I was there. She cans strawberries, raspberries, and blueberries, so the meals feature ☛ homegrown vegetables and fruits. They also have their own chickens and you cannot get fresher eggs. Wilma bakes all her own breads and desserts. One entree is served each night. Homemade soup or fresh fruit cocktail starts your dinner. The entree may be pork chops in a sweet and sour sauce, or baked ham, or an Italian dish, with salad and dessert.

The rooms are very clean and neat. There are bunk rooms for skiers. In the evening, find a book to read or play bumper pool or Ping-Pong in the game room. You also can sit in the living room and enjoy the sight and sound of the interesting fountain.

The Mad River flows by the inn and is wonderful for you fishermen. There are three ski areas nearby, Sugarbush, Sugarbush North, and Mad River Glen. Camel's Hump is on the list of inns involved in hiking and bicycling from inn to inn. There are short trails through farm country. This I would love to do.

How to get there: Take Exit 9 off I-89 and go left on Route 100B. The inn is on your left.

E: Maybe I could take a friendly cow for a walk.

Were it not for a night's rest in a country inn tomorrow would be but another day.

olive Metcalf

The Four Columns Inn
Newfane, Vermont
05345

Innkeepers: Jacques and Sandy Allembert
Telephone: 802-365-7713
Rooms: 9 rooms, 3 suites, all with private bath and air conditioning.
Rates: $60 to $90, double occupancy, continental breakfast included. Ski packages available.
Facilities: Inn closed in April and November 1 to Thanksgiving. Restaurant closed Tuesdays. Lunch July through October; dinner, jacket required. Bar. Swimming pool. Hiking, ice skating, and skiing nearby. MasterCard and Visa accepted.

The inn is located on the most photographed town common in Vermont. The area is just beautiful and so is the inn. Sandy and Jacques are truly marvelous innkeepers. They are friendly and so is their staff.

The rooms are full of antiques. The Victorian Room has a brass bed. Another room has a canopy bed with a lace top, and four poster beds are in others. Handmade rag rugs are all over and ☞ plants in your room are a wonderful touch. Big towels and good pillows and mattresses; all these things make up a fine inn. The third floor suite has a lovely porch with wicker furniture facing the common. A nice place to sit and watch the world go by.

The inn has nice living rooms where you can gather to visit with other guests, read, watch television, or just relax. The dining room with a fireplace has blue and white napery. A ☞ beautiful armoire is used to display the superb wines served here.

The inn was given three, well-deserved stars in the Mobil Travel Guide for its food and rooms. Jacques managed several restaurants in New York City before becoming an innkeeper. He always gave his diners the very best and he continues to do just that here in Newfane. Chef Gregory was a protégé of the former owner, who was a fine chef himself, and he stayed on with the Allemberts. He is inventive and loves to use local fare. He buys ☞ Vermont raised milk-fed veal and does his own butchering. I've had the veal here and it is heavenly. One of the chef's appetizers is ☞ charred raw tenderloin with cayenne mayonnaise, which is oh, so good. One dinner offering is boned, sliced double breast of duck with a rhubarb and radish sauce. You can't miss with food like this. The dessert cart is sinful. How do you choose between white or chocolate mousse?

The lounge has a pewter bar, which is very unusual. There is a piano here, plants, and more country charm than you can shake a stick at. Do I like it here? Just wish I lived closer.

How to get there: The inn is 220 miles from New York and 100 miles from Boston. Take Exit 2 from I-91 at Brattleboro to Route 30 North. The inn is in Newfane, 100 yards off Route 30 on your left.

E: Max is a big, beautiful German shepherd who watches over a wonderful set of twin boys, especially at the inn's lovely swimming pool. Down at the stream is a hammock waiting for you.

Old Newfane Inn
Newfane, Vermont
05345

Innkeepers: Eric and Gundy Weindl
Telephone: 802-365-4427
Rooms: 10, 8 with private bath.
Rates: $65 to $85, double occupancy, continental breakfast
  included.
Facilities: Closed April to mid-May, late October to mid-December, and on Mondays. Lunch in summer and fall,
  dinner, bar. Parking. Skiing nearby. No pets. No credit
  cards accepted.

The inn is well named, for old it is, 1787 to be exact. It
has been carefully kept, however, and the weary traveler will
find great comfort and fabulous food.

Almost all the rooms have twin beds. The rooms are
large and tastefully furnished. Gundy has beautiful taste in
her decorating. There is an informal bar and lounge, and the
dining room has tables with pink cloths over white ones. Very
effective. There is a huge brick wall with fireplace in the din-

ing room that gives a wonderful feeling of warmth and good cheer. The ☞ floors here are polished to a turn and beyond. And not just run-of-the-mill glassware for the inn. ☞ The drinks I had before lunch were served in crystal.

Eric is a fine chef. His soups are a bit different and very good. I have tried both the cold strawberry and creamed watercress. Loved them both. By the way, I hate calves liver, but Eric asked me to try his. What magic he performed I do not know, but I ate every bite. Veal is king here. Eric butchers his own, so he gets the exact cuts he wants. Of course, the menu also has seafood, lamb, fowl, and fine steaks. The dessert menu reads like poetry from the flaming suzette and jubilee to a fabulous omelette surprise. There are also some cream pies that demand that you do not even think of calories.

How to get there: Take Exit 2 from I-91 in Brattleboro, and follow Route 30 north. The inn is on Route 30, on the left in Newfane.

E: *Gundy arranges pillows on the beds just beautifully.*

> *Come away, O human child!*
> *To the waters and the wild*
> *With a faery hand in hand . . .*
> *—William Butler Yeats*

Olive Metcalf

The Inn at Norwich
Norwich, Vermont
05055

Innkeepers: Barbara and Eugene Bellows
Telephone: 802-649-1143
Rooms: 26, all with private bath; 2 suites with kitchen facilities; television and phone in all rooms.
Rates: $66 to $86, double occupancy, EP.
Facilities: Open all year. Breakfast, lunch, dinner, Sunday brunch, bar. Swimming, canoeing, golfing, and skiing nearby. MasterCard and Visa accepted.

It's nice to have old innkeepers back in a fine inn like this one. The Bellowses had the Bee and Thistle in Connecticut for a few years.

Right on the sign for the inn it says, "Since 1797," and it is truly said, because travelers up the beautiful Connecticut River Valley have been finding a warm welcome at this grand old house ever since. It is just a mile away from Dartmouth College, and alumni, skiers, tourists, and commercial travelers find a special homelike atmosphere here that is dignified but a lot of fun.

There's a nice new bar and lounge area named ☞ the Jasper Murdock Tavern, after the inn's first owner. The dining rooms are lovely, with good napery and comfortable Thomasville chairs. The big bow window in the main dining room is a delight, but I still love to eat on the flower-filled porch. It's a nice place to watch the snow in winter.

The food is glorious. Sunday brunch has a new one on me: ☞ Pojarski. Come and see what it is. Lunch has some different items, such as Ham Salad in Puff Pastry or Veal Strips Béarnaise, and then on to dinner. Ambrosia. One appetizer is Baked Brie with Almonds. Nice and different. The ☞ roast duck is completely boned, a real treat. The desserts are wonderful. Their wine list is one of the most extensive I have seen.

The rooms have new beds and mattresses. There are canopied beds and some iron and brass beds. All are beautiful.

How to get there: Take Exit 13 from Route I-91. Go west a bit less than a mile to the center of town. The inn is on your left.

E: *You can come to Norwich by air, car, bus, or rail, or walk if you must, but do come.*

Choose your inn, and enter in the world of relaxation.

olive Metcalf

Johnny Seesaw's
Peru, Vermont
05152

Innkeepers: Gary and Nancy Okun

Telephone: 802-824-5533

Rooms: 30, all with private bath; ski bunk rooms; cottages with fireplaces.

Rates: In summer, $15 to $27, per person, EPB; in winter, $35 to $60, per person, MAP.

Facilities: Closed end of skiing to Memorial Day, and end of foliage until Thanksgiving. Breakfast, dinner, liquor license. Parking. Television, game room, swimming, tennis. Skiing, hunting, golfing, horseback riding, and fishing nearby. MasterCard and Visa accepted.

Skiing Magazine says this inn has the best Yankee cuisine in New England. The food is good, ☞ tasty country food prepared with imagination, featuring home-baked bread and homemade soup. Val is the fine lady chef who turns out all this fine fare.

The inn has a unique character, mostly because of the guests who keep coming back. It is set 2,000 feet up, on

Bromley Mountain. The sixty-five-by-twenty-five-foot pool, marble-rimmed, is a great summer gathering place, and the tennis court is always ready. There are six nearby golf courses, and riding is offered at the Ox Bow Ranch near Weston.

For the many skiers who come to Vermont, Bromley's five chairlifts and GLM Ski School are right next door. Stratton and Magic Mountains, the Viking Ski Touring Center, and Wild Wings X-C, are but a few minutes away.

For fishermen and hunters, or those who wish to take up the sport, the Orvis Fly-Fishing and Wing Shooting Schools in nearby Manchester have classes. The sportsman classes are held twice weekly, in three-day sessions through October, and participants may stay at the inn. The nearby towns boast many attractive and interesting shops.

How to get there: The inn is 220 miles from New York, 150 from Boston. From Route 7 take Route 30 right at Manchester Depot. The inn is 10 miles east, on Vermont Route 11. From I-91, follow Exit 6 to Route 103 to Chester. The inn is 20 miles west, on Vermont Route 11.

E: ☛ *The circular fireplace in the lounge really attracts me, to say nothing of the cushioned platform along one side of the room.*

Cats, birds, flowers, and dogs
in companionate confusion are to be found
where hospitality has bested the world of commerce.

olive Metcalf

Wiley Inn
Peru, Vermont
05152

Innkeepers: Toni and Patrick Smith
Telephone: 802-824-6600
Rooms: 17, 9 with private bath.
Rates: In winter, $76 to $90, double occupancy, MAP. Rest of
   year, $35 to $60, double occupancy, EPB.
Facilities: Open all year. Breakfast, dinner. BYOB. Game
   room, heated swimming pool. Hiking, horseback riding,
   fishing, skiing, and Alpine Slide nearby. MasterCard and
   Visa accepted.

   It is always nice to have an inn back in the book. I feel
Toni and Patrick, the new innkeepers, will do justice to this
nice inn.
   Two of the guest rooms have fireplaces. The Bromley
Room has wonderful photographs of the mountain. The
game room is full of fun things to do. The ☞ player piano has
tons of rolls to play. There's a real, old-fashioned ☞ juke box

that has only music of the forties, and that's nice. Lots of games and magazines are here for you to enjoy.

There is a plaque in the game room that I just love. It reads:

> *Oh how I wish I could foresee*
> *What is about to happen to me*
> *For here I am about to descend*
> *I pray the Lord I do not upend.*
> —The Skiers Prayer

This is a BYOB inn; however, the set-ups are here for you. There is another fireplace in the dining room. This surely feels good on a cold night.

No matter what season, there are things to do at the Wiley Inn. In the summer, swim in the inn's heated pool. The Long and Appalachian trails are nearby; so are horseback riding, fishing in the Battenkill River, and the Alpine Slide at Bromley. In spring, watch the maple sugaring to see how the syrup is made. Fall, the foliage is king, and in winter there are Bromley, Stratton, Magic Mountain, Snow Valley, and Timber Ridge for you downhill skiers. Cross-country ski-touring centers are within minutes. Go and enjoy.

How to get there: From I-91, take Exit 6 to Route 103 to Chester, Vermont. Go left onto Route 11 and the inn is 20 miles west in Peru.

E: A cat called Kitty and a black Labrador retriever called Tessie are never in your way.

The Pittsfield Inn
Pittsfield, Vermont
05762

Innkeepers: Tom and Sue Yennerell
Telephone: 802-746-8943
Rooms: 8, 2 with private bath.
Rates: $38 to $45, per person, double occupancy, MAP.
Facilities: Closed mid-April to mid-May. Breakfast, dinner, bar, lounge. Tennis, racquetball, swimming, golfing, horseback riding, skiing, and theater nearby. Master-Card and Visa accepted.

Tom and Sue are young, ambitious, and nice innkeepers of an inn and tavern that have been here since 1835. The town is small with a one-room post office and a bandstand on the village green, but within minutes there are tennis, racquetball, swimming, golfing, horseback riding, rivers for fishing, and summer theater. In winter there is downhill skiing at Killington or Pico ski areas, as well as ski touring and cross-country skiing. ☛ This inn is a pleasant home base for anything you care to do.

The inn's combination living room, bar and lounge has a woodburning stove, an upright piano—just waiting for you to play—and lots of games. The bar is of ☞ antique marble.

Guest rooms are warmly decorated with bright wallpapers, interesting antiques, and quilts on the comfortable beds. These young innkeepers are really doing a nice job. Some rooms are small and some are large. One is in my colors, lavendar and white. They are all very clean.

The dining room is bright and airy. The food is good. One appetizer caught my eye, Crepes Suehoise, homemade crepes filled with smoked salmon, eggs, and herbs, and topped with a dill sauce. The house special is lean loin of pork stuffed with an old New England-style sausage and glazed with an onion and sage gravy. Desserts are freshly made every day.

The Tweed and White rivers are close by, so come on up all you fishermen. They are full of trout and salmon. Ski touring is close by, and so are downhill and cross-country skiing. The inn is part of an inn-to-inn hiking system. You also can bike or ski from inn to inn. This is fun to do.

How to get there: The inn is 20 miles northeast of Rutland. Take Route 4 east and Route 100 north to the village of Pittsfield. The inn is right on the green.

☒

E: *I truly am a chocoholic and the chef made me* ☞ *chocolate covered strawberries surrounded by Bavarian cream and with whipped cream on the top sprinkled with blueberries. What a way to live.*

The Golden Stage Inn
Proctorsville, Vermont
05153

Innkeepers: Tim and Shannon Datig and family
Telephone: 802-226-7744
Rooms: 10, 2 with private bath.
Rates: $50, per person, double occupancy, MAP.
Facilities: Closed April and November. Breakfast, dinner,
  beer and wine license. Swimming pool. Bike tours. Hik-
  ing, skiing, Alpine Slide, and gondola rides nearby.
  American Express, Mastercard, and Visa accepted.

The Golden Stage Inn still is known locally as the Skinner place, for Otis, the actor, and his daughter Cornelia Otis
Skinner, the author. The house was built over 200 years ago,
shortly after Vermont's founding. It was once a stagecoach
stop, and is reputed to have been a stop on the underground
railway.

Tim and Shannon are the reason the food served here is
good. ☛ She is the chef and Tim is the baker. Everything is
homemade, hearty, and traditionally New England.

Four acres of rolling lawns, beautiful gardens, and trees are just what you need for a picnic, a long walk, or for being alone. Surrounding this haven of loveliness are thousands of acres of forests to hike in and four mountains noted for their good skiing. They are Okemo Mountain, Mount Ascutney, Bromley (fun in summer, too, with its exciting Alpine Slide down the mountain), and Killington Peak, which has year-round gondola rides, the longest in the U.S. Killington often has the longest ski season in the East.

The porches of the inn are lovely and the views of the Black River valley and Okemo Mountain any time of the year are breathtaking.

☛ Biking from inn to inn is another way to see this wonderful country. While you bike to the next inn, a support van transfers your luggage. This is my idea of neat.

The public rooms with the cozy fireplace in the living room are very comfortable after a day of just doing your own thing. Maybe all you want to do is sit and knit or read. This inn is a nice place to do it.

How to get there: Take Route 103 North out of Chester and just before you get to Ludlow you will see the Golden Stage Inn. From I-91 take Exit 8 onto Route 131 West to Proctorsville.

E: *I like birds, too, especially parrots. Roger is a yellow-naped Amazon one.*

olive Metcalf

Okemo Lantern Lodge
Proctorsville, Vermont
05153

Innkeepers: The Racicot Family
Telephone: 802-226-7770
Rooms: 7, one with private bath.
Rates: $46 to $52, per person, MAP.
Facilities: Open all year. Breakfast, dinner, beer and wine license. Golf, tennis, bicycling, skiing, and skating nearby. All major credit cards accepted.

The first thing you notice when you enter the inn is a monster of a spinning wheel in the front hall. In the living room there is an exquisite old pump organ. This room is all comfort, armchairs, couches, a crackling fire to warm your toes, and an enticing chaise in front of a sunny bay window.

All of the guest rooms are attractive, and one has a lovely, eyelet-canopied bed.

Joan is "chief cook and bottle washer." The aromas of ☞ freshly baked bread, freshly perked coffee, and home-smoked bacon will awaken you. If you have a special occasion a champagne breakfast in bed is a nice treat.

There is so much to do in this area year round. Spring is the time to watch the maple sugaring or just go fishing in one of the well-stocked lakes or streams. In summer golf, tennis, hiking, and bicycling are close at hand. Fall is foliage and cider. Winter brings skiing and skating, or you could also curl up with a good book by the fire.

How to get there: Take I-91 to Exit 6 in Bellows Falls. Go north on Route 103 to its junction with Route 131 and turn right. The inn is on the left in a quarter of a mile.

E: *Tumble in the Rumble, as it says in their brochure. In good weather a ride in the* *rumble seat of a 1935 Plymouth complete with a raccoon coat on the driver and assorted appropriate coats for the guests is my kind of fun.*

Spring flowers add the final brush strokes
at the edges of the granite walk
to the inn's front stoop.

Woodstock ?.

Olive Metcalf

The Quechee Inn
Quechee, Vermont
05059

Innkeepers: Michael and Barbara Yaroschuk
Telephone: 802-295-3133
Rooms: 22, all with private bath and television.
Rates: $65 to $135, double occupancy, EPB.
Facilities: Closed April and first two weeks in December. Breakfast, dinner Wednesday through Sunday, bar. Cross-country skiing learning center, fly fishing lessons, bicycles and canoes to rent, downhill skiing, golf, tennis, squash, swimming, boating, fishing, and hiking. American Express, MasterCard, and Visa accepted.

The first time I saw and heard Quechee Gorge I was standing on the bridge that spans it. Now I know another way to see this remarkable quirk of nature. The inn is but one-half mile from it, and ☞ the innkeepers will show you how to see it from an unusual angle.

Quechee Inn was a private home from 1793 until 1976. Beautifully converted to an inn, it reflects the care the inn-

236

keepers give it. Some of the rooms have the largest ☞ four-poster, king-sized beds I have ever seen, and others have comfortable twins. Seven more guest rooms, in the wing off the original building, have picture windows overlooking the meadow and lake. All rooms are equipped with color cable television.

Barbara has lovely stencils in the dining room and a beautiful awning over the porch. Adjoining the dining room is a small library and conference room wired for audio-visual equipment. It's a real treat to be able to have a business meeting at a place like this. The living room has an abundance of comfortable chairs and couches, a piano, color television, books, and a fireplace. One feels at home here any season of the year.

The Yaroschuks do things so well. Christmas is a good example. The ☞ guests help decorate the tree, and on Christmas Eve they have an open house for inn guests and townspeople who join in singing Christmas carols and enjoying the baked goodies. On Christmas Day all sit down to an old-fashioned family dinner.

The inn guests have ☞ full club privileges at the Quechee Club. The golf courses are breathtakingly scenic and are great tests of golf. If you do intend to play, let the inn know when you call for reservations so they can arrange a tee-off time for you. You may also play tennis and squash here.

And then there's Governor Marsh, a wonderful golden retriever, who helps run the inn.

How to get there: From I-91 take Route 89 north to Exit 1. Go west on Route 4 for 1.2 miles, then right on Club House Road for one mile to the inn.

E: *Old-fashioned New England dining with homemade breads, ☞ sticky buns, and regional specials such as trout and venison make a visit here a must.*

Saxtons River Inn
Saxtons River, Vermont
05154

Innkeeper: Averill Campbell Larsen
Telephone: 802-869-2110
Rooms: 19, 9 with private bath; 2 suites.
Rates: $30 to $60, double occupancy, continental breakfast
    included.
Facilities: Closed January through March. Dinner every day
    except Tuesday, Sunday brunch, bar. Antiquing, skiing,
    golfing, canoeing, music, museums, and theater nearby.
    No credit cards honored, but personal checks accepted.

    Blessings on the Campbell family, and especially on
Averill Campbell Larsen, who was responsible for renovating
this turn-of-the-century inn and revitalizing the little village
of Saxtons River. I've been saying this a long time and I still
mean it.

    Cross the wide front porch and come through the gra-
cious front door. To the right is a little breakfast room, to the
left, the ☞ copper bar. Straight ahead is the dining room.

Tiffany chandeliers light the flower-bedecked tables, and some of the freshest, most original food is brought out from the spick-and-span kitchen to please even the most particular diner.

The menu changes, of course, with what is fresh and good in season. If you are really not hungry you can have ☞ soup, salad, and bread for a most nominal price. If you are starving, begin with soup—how about some West African Peanut Soup?—or Mushrooms Maison or Picadilla, wheat tortillas filled with hot sausages, olives, spices, tomatoes, and cheddar cheese. Then go on to a main course of Chicken Satay with an Indonesian Peanut Sauce, Szechuan Shrimp, or Spanakopeta, a spinach and feta cheese pie. But be sure to save room for dessert. They are all appallingly good, and are outlawed by every diet club in the country.

☞ The guest rooms are spectacular, handsomely decorated with a combination of old furniture and crisp new fabrics. Your innkeeper has traveled around the world and knows what is needed for creature comforts, including pleasant places to read, with lights in the right places. She has slept in every one of her guest rooms, an acid test, and she has her own aerie at the top of the tower, five stories above the world of Saxtons River.

How to get there: From I-91 take either Exit 5 or 6 at Bellows Falls. Pick up Route 5, and proceed to Route 121. Saxtons River is on Route 121, and the inn is on Main Street in the center of town.

E: *I love to read in bed, and this is the most comfortable place for doing it.*

Olive Metcalf

The Londonderry Inn
South Londonderry, Vermont
05155

Innkeepers: Jim and Jean Cavanagh
Telephone: 802-824-5226
Rooms: 25, 20 with private bath.
Rates: $26 to $60, EPB.
Facilities: Inn open all year. Restaurant closed late October
   to mid-December, and April to late May. Lunch summer
   and fall, dinner, bar. Pool tables, Ping-Pong, swimming.
   Skiing, horseback riding, and hiking nearby. No credit
   cards honored, but personal checks accepted.

The inn sits high on a hill overlooking the village of
South Londonderry. It is central to three big ski areas, Bromley, Magic Mountain, and Stratton.

In summer there is a large heated swimming pool.
Nearby they have horseback riding, hiking, and bicycle trails.
Any time of the year there is pool to be played on the inn's
two ☞ vintage pool tables. In addition, there are many com-

240

fortable places to relax, read a book, do needlepoint, or just enjoy a blazing fire on the hearth.

The inn dates back to 1826 when it was a farmhouse. The rooms have twin, double, and king-sized beds with down comforters, down pillows, and large thirsty towels. Jean also puts fresh flowers in the rooms. These little touches are far too often overlooked by innkeepers.

The inn has a nice lounge and a service bar off the living room, so you can be comfortable by the fire before dinner with your favorite cocktail in hand. The menu changes nightly, but always includes four to eight entrees served with fresh vegetables, four or five appetizers, at least one home-made soup, and great desserts.

Honey is the inn dog you will love.

How to get there: Take Exit 2 from I-91 at Brattleboro, and follow Route 30 north to Rawsonville. Then take Route 100 to South Londonderry. The inn is on your left.

☀

E: *The dessert names are really creative, FBI Cake, Orient Express Torte, and Hungarian Rhapsody.*

If you have never been drawn shivering
from the warmth of a good bed
by the sizzling lure of bacon on the grill,
you have never been in a country inn.

Butternut Inn
Stowe, Vermont
05672

Innkeepers: Jim and Deborah Wimberly
Telephone: 802-253-4277
Rooms: 18, all with private bath.
Rates: $24, summer; $28, fall; per person, double occupancy, EPB. In winter, $48, per person, double occupancy, MAP.
Facilities: Closed mid-April to mid-May, and November to mid-December. Breakfast, dinner, afternoon tea. BYOB. Heated swimming pool. Skiing nearby. MasterCard and Visa accepted.

Through the red door and into a charming country inn, this is Butternut, located part way up a mountain road ☛ with a wonderful view of Mount Mansfield. It really does not matter what season you arrive, as they are all spectacular. Stowe is the ski capital of the East for downhill skiing, and there is excellent cross-country skiing as well. In the fall the mountains look as if they have been painted. In the summer the inn has a ☞ solar-heated swimming pool, and there's a lovely mountain stream babbling along nearby.

The inn has a family room with a good library, Ping-Pong, pool table, and board games. Next to it is an unlicensed bar, so bring what you want, and a beautifully carved piano. Hopefully there is one in every crowd who can play. The dining room is beyond, cozily warmed by a potbelly stove. Lovely stained glass Tiffany lamps hang over the tables. All in all this is an inn with most everything.

Food is served family style, with one entree each evening. Everything is ☞ homemade and so good. Deborah is the chef. There is a fine salad bar, something I really do like. Afternoon tea is served with Deborah's yummy butternut cookies.

The rooms are delightful. On the third floor are large family rooms, and everywhere the inn is very clean.

How to get there: From Stowe take Route 108 to the inn on the left.

ᕮ

E: *This would be a nice place to come to see the fall colors change.*

A night at an inn adds a tinge to the coming day
that cannot be described, only enjoyed.

Charda
Stowe, Vermont
05672

Innkeepers: Karl and Joan Jokinen
Telephone: 802-253-4598
Rooms: 11, all with private bath.
Rates: In summer, $35 to $60, double occupancy, EP; in winter, $28 to $30, per person, EPB.
Facilities: Open all year. Breakfast, dinner, bar. Skiing. All major credit cards accepted.

Nice to have old innkeepers back. This lovely couple retired for a few years from an inn in Connecticut, and now are back at it in Stowe. They bought a favorite inn of mine. Charda looks just like it belongs in the Alps. It has such a splendid view of Mount Mansfield and Spruce Peak.

The rooms have always been ☛ clean and comfortable, but Joan has really spruced them up for eye appeal. Bright colors add such a lot. The old barn that was turned into rooms is charming.

The dining room is lovely, and there's a small bar in its

center with great espresso and cappuccino machines to turn out heavenly coffees. The menu is a joy. Steak, of course, and pork and duck. ☞ Braised Hungarian Beef Goulash, served with homemade spaetzle, is a winner, and so is Szekely Goulash, Transylvania style—pork pieces baked with sauerkraut. The appetizers are also very gourmet; small stuffed cabbages, Hungarian stuffed mushrooms, and many more. The dessert lift is yummy: Black Forest Cherry Torte, apple strudel, peach melba, and, of course, ☞ they have Palacsinta.

There's a heavenly porch that is used for breakfast and cocktails in season. What a view!

How to get there: Take I-89 to Route 100 and go north. The inn is on the left, north of Stowe.

♒

E: *They have a motto! A guest arrives, but a friend returns.*

> *Innkeeping takes twenty-five hours*
> *of every twenty-four, but done right*
> *it makes a wonderful life.*

Edson Hill Manor
Stowe, Vermont
05672

Innkeepers: The Heath Family
Telephone: 802-253-7371, 802-253-9797
Rooms: 11, 5 with private bath, in the manor; 6, with 2 baths, in the annex; 8, all with private bath, in the carriage house.
Rates: $48 to $85, per person, MAP.
Facilities: Closed mid-April to mid-June, and November. Breakfast, lunch in winter only, dinner, fully licensed bar, après-ski lounge. Pool, tennis court, fishing, horseback riding and instruction, cross-country skiing with rentals and instruction. Ice skating and golf at Stowe Country Club nearby. No credit cards honored, but personal checks accepted.

Here you are, halfway between Stowe and Mount Mansfield, 1500 feet above the hubble-bubble of that lively village of Stowe that is growing every year. Here is truly luxurious living, in a house that was built in 1939 for a family that loved to ski and ride.

☛ The swimming pool here is beautiful. It won an award from Paddock Pools of California. The stocked trout pond is a must for anglers, and you can use the inn's boat. How nice to go catch a fish and have it for your breakfast. When the snow comes, ☛ the stables turn into a cross-country ski center, so there you are, practically taking off from the inn door.

This attractive house has been run as an inn since 1953, and there are still homelike touches. The pine paneled living room has an aura of quiet elegance that reflects the feeling of gracious living all too often missing from our busy lives.

Downstairs are bar and lounge. ☛ A skier's lunch is served here. Hot soup of the day, chef's salad, hot chili, and good sandwiches. A special on cold days is hot mulled cider.

The inn has always had nice guest accommodations, but now there are eight new rooms with beamed ceilings, brick fireplaces, and private baths.

This is a beautiful inn. Many of the paintings were done by ☛ Effie Juraine Martin Heath, the grandmother of the family. The view is spectacular, and Bow, the inn's golden retriever, is a must-see beauty.

A note of particular interest to all you moviegoers is that Edson Hill Manor was the winter filming location for Alan Alda's "The Four Seasons."

There are so many different rates and packages for so many different activities, I suggest you write for the complete set of brochures.

How to get there: Take Route 108 north from Stowe 4.9 miles, turn right on Edson Hill Road, and follow the signs uphill to the Manor.

E: *The old Delft tiles around many of the fireplaces are so appealing. Look closely at the living room curtains. Somebody shopped hard for that material.*

Foxfire Inn
Stowe, Vermont
05672

Innkeepers: Irene and Art Segreto
Telephone: 802-253-4887
Rooms: 5, all with private bath; chalets.
Rates: $48 to $56, double occupancy, EPB.
Facilities: Open all year. Breakfast, dinner, bar. Parking.
   Downhill and cross-country skiing, fishing, skating, and
   hiking nearby. American Express, MasterCard, and Visa
   accepted.

   The Segretos want to welcome old and new friends, and
there are myriads of them, to their inn. The house is over 150
years old and has been restored to easy comfort by these en-
thusiastic innkeepers. And there is so much to do here, from
the finest skiing in the East to great lounging by the pool.
   There is a beautiful inn dog, Coby, a "formerly white"
Samoyed who smiles his secret smile to greet you. Irene says
he is just impossible to keep clean, but he did not look that
dingy to me. Could be the contrast with the snow.

Irene has created a garden room that is a great spot for breakfast and dinner. It is all white lattice with loads of hanging plants. This is a gazebo to end them all.

The best Italian kitchen in New England may seem a bit misplaced so far north in Vermont, but it is here. Taste, and you will agree. The ☞ tomato sauce is an old family recipe brought over from Naples. And do try things like Baked Broccoli, which is a combination of tomato sauce, ricotta cheese, and broccoli. There are seven different and delicious veal dishes. Boneless breast of chicken is prepared five ways, and the Eggplant Parmigiana has a special place in my heart. Shrimp Marinara I can still taste. As the front of the menu says, here you discover "The Italian Art of Eating."

And when you can push yourself away from the table, you have Stowe at your door, with antiques, shops, skiing, skating, walking, hiking, fishing, and more.

How to get there: Take I-89 to Route 100 north into Stowe. The inn is on the right, 1½ miles north of town.

E: *Pass me another tortoni, please. I am settled in for the season.*

> *A cricket on the hearth of a country inn*
> *is music beyond the angels.*

Olive Metcalf

Green Mountain Inn
Stowe, Vermont
05672

Innkeeper: Lewis Kiesler
Telephone: 802-253-7301
Rooms: 57, all with private bath, color television, and telephone.
Rates: $40 to $75, single; $45 to $85, double occupancy; EP.
Facilities: Open all year. Breakfast, lunch, dinner, lounge. Beauty shop, gift shop, health club with sauna, whirlpool, massage, and exercise machines. Racquetball and complete health program. Skiing, heated swimming pool. All major credit cards accepted.

This lovely inn turned 150 years old in 1983, and to properly celebrate the event, ☞ it was completely restored. There are period wallpapers, paints, and stencils, new smoke alarms and sprinkler systems, and an all-new handcrafted reproduction furniture line, named after the inn by the manufacturer.

☞ The Health Club is new. What a place! It has everything you could want in it. Massage, sauna, whirlpool—such luxury. Inquire about the inn's complete health package, which includes diet. If the health club isn't for you, there's a ☞ heated outdoor swimming pool with a sun terrace, a glorious spot on a summer day.

The Whip is the lounge area, which provides a casual setting for the food that is served all day. A beautiful, huge fireplace is along one wall, and the beer tap is the most unusual I've seen. It is colorful ceramic and serves three different beers.

The dining room is charming. At lunch the chicken salad plate was beautifully served and delicious. Dinner was even better. ☞ Everyone who works here makes you feel right at home.

After you've had an active day on the ski slopes, the public rooms are a great place to relax. The library has a chess set at the ready. The connecting parlor with a roaring fire in the fireplace has the daily newspapers, including the *New York Times.*

The guest rooms have twin beds or canopy-covered queen-size beds, with comfortable mattresses. All are well appointed, with lots of towels and extra pillows.

This inn really has everything.

How to get there: Take I-89 to Route 100 north into Stowe. The inn is at the intersection of Routes 100 and 108.

E: *This is the ski capital of the East. How nice to relax in this lovely country inn.*

Clive Metcalf

Ten Acres Lodge
Stowe, Vermont
05672

Innkeepers: Dave and Libby Helprin
Telephone: 802-253-7638
Rooms: 14, 10 with private bath; two guest cottages.
Rates: In summer and fall, $37 to $62, double occupancy,
   EP. In winter, $38 to $60, per person, EPB; $56 to $78,
   per person, MAP. Guest cottages higher.
Facilities: Open all year. Breakfast, dinner, bar. Pets in cot-
   tages only. Heated swimming pool, tennis court, cross-
   country skiing. Downhill skiing nearby. All major credit
   cards accepted.

   The living rooms at Ten Acres Lodge are the most inviting and comfortable these bones have enjoyed in many a
mile. You find soft couches and chairs, large fireplaces, ☞
bookcases full of good reading, and windows that look out on
sheer beauty year round. In summer, dairy cows graze in the
rolling farm fields across the road, and in winter, cross-country ski trails crisscross the hillside. Around the inn are

maples more than 100 years old that provide lazy New England shade.

The dining rooms are beautifully appointed from the poppy-colored wallpapers to the napery. The food is thoughtfully prepared. The ☞ menu changes every night. There are things for starters like fresh artichokes and scallops with saffron mayonnaise or garlic sausage with roasted red peppers. And this I love, fried brie with apples. The menu has a variety of fish, veal, steak, and lamb entrees, all skillfully cooked by the chef.

The very comfortable guest rooms are carpeted and pine-paneled or wallpapered with pine trim. The beds are queens and doubles, covered with ☞ lovely homemade spreads. The guest cottages have their own kitchens, working fireplaces, and terraces that look out at all the wonderful scenery that surrounds Stowe.

The inn has a neat bar and a game room all set for a game of backgammon, chess, or checkers. Outside, you are in the ski capital of the East. The mountains are just beautiful. Go and enjoy.

How to get there: From Route 100 North in Stowe, turn left at the three-way stop onto Route 108. Proceed approximately 3 miles, then bear left onto Luce Hill Road. Ten Acres is located in approximately ½ mile, on the left.

E: The twin couches in front of one of the fireplaces beckon me.

Tucker Hill Lodge
Waitsfield, Vermont
05673

Innkeepers: Emily and Zeke Church; Carter Parkinson
Telephone: 802-496-3983
Rooms: 20, 14 with private bath.
Rates: $47 to $59, per person, double occupancy, MAP.
Facilities: Open all year. Dinner served in season. Sunday
    brunch only through October, cross-country lunches,
    bar. Swimming pool, ski touring center. Fishing, tennis,
    and golf nearby. All major credit cards accepted.

You will find Tucker Hill Lodge nestled on a wooded
ridge overlooking the road that winds up to the Mad River
Glen Ski Area. ☛ Route 17, by the way, is one of the most
spectacular roads you will ever find.

The inn is cozy, ☛ fresh flowers in your room, handmade quilts on most of the beds, comfortable living rooms
and caring innkeepers.

The menu changes every day, and the food is excellent,
with inventive dishes like shrimp and watercress salad with a

vinaigrette gourmande dressing, or avocado and grapefruit salad with a dressing of grapefruit and lemon juices, scallions, and olive oil. The veal is tender and light. One way it is served is with asparagus sauce, another is with lemon sabayon sauce. I like the different touches the chef has up here. They also serve interesting fish dishes like poached tilefish with shrimp and leeks, or poached monkfish with a tomato beurre blanc sauce. Of course, beef and chicken are on the menu too. And would you believe a coffee called Dastardly Mash? Come on up and try it.

There is a lot doing up here. A ski touring center is right here at the inn. In addition, there is a Robert Trent Jones golf course nearby, plus swimming, tennis, fishing, and more. Or you can just relax in this lovely inn. Do remember to pat Blue, the inn dog.

How to get there: Turn west off Route 100 onto Route 17 in Waitsfield in the Mad River Valley. Go 1½ miles west; the sign for the lodge will be on your left.

E: *I cannot think of a nicer place to sit than on the deck, under the trees, sipping something long and cool, or I'll take the menu, one item at a time, from Tabouli, Seviche, to Roast Pork with Mustard sauce. Yum, yum.*

To find a good inn as darkness glowers on the horizon, there is no treasure to match it.

White Rocks Inn
Wallingford, Vermont
05773

Innkeepers: Jeffrey and Jennifer Cook
Telephone: 802-446-2077
Rooms: 4, one with private bath.
Rates: $20 to $35, per person, double occupancy, EBP.
Facilities: Open all year. Dinner, Sunday brunch, bar. Horse-
    back riding. Canoeing. Fishing, cross-country skiing,
    and downhill skiing nearby. MasterCard and Visa ac-
    cepted.

Behind the inn is one of the most magnificent barns I
have ever seen. Around the inn are simply beautiful trees.
There are eighty acres for you to roam. What a heavenly
place to go for a ☛ horseback ride.

Otter Creek borders the property and is a delightful
creek for canoeing. It flows north through farm country to
Lake Champlain. Just south of the property, the creek is a
good place for fishing. Jeffrey is an ☛ avid fisherman and he

is always scouting around the area for new fishing spots. He's happy to direct you to them.

The inn is old. There are wide-board floors and very comfortable beds. A lovely ☞ Victorian parlor is just right for cocktails. Do you remember the old roll-top desks? Well, they have one in the small private dining room. There is an old butter worker in one corner of the room. A very interesting antique that used to work.

The menu is full of mouthwatering dishes. Breakfast includes ☞ Eggs à la Mer, poached eggs over rich seafood topped with hollandaise sauce, or Pancake Souffle, a large pancake with sautéed bananas and honey. Sunday brunch is equally good with a variety of dishes. For dinner, one of the appetizers is so good—mushroom caps stuffed with spinach and seafood. Entrees include duck, crisp-roasted with a chambord sauce, or tournedos with a tangy mustard and horseradish sauce. Doesn't this sound too good to be true? Come on up and try it all.

How to get there: Going north on Route 7, the inn is on the left before the town of Wallingford.

ᕼ

E: *Fresh vegetables from their own garden are so nice.*

> *"There is nothing which has*
> *been contrived by man by which*
> *so much happiness is produced*
> *as by a good tavern or inn."*
> —Samuel Johnson

The Inn at Weathersfield
Weathersfield, Vermont
05151

Innkeepers: Mary Louise and Ron Thorburn
Telephone: 802-263-9217
Rooms: 10, all with private bath; 2 suites.
Rates: $36 to $40, per person, double occupancy, EPB plus afternoon tea; or $55 to $60, per person, double occupancy, MAP plus tea.
Facilities: Open all year. Breakfast, afternoon tea, dinner, tavern. Horse and carriage stalls. Tennis, sauna, pool table, Ping-Pong, exercise equipment. No children under 8. MasterCard and Visa accepted.

This beautiful old inn was built circa 1776 and has a wonderful history. At one point during the Civil War it was an important stop on the Underground Railroad, hiding slaves en route to Canada. The inn is set well back from the road. Your rest is assured.

Everything that Mary Louise and Ron do to improve this lovely inn is done with class and lots of care. In the new wing are five redone rooms with sensational ☞ old bathtubs. These are real honest-to-goodness Victorian bathrooms. There are Rumford fireplaces in all of these rooms and in a lot of the other rooms as well. Each suite has two rooms and can hold four people. All the rooms are beautiful with ☞ fresh flowers, fresh fruit, canopy beds, electric sheets, and feather pillows.

Over the years Ron has built an extensive and good wine cellar. The new tavern is handsome and so is the greenhouse dining area. Mary Louise found some old stencils to use and her quilt collection is a beauty.

The food is imaginative and different. Cider jelly is made nearby and used in some cooking. I never had had it before, so I bought some and used it as a baste on lamb chops at home. Delicious! Chicken Weathersfield is just one of Mary Louise's recipes that does wonderful things with boneless breast of chicken. The inn has many mulberry trees from which the owners make a sweet and sour mulberry sauce, one use for which is on stuffed pork chops.

Daughter Heather and husband, Jack, are potters. Their fine work is used in the inn, and certain pieces are for sale here.

There is a ☞ horse and carriage that will take you to the old swimming hole. The area here is full of berries. In winter you may go for a sleigh ride. All of this and a beautiful country inn.

How to get there: Exit 7 from I-91. Take Route 106 north to Perkinsville. About one-half mile short of the village you will find the inn on your left set well back from the road.

☖

E: *A wassail cup is served from a cauldron in the keeping room fireplace. High tea is a special I love along with a gaggle of inn dogs known as "Mom's Moldy Muppets."*

Grandmother's House
West Arlington, Vermont
05250

Innkeeper: Mrs. Walter Finney
Telephone: 802-375-2328
Rooms: 5, 3 double, 2 single, with 2½ baths.
Rates: $50, per person, MAP. Reservations and deposit requested. Minimum stay of two nights.
Facilities: Open all year. Breakfast and dinner for house guests only. No bar. Parking. No pets. Fishing, tennis, swimming. Skiing, museums, and summer theaters nearby. No credit cards accepted.

One of the nice things about Grandmother's House is that it never changes, nor does it ever need to.

Of course you must go over the river and through the covered bridge to reach Grandmother's House. When you arrive, you may find a hand-lettered sign on the door saying, "Grandmother Washing Hair. Holler loudly." Mrs. Finney, official Grandmother to the world, has a whole file of signs for any occasion. She prefers her guests to stay more than one night. If you stay awhile, you can really begin to relax.

Nearby are many antique shops, but Mrs. Finney doesn't need to go to them. Her house is filled with beautiful things, and one of her prizes is a tiger maple four-poster, made by her (we think) great-great-grandfather.

☛ This is a superb place for fishermen because the Battenkill River is close at hand. You can loaf under the great shady maples, take a swim under the covered bridge, play tennis, croquet, or horseshoes, take long walks along country lanes, or ski in winter. Once upon a time Norman Rockwell, the artist, lived in this house, and you are right across the lane from a dear little Methodist church.

How to get there: Turn off Route 7 in Arlington onto Route 313. Go 4 miles to a covered bridge on the left, and cross that bridge to Grandmother's House. Or, take Route 22 from Cambridge, New York, to Route 313. Go 12 miles, and the covered bridge will be on your right.

E: *Look at the figures holding the plants on each side of the porch. They came from Mrs. Finney's grandmother's conservatory. They are charming.*

*I have enjoyed the hospitality of a good inn
and I am ready for the day ahead.*

Olive Metcalf

Deerhill Inn
West Dover, Vermont
05356

Innkeepers: Eileen and Ron Armonath
Telephone: 802-464-3100
Rooms: 17, 16 with private bath.
Rates: $110 to $155, double occupancy, MAP.
Facilities: Closed Easter to Memorial Day. Breakfast, dinner, lounge, full license. No pets. Not recommended for small children. Swimming pool, tennis. Golfing and skiing nearby. All major credit cards accepted.

The setting for the Deerhill Inn is perfect. Surrounded by lovely maple and fruit trees, it is perched on a hill with views of the countryside's beautiful mountains and lush meadows. It is nice and quiet up here. This is good country for hiking or cross-country skiing. Nearby are Mount Snow, Carinthia, and Haystack for downhill skiing. In summer you're sure to enjoy the inn's swimming pool and tennis court. The Mount Snow 18-hole golf course is close at hand.
　　There are several large living areas with ☛ fireplaces

and comfortable furniture. There also is a small, well-stocked library. The views of Mount Snow from any place in this lovely inn are beautiful and so tranquil.

The guest rooms are clean, bright, and handsomely furnished. There's a choice of twin, double, queen, and king beds, and there are four lovely canopy beds. All very restful.

I love romantic dining, and here at the Deerhill it is by candlelight with attractive pink and white napery. The food has a touch of Europe blended with the best of Vermont. The escargots are served with garlic and herbs under puff pastry in a ramekin. I love garlic, and these escargots are good. The fresh sole with lime butter is nice and different. So is the duck that has a date and port sauce. And it is rare to have rack of lamb for one person. A really nice touch.

How to get there: Take Route 9 to Wilmington; turn north onto route 100 at the traffic light and continue to West Dover village. Pass the church and post office; at the antique store turn right onto Valley View Road. The inn is 300 yards up the road on the right-hand side.

E: Eating my way through New England is fun with food like this.

The Inn at Sawmill Farm
West Dover, Vermont
05356

Innkeepers: Rodney, Ione, Brill, and Luz Williams
Telephone: 802-464-8131
Rooms: 12 rooms, all with private bath, in the inn; 10 cottage
rooms, all with private bath and fireplace.
Rates: $140 to $200, double occupancy, MAP. In foliage season and between Christmas and New Year's Day, $10
higher.
Facilities: Closed the Sunday after Thanksgiving to mid-December. Breakfast, dinner, bar, lounge. Swimming pool,
tennis court, trout and two bass fishing ponds. No pets.
No children under 10. No credit cards accepted.

The Williams have transformed an old Vermont barn
into the gayest, warmest, most attractive inn that I have seen
in many a country mile. Ione is a professional decorator and
Rod is a noted architect, which makes for a wonderful mar-
riage of talents for just a perfect inn. The Williams' son, Brill,
runs the kitchen and he does a superb job of it. Brill's lovely

wife, Luz, is in charge of the inn's gift shop, and she has filled it with beautiful things, some from her ☞ native land, Colombia.

The inn's copper collection is extensive. The ☞ oversized fireplace in the living room is surrounded with it and there's a huge copper-topped coffee table that's a beauty. They also have a handsome brass telescope on a tripod for your viewing of Mount Snow. A most incredible bar of solid copper also lives here. This is in the Pot Belly Lounge.

Accommodations are very different, with some Victorian rooms, some done in Chippendale, and all with the flavor of New England at its best. The cottage rooms have fireplaces. The accommodations upstairs in Spring House have a living room with fireplace, bedroom, and bath in the most glorious colors imaginable. I was in Farm House and my room was done in the softest pastels, with a king-sized bed and a lovely dressing room and bath. They are all color-coordinated with thick towels and extra pillows. ☞ Little boxes of Godiva chocolates are in each room. A very nice touch.

Dinner is beyond belief. Brill is a fine chef. There are twelve appetizers. ☞ Coquille of Crabmeat Imperial under glass was my choice. Brill's wife, Luz, who joined me for dinner, had thinly sliced raw sirloin of beef with shallot and mustard sauce. Of course I tasted some of hers. Outstanding. The soups are inventive and good. One entree is Medallions of Pork Tenderloin with cognac, cream, and walnuts. There are many more. They are perfectly complemented by wines from Brill's impressive wine cellar. Desserts are all homemade. Breakfast also is special. Fresh orange juice and homemade tomato juice are just starters. The staff who serve all these goodies are very courteous.

How to get there: Take I-91 to Exit 2 in Brattleboro. Take Route 9 west to Wilmington, and then follow Route 100 north 6 miles to West Dover.

E: *The inn makes a specialty of special times. Do try to get up here for Christmas. It's something you will never forget.*

Olive Metcalf

Snow Den Inn
West Dover, Vermont
05356

Innkeepers: Milt and Jean Cummings
Telephone: 802-464-9355
Rooms: 8, all with private bath.
Rates: $23 to $43, per person, double occupancy, EPB.
Facilities: Open all year. Breakfast, dinner in winter, BYOB. Downhill and cross-country skiing, golf, tennis, swimming, boating, and music festival nearby. American Express, MasterCard, and Visa accepted.

The Snow Den Inn was built in 1885 by the Davis family as a farmhouse. It was a family house until 1952 when it was converted to an inn.

Snow Den is a good name for an inn up here in snow country. There is so much to keep you busy and happy in this area. The inn is two miles from Mount Snow, and two minutes from the Mount Snow Golf Course and Country Club. ☞ Facilities at the club are available to guests at Snow Den. The Marlboro Music Festival is nearby, and so are summer playhouses, craft shows, and fairs. Cross-country skiing is only minutes away, and the Stratton, Magic, and Bromley ski areas are 45 minutes away.

The inn is informal and comfortable. The den is large, and has a fireplace and a picture window that overlooks Mount Snow. This is a good place to relax after a busy day. The bedrooms are large. ☞ Five of them have color television and fireplace. On a blustery winter night this is heaven.

Milt is the chef. One entree is served each night. Breakfast is yummy, with French toast, eggs, crisp bacon, and homemade zucchini nut bread.

And to make things warm and wonderful, there is a ☞ nice wood stove in the dining room.

How to get there: Follow Route 100 from Wilmington to West Dover. The inn is on your right in the middle of the village.

E: *Milt and Jean have been here since 1976, so you know they are old hands at innkeeping.*

> *"Does the road wind uphill all the way?*
> *Yes, to the very end.*
> *Will the day's journey take the whole day long?*
> *From morn to night, my friend."*
> —Christina Rossetti

West Dover Inn
West Dover, Vermont
05356

Innkeepers: Donald and Madeline Mitchell
Telephone: 802-464-5207
Rooms: 12, 10 with private bath and television.
Rates: $45 to $90, double occupancy, EPB.
Facilities: Closed the first two weeks in May and after foliage
    season. Lunch and dinner, summer and foliage season;
    dinner in ski season; bar. No children under 8. Skiing,
    hiking, golfing, and more nearby. All major credit cards
    accepted.

☛ The Mitchells are to be complimented for restoring
this fine old inn. An inn since 1846, it became the site of the
town offices and had many changes before 1889, when the
first addition was completed. It was known as the Green
Mountain Inn until 1955.

The rooms are airy and decorated with antiques and
hand-sewn quilts. They all have a view of the mountains.

Henry and Iodine are the inn cats. I love their names. Smoky is the inn dog.

The dining room is named Capstone, and the menus are very inviting. Lunch suggestions include sandwiches, burgers, soups, salads, and very inventive omelettes. On the dinner menu under appetizers is Sole Paupiette. Delicious. There are good American entrees like Yankee Pot Roast and Lamb Houstonian, and, of course, the catch of the day.

The inn's location is a perfect base for whatever you care to do—swimming, sunning, leaf peeping, skiing, hiking, shopping, and much more. You could also come here to just relax and enjoy.

How to get there: Take Exit 2 for I-91 at Brattleboro, Vermont, then take Route 9 west to Route 100 north. In West Dover you will find the inn on your right in the village.

☼

E: ☛ *The magnificent old organ in the parlor is a dream.*

*Let us escape for a day, or better a week,
and hide away in a country inn.*

Olive Metcalf

The Inn at Weston
Weston, Vermont
05161

Innkeepers: Stu, Sue, and Molly Douglas
Telephone: 802-824-5804.
Rooms: 13, 7 with private bath.
Rates: $38 to $52, per person, MAP. EPB rates available.
Facilities: Closed mid-April to mid-May, midweek in November, and December 1 through December 15. Dining room closed Wednesdays, except in foliage season. Breakfast, lunch in winter on Saturdays, dinner, Sunday brunch, bar. Television in game room. Wheelchair ramp available for dining room and one ground-floor bedroom. Cross-country skiing from inn door. Downhill skiing, hiking, summer theater, and museums nearby. No credit cards accepted.

If you walk in the front door of this lovely inn, you are in Sue Douglas' kitchen, and Sue is the chef. She greets you with a warm smile and great culinary treats. The last time I was here, the fare was ☞ Poached Salmon with Mustard

Sauce, Veal Provençale, Braised Duck with honey, black cherries, and cassis sauce, Monk's Breast of Chicken with mushrooms, fruits, and crème fraiche, and a different vegetarian entree each night.

Stu is the breakfast chef, and he makes marvelous ☞ whole wheat, cornmeal, and rye pancakes, or French toast made from Sue's homemade breads. It is all served with Vermont bacon and maple syrup. The homemade apple butter contains ☞ whole slices of apple, and the blueberry muffins are so good. Sunday brunch is delightfully creative.

The rooms are small, and very very pleasant with antique beds that are comfortable. The dining room has so much charm and warmth, with walls of real barn siding, and the dining porch is a most popular place to dine in summer and fall. Everyone who works here ☞ smiles. They are a happy group. As the Douglases say, "This is where friendships begin," and they really do. If you are on a special diet, tell Sue and she will try to help you stay within it.

Weston is the home of the Vermont Country Store and Vermont's oldest, continuously operated, summer theater. These, plus craft shops, museums, and the lovely village green are all within a pleasant stroll. The inn is close to several ski areas, so do come and enjoy.

How to get there: Off I-91, on Exit 6, take Route 103 to Chester. Follow Route 11 to Londonderry, and turn right on Route 100 to Weston. The inn is in the Village.

☒

E: *Afternoon tea is served at 4, with hot spiced cider and Sue's homemade goodies—Wow!*

Windham Hill Inn
West Townshend, Vermont
05359

Innkeepers: Linda and Ken Busteed
Telephone: 802-874-4080
Rooms: 15, all with private bath.
Rates: $52 to $55, per person, double occupancy, MAP.
Facilities: Closed April and November. Breakfast, dinner, full
    license. All the activities of all seasons. MasterCard and
    Visa accepted.

At Windham Hill Inn you are sitting on the top of the world. It is beautiful up here. The West River Valley stretches as far as the eye can see. Built originally about 1825, it was a working dairy farm, and in 1962 was converted into an inn, which it has remained.

The family-style meals are memorable. Linda is the chef, and she makes all her own ☛ breads and desserts as well as her soups and appetizers. Ken is the breakfast chef, and together this pair make a great team. In season all the vegetables are fresh, most from the inn's gardens.

The rooms are charming. Linda and Ken recently renovated the lovely old barn on the property to add five more guest rooms to the inn. They are very unusual, plus their views are spectacular. Two of the rooms in the house ☞ have their own balconies.

The living room is full of Victorian wicker and has a good New England wood stove. Off of this is a lovely balcony that overlooks the world. The whole inn feels like home. There are plants everywhere. I found a large stack of old *Life* magazines, something I love. They also have a well-stocked library.

There is much to do here, a practice ski slope, floodlit ice-skating pond, tobogganing, sledding, snowshoeing, and cross-country skiing. Nearby are Stratton Mountain, Big Bromley, Magic Mountain, Mount Snow, Snow Valley, Maple Valley, and Timber Ridge. A schuss-boomer's dream come true.

As the innkeepers say, the inn continues to be one of the best kept secrets in Vermont.

How to get there: Take Exit 2 off I-91 in Brattleboro, then Route 30 for 21 miles to West Townshend. At the Country Store turn right, up the hill, onto Windham Road. Look for the inn's sign on the right in 1½ miles.

Ⴤ

E: *The peonies were in bloom. They have some in two colors. Another garden sight I have never seen before was their magnificent* ☞ *Fringe tree.*

Brook Bound
Wilmington, Vermont
05363

Innkeeper: Jim McGovern
Telephone: 802-464-5267
Rooms: 15, 10 with private bath; 2 housekeeping chalets.
Rates: $50 to $60, double occupancy, EPB.
Facilities: Open all year. Breakfast only meal served. Dinner
    served at the Hermitage nearby. BYOB. Recreation
    room, pool table, Ping-Pong, swimming, tennis. Music
    and skiing nearby. No credit cards accepted.

In the beautiful Green Mountains of southern Vermont,
off a country road in a lovely quiet setting with commanding
views of Haystack and Mount Snow, there is this warm and
friendly inn waiting to welcome you.

The grounds are spacious, and the ☞ pool is heated. It
sits up above the inn with the tennis courts beyond. There
are glorious big trees all over, and in the fall they are a sight
to behold.

Breakfast is the only meal served at Bound Brook, but the Hermitage, which is also owned by Jim McGovern, is nearby, and a great spot to have some dinner. Setups are provided for your drink at Bound Brook, and in the winter it all happens around a neat fireplace. The inn has a refrigerator especially for guests to keep luncheon food and snacks or drinks. This is a nice thing to do.

Two chalets are close by. The smaller one holds up to six people and the larger one can accommodate nine. You do your own cooking and housekeeping.

The inn is close to several ski areas for both downhill and cross-country skiing. There is so much to do in this area any season of the year that it would take pages just to list everything.

You are only twelve miles from the Marlboro Music Festival or the Brattleboro Music Center's Bach program. A real turn-on for a music lover.

How to get there: From Wilmington take Route 100 north and turn left on Cold Brook Road. Go 2.2 miles to the inn.

❦

E: *Cross-country ski trails connect the Bound Brook to the Hermitage, so you can go right out the front door.*

A warming fire, a strong drink, a genial innkeeper . . . and winter is somewhere in the hills but is not here.

Olive Metcalf

The Hermitage
Wilmington, Vermont
05363

Innkeeper: James McGovern
Telephone: 802-464-3759
Rooms: 16, all with private bath, 11 with fireplace.
Rates: $70 to $80, per person, double occupancy, MAP.
Facilities: Open all year. Breakfast, lunch in season, dinner.
  Accessible to wheelchairs. Sauna, wine cellar, game bird
  farm, trout pond, tennis, hiking, cross-country skiing
  from the door. All major credit cards accepted.

High on a windy hill facing Haystack Mountain, you will find a unique and heartwarming country inn, The Hermitage. The owner is a man for all seasons who knows what he is doing. He also has a certain charm, maybe it is the quick smile or a fleeting twinkle as he says, ☛ "No piped-in music in *my* inn." You might, though, find a classical guitarist some night, or someone at the piano in the lounge.

Come in the very early spring, and you will find maple sugaring going full blast. There are four sugarhouses on the property, and Jim McGovern makes 700 gallons of maple syrup in an unexceptional year. In summer the big kettles are kept simmering, making homemade jams and jellies. Along with this talent for making the most of nature's bounty, Jim is an oenophile (wine lover), and has a wine cellar with a stock of 30,000 bottles. You are never at a loss for the perfect wine to enjoy with this inn's first-rate food.

Dining at the Hermitage is truly gourmet and includes homegrown game and fresh vegetables. The dining rooms are lovely. The newest addition is the Delacroix Room named for Michael Delacroix whose paintings are featured throughout the inn. There's a fireplace to warm you while you enjoy some of Jim's wines.

Jim raises as many as sixty different species of game birds. Most of them, such as pheasant, partridge, duck, quail, turkey, and goose, are raised for gourmet dining. Jim also has show birds, brilliantly colored species of ducks and peacocks and a pair of black swans. He has an incubator for the eggs and I watched the babies breaking out of the eggs. Cognac and Burgundy, two friendly English setters (Jim also raises them), may come by to say hello, but they are likely to be distracted by a passing gaggle of geese that will fly off in a flurry of wings.

The comfortable rooms, eleven with their own working fireplaces, are furnished with antiques and, oh, those brass beds. In the carriage house you will even find a sauna.

How to get there: Take Route 9 to Wilmington, follow Route 100 north 2 miles to Coldbrook Road on the left. The Hermitage is 3 miles down Coldbrook Road.

E: *The wine cellar, with its two crystal chandeliers, marvelous selection of wine and gifts, turned me on. What to do with your old claw-footed bathtub? Use it to store wine. There is also an old bassinet used for the same purpose.*

Olive Metcalf

The White House
Wilmington, Vermont
05363

Innkeeper: Robert Grinold
Telephone: 802-464-2135
Rooms: 8, all with private bath, 2 with fireplace; one suite.
Rates: $70 to $80, per person, MAP.
Facilities: Open all year. Breakfast, dinner, Sunday brunch.
Skier's lunch in winter. Bar, lounge, swimming pool inside and out, health spa with sauna, steamroom, whirlpool. Cross-country and downhill skiing nearby. Credit cards accepted, but personal checks preferred.

You would expect an inn named the White House to be elegant and, believe me, this one is. Built in 1914, the Mansion has much to offer.

The gallery on the main floor has an extremely unusual wallpaper that was printed in Paris in 1912. There are high ceilings throughout the inn and the living room is large with a fireplace and beautifully covered (blue, of course) couches and chairs. So nice to come back to after a day on the ski trails.

There are two dining rooms, both of which are very elegant, and a small private dining room. The food served in this three-star inn is superb, but would you expect anything else in the White House? Here's just a sampling of what they offer. There are nine appetizers, including brandied grapefruit and interesting soups. The one I liked best was shrimp stuffed mushrooms. Entrees are numerous and varied with always a special one or two. All are oh, so good and served with excellent salad and breads. Of course, all the desserts are homemade. I get hungry just writing about Bob's inn.

The grounds are sumptuous, with a lovely rose garden and fountain, and below this is a sixty-foot swimming pool. There's another small fountain outside the lounge, and from this delightful room you watch spectacular sunsets over the Green Mountains.

The Health Spa is what you need after a day of fun; exercise and massage room, sauna, whirlpool, steamroom, and showers. There's also an inside pool to relax in. Ah, what an inn.

How to get there: From Route I-91 take Route 9 to Wilmington. The inn is on your right just before you reach the town.

E: *Intrigue! Why did the original owner of the house put in a secret staircase? You will have to ask where it is.*

*The warmth of a country inn
can only be likened to
a well-made down comforter.*

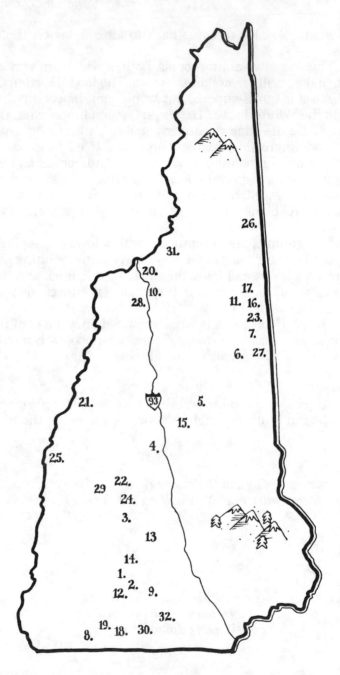

Numbers on map refer to towns numbered
on index on opposite page

New Hampshire

Uplands Inn
Antrim Center, New Hampshire
03440

Innkeepers: Fred and Judy Heyliger
Telephone: 603-588-6349
Rooms: 7, one with private bath.
Rates: $38 to $58, double occupancy, EPB.
Facilities: Open all year. Dinner by reservation. BYOB. No
    pets. Cross-country skiing, hiking. Swimming and boat-
    ing nearby. No credit cards accepted.

One of the first things I saw when I was looking around
the inn was an ☞ absolutely magnificent, huge bookcase
with glass doors. I have never seen anything like it.

There are two sitting areas with fireplaces, a lovely dining room, and, when the weather permits, a screened-in dining porch. The Captain's Room has a king-sized canopy bed
and large sitting area with a private bath. There is a Victorian
daybed and matching rocker in here. The other guest rooms
are small to medium in size, well furnished, comfortable, and
clean.

Judy has a large garden and a greenhouse in which she starts her plants early. All ☞ vegetables are truly fresh. Fred is the breakfast chef and Judy is the dinner chef. All soups, breads, and desserts are homemade. She makes a herbed minestrone soup from her garden, which is delightful, curried chicken crepes, beef stroganoff, and much more. There is one entree each evening.

The inn has a sixty-five-acre backyard of pastures and woods with views of the village and mountains to the south. At the top of Meeting House Hill is the site of the original Antrim Village. All that remains is the village cemetery.

Close by is beautiful Lake Gregg or Pierce for boating or swimming; hiking or picnicking on Mount Monadnock; golfing, tennis, and theater in Peterborough; a lot of downhill or cross-country skiing; and just a beautiful, peaceful countryside.

How to get there: From Route 202 take Route 31 north. Two-and-one-half miles north to the village, turn right on Miltinmore Road at the grange.

E: *Fresh flowers in your room are so nice.*

I was lost, I was tired, I was discouraged,
and then I found a friendly inn.

Olive Metcalf

David's
Bennington, New Hampshire
03442

Innkeeper: David Glynn
Telephone: 603-588-2458
Rooms: 2, each with private bath.
Rates: $45, double occupancy, EP.
Facilities: Closed Mondays, and December 1 to April 1.
Breakfast for house guests only. Lunch, dinner, full license. No credit cards honored, but personal checks accepted.

I think David can feed about forty people, but he has overnight accommodations for only four. The rooms with their beamed ceilings and wide "illegal board" floors (so called because in those days boards over twelve inches in width were for the exclusive use of the King of England) are nice and cozy. The house belonged to David's grandmother, and he has fully restored it to its circa 1788 self. The walls have the original stencils by Moses Eaton, a famous man in his time. These designs have been duplicated throughout the whole inn.

Now for the best part, and that is David's food. His fame stretches many miles in all directions. There were three of us enjoying his food, and, of course, I tried as much of it as I could. The Fresh Salmon Pie with an egg sauce was lighter than eating butterflies. The chicken and the lobster pies were sinfully delicious. The menu goes on, but I had to stop, well, not quite yet. We had one each of New England Deep-dish Apple Pie à la mode, Apricot Rum Cake à la mode, and David's Meringue Shell Vanilla Ice Cream with chocolate or strawberry sauce. I could hardly make it to the door. This is superb food. All breads and pastries are made here, and all of the vegetables are fresh.

There are jars of David's relishes, jams, and jellies for sale. Do take some home with you.

How to get there: Going north, exit from I-91 at Brattleboro and take Route 5 north to Route 9. Stay on 9 until North Branch, then turn right onto Route 31, which will take you into Bennington. David's Restaurant and Inn is across from the Town Hall in Bennington Square.

☀

E: *The old carriage seat in the tiny sitting room intrigues me. From the surrey with the fringe on top?*

olive Metcalf

The Massasecum Lodge
Bradford, New Hampshire
03221

Innkeepers: Mary Jo and Jim Shipe
Telephone: 603-938-2136
Rooms: 7, 5 with private bath, one cottage.
Rates: $35 to $42, double occupancy, EP. Special packages
   for groups.
Facilities: Open all year. Breakfast, dinner for four or more
   guests. BYOB. Swimming, croquet, badminton, horseshoes, boating, fishing, golfing, hiking, ice-fishing, skiing. No credit cards accepted.

The town of Bradford was settled about fifteen years
prior to the American Revolution. This lodge was built as a
farmhouse by Isaac Davis, who is reputed to have been the
first settler in Bradford. About one hundred years later, in
1850, the Massasecum Lodge was opened to guests.

The grandfather's clock in the entry was made by Robin
Roberts 175 years ago, and still keeps perfect time. A marvelous, 75-year-old ☛ Brunswick pool table is in the dining

area. To play, jackets are required, but no top hats; all in fun, of course. I had such a good time playing a few games with Jim. There's a piano, and hopefully a guest who can play. It's cozy and warm in here in the cool weather months, thanks to a good woodburning stove. There are a few of them in the inn.

Mary Jo is the chef, and she prepares one entree each evening. Vegetables come from the lodge's gardens, and desserts and breads are all made in the inn's kitchen. Mary Jo served baked stuffed Rock Cornish hens to my friend, Lucy Goodale, and me. First we had ☞ homemade cauliflower and cheese soup that was excellent, and for dessert we had pumpkin ice cream. We ate every bit.

There is a view of the lake from some of the guest rooms. Other rooms look out on the surrounding mountains. All the guest rooms are comfortable and clean.

The lodge provides many activities for the guests. Aside from playing lawn games, swimming, and "cooking out" down at the private sandy beach, guests often walk over to the lovely waterfalls or hike over the 160 acres of woods and fields. The inn has its own boat for a row on the lake. Sailboats can be rented nearby. In the spring you can go fishing for brook trout, perch, pickerel, and bass. Skiing and ice-fishing are fun activities for the winter.

Do come, and bring along the kids. Massasecum is a family lodge, with children always welcome.

How to get there: Go up I-93, exit west on I-89, and exit west on Route 202/9 to Route 114 at Henniker. Proceed north on Route 114 about 6 miles. The inn is on the left.

☕

E: *There are three of them. Mother Cat, a calico, White Cat, and Coon cat. Very simple.*

Olive Metcalf

The Pasquaney Inn
Bridgewater, New Hampshire
03222

Innkeepers: Marge and Roy Zimmer
Telephone: 603-744-2712
Rooms: In summer, 28; in winter, 18; 10 with private bath.
Rates: $19 to $25, per person, double occupancy, EP; or $36
    to $45, per person, double occupancy, MAP.
Facilities: Closed October 15 to Christmas. Breakfast, din-
    ner, box lunches. Recreation barn, lawn games, lake
    swimming, boating, fishing, hiking, cross-country ski-
    ing. Golf, tennis, and downhill skiing nearby. Master-
    Card and Visa accepted.

The sideboard in the lobby of the inn is a 1790 Baltimore
Hepplewhite, a thing of beauty. The living room, with a fireplace, looks out over Newfound Lake, as does the dining
room. Dining at the inn is informal and relaxed, with all
meals served family style. ☛ Vegetables, always fresh, come
from either the inn's ample gardens or the local markets.

Best of all, the desserts and the breads are all done in the inn's own pastry kitchen.

Guest rooms are bright and attractive, some with a lake view, and the others with great views of the surrounding mountains. There are private and shared baths, and be sure to specify your wants when you make a reservation.

Basically Pasquaney is a family inn, with children always welcome. The recreation barn has a basketball court, shuffleboard courts, Ping-Pong, and a ☞ full, square dance floor with an old-fashioned caller's balcony. There is a calico cat called Mother Cat, and two other felines called simply Cat.

There is much to do here, no matter what season of the year. The inn has its own sandy beach on the lovely lake, also little skiffs for those who wish to take a row around the cove. Sailboats can be rented nearby. Golf and tennis are also near at hand. Winter brings skiing, spring means fishing for land-locked salmon or trout, and fall is that glorious foliage season. Newfound Lake is very reminiscent of the lake district of northern England, and beautiful.

How to get there: From I-93, take exit 23, turn left onto Route 104, then right onto Route 3A. The inn is on the right across from Newfound Lake.

☒

E: *The inn prepares box lunches for hikers, skiers, and motor trippers. Nice touch.*

Corner House Inn
Center Sandwich, New Hampshire
03227

Innkeepers: Jane Kroeger and Don Brown
Telephone: 603-284-6219
Rooms: 4, one with private bath.
Rates: $22 to $30, single; $32 to $40, double occupancy; EPB.
Facilities: Closed a few weeks in the spring and in the fall. Lunch, dinner, BYOB. Skiing and hiking nearby. American Express, MasterCard, and Visa accepted.

This is a very interesting town. Different. The inn is centrally located so you can walk to everything. The ☞ New Hampshire League of Arts and Crafts is here as well as pottery shops, galleries, and museums. There are five major ski areas within a short driving range.

The inn has been operating as an inn for over 100 years. To keep pace with its history, the waitresses are in colorful period pinafores. The food they serve is excellent. The kitchen is famous for its ☞ crepes, and several different ones are prepared each day. I have tried a few and, wow, are they good. They also do fabulous things with soups. Another great inn specialty is ☞ dessert; apple crisp or apple pie stand out, and I dare you to eat just one of their cookies and not go back for more.

Of special note is the inn's house salad dressing. It is a ☞ buttermilk-dill combination. One of my party usually hates salad, but he ate it down to the last wisp of lettuce.

Roast duck is unusual. It is glazed with a variety of fruit sauces. And a new one on an old "inn creeper" like myself was Crab 'n Scallop Pie topped with puff pastry. Well, that tells enough about this good New Hampshire food.

The rooms are very comfortable. Bay windows in the living room, a spinning wheel, and plants give that touch of comfort you love in an inn. The carriage house is now the main dining room.

How to get there: Up I-93 to Exit 24, thence Route 3 to Route 113. Route 113 goes directly to Center Sandwich.

E: *Good inn animals are here. The cat is Anna and the dog, a golden retriever, is Cousteau.*

For one night at least
let me escape from all those things
the Puritans tell me I must face.
Let me find a friendly inn.

Stafford's in the Fields
Chocorua, New Hampshire
03817

Innkeepers: Ramona and Fred Stafford
Telephone: 603-323-7766
Rooms: 14, 8 with private bath; cottages.
Rates: $50 to $85, per person, double occupancy, MAP.
Facilities: Open all year. Breakfast, dinner, Sunday brunch, liquor license. Trail lunches available. No smoking dining room. Parking. No pets. Clay tennis court, cross-country skiing. No credit cards accepted.

At the end of a quiet country lane sits a really lovely country inn. It comes with a babbling brook, has forests at hand, and overlooks some rolling fields. You will also find a barn with truly unusual acoustics. ☞ Square dancing is fun here in the summertime.

Ramona Stafford likes to cook in a sort of French country style with wine and herbs and spices and, best of all, with great imagination: Pork Tenderloin with Prunes, and Stuffed Chicken Breast with almonds and raisins. The daughter of

292

the house, Mono, is responsible for the really sinful ☞ desserts. Mother and daughter hold cooking classes. Oh, to live near them.

Breakfast is the way to start your day. Omelettes are different, sour cream with green chives, mild country cheddar, or cheddar and salsa. For Sunday brunch a real special is ☞ Eggs Hussard with Marchant du Vin. It translates to a wine merchant or a wine sauce in the vernacular. You could also try eggs Benedict or blueberry pancakes. You will not go wrong. Ramona serves well-balanced meals.

The inn is immensely comfortable with cross-country skiing right on the fields, and just utter peace. As Fred Stafford says, there is an inexhaustible supply of "nature things to do." Just sitting, watching the swallows swoop or a leaf spin slowly to the ground restores what you may have lost in the hustle and bustle of today's world.

Turn in the lane some snowy evening and see Stafford's glowing in the field, waiting to welcome you from a world well left behind.

How to get there: Take Route 16 north to Chocorua Village, then turn left onto Route 113 and travel one mile west to the inn. Or, from Route 93, take Exit 23 and travel east on Route 104 to Route 35, and then to Route 16. Proceed north to Route 16 to Chocorua Village.

E: Bulah, a Brittany spaniel, lives here.

Darby Field Inn
Conway, New Hampshire
03818

Innkeepers: Marc and Marily Donaldson
Telephone: 603-447-2181
Rooms: 16, 14 with private bath, 2 with semi-private bath; one suite.
Rates: $50 to $70, per person, double occupancy, MAP.
Facilities: Closed in April and first three weeks in November. Breakfast, dinner, bar. Television, library, swimming pool, skiing, hiking. American Express, MasterCard, and Visa accepted.

Set high atop Bald Hill in New Hampshire's White Mountains with spectacular views of this wonderful country is Darby Field Inn. Located 1,000 feet above Mount Washington Valley and only three miles from Conway Village, the inn delights wanderers adventurous enough to leave the beaten path.

The inn borders the ☛ White Mountain National Forest

where guests are welcome to cross-country ski, snowshoe, hike, or walk to nearby rivers, waterfalls, and lakes.

Rooms are charming, some with four-poster beds, patchwork quilts, and braided rugs. Most rooms have private baths, and they are tucked away wherever space was available. How do you feel about an L-shaped shower stall?

Downstairs the inn's huge ☞ cobblestone fireplace is the center for warm conversation. If you want a bit livelier time come into the pub, which sometimes features local singers.

Candlelight dinners begin with fine wine and a smashing sunset view up the valley. The food reflects the careful preparation of the chef. You'll always find a chef's special and fresh fish du jour. Whatever you order up here it will be excellent. Desserts are interesting. You must try Darby Cream Pie, quite different. The ☞ Irish Revolution will really end your day nicely.

Darby Field, a notorious Irishman, was the first white man to ascend Mount Washington. Had the inn been here in 1642, it is doubtful whether Mr. Field would ever have passed the pub.

How to get there: **Turn** on Bald Hill Road a half-mile south of the Kancamagus Highway on Route 16, then go one mile up the hill and turn right onto a dirt road. The inn is one mile beyond.

E: *The inn dogs are Malamutes, Lupo and Chuska. Beautiful animals.*

> *A good innkeeper, a good cook,*
> *and an affable barkeeper*
> *are as standard in a country inn*
> *as a fire engine in a fire house.*

olive Metcalf

Fitzwilliam Inn
Fitzwilliam, New Hampshire
03447

Innkeepers: Charles and Barbara Wallace
Telephone: 603-585-9000
Rooms: 25, 12 with private bath.
Rates: $24 to $28, single; $28 to $32, double, EP.
Facilities: Open all year. Breakfast, lunch, dinner, bar. Television, sauna, swimming pool, cross-country skiing. All major credit cards accepted.

"The more plastic motels that are built, the more people are going to be driven back to a warm country inn, without wall-to-wall carpeting, but with something else." Enoch Fuller said this. And the Fitzwilliam Inn, which he owned and operated until his death in 1973, is indeed a warm country inn. The Fitzwilliam Inn is still the same old-fashioned New England inn that has been offering food, grog, and lodging to weary travelers since 1796.

If sleigh riding is your idea of a great winter sport, book yourself in at Fitzwilliam. ☛ In summer there is square dancing in the village, and there are many antique shops in this little town. The bar is a great little taproom, where hot winter drinks are called Broken Legs. Meals are hearty New England affairs, with a wonderful homemade ☞ pumpkin bread, and homemade desserts. All menus are tacked to little breadboards.

The Wallaces like to have music at the inn, so there are concerts on a regular basis year round. In summer you can enjoy the beautiful pool, after ☞ the sauna, and then lunch on the patio. All this, with the charm of a centuries-old inn, lovely antiques, and a cordial welcome from the innkeeper.

The men's room is a must. It has a blackboard for graffiti and a great red rocking chair for relaxing.

How to get there: The inn is 205 miles from New York, 65 miles from Boston. Vermont Transit buses stop at the door. It is on Route 119, just west of the intersection of Route 12.

E: *Over the fireplace hangs this word puzzle. The Wallaces will have to unscramble it for you.*

> *If the B mt put:*
> *If the B. putting:*
> *Don't put: over A - der*
> *You'd be an*it!*

Olive Metcalf

The Inn at Crotched Mountain

Francestown, New Hampshire

03043

Innkeepers: John and Rose Perry
Telephone: 603-588-6840
Rooms: 14, 5 with private bath, 4 with fireplace.
Rates: $30 to $60, double occupancy, EP.
Facilities: Closed first three weeks in November. In winter, open only on weekends and holidays. Breakfast, dinner, bar. Tennis, swimming pool, cross-country skiing. Golfing, fishing, and summer theater nearby. No credit cards accepted.

This 150-year-old colonial house is located on the northern side of Crotched Mountain. There is a forty-mile view of the Piscataquog Valley, complete with spacious skies. Both innkeepers have gone to ☞ school to learn their trade, and what a charming house to practice it in. They are both pretty special themselves. Rose is from Singapore, and John is a Yankee.

Come and stay, there are many things to do. There are three golf courses in the nearby valley, fishing is great, and there is a wading pool for the young, as well as a thirty-by-sixty-foot pool for real swimmers. Two areas provide skiing, one at the front door, and another down the road. Two clay tennis courts eliminate that tiresome waiting for a playing area. And come evening there are two summer theaters, one at Peterborough and another in Milford.

There are two English cockers who live here, Kong and Anan. Anan is Kong's daughter. There are numerous streams, ponds, and lakes for fishing and mountains for hiking. Golf is nearby. Come and enjoy this wonderful countryside with Kong and Anan. They would love to have you.

How to get there: Take 101A from Nashua to Milford, Route 13 to New Boston, and Route 136 to Francestown. Take Route 47 2½ miles, then turn left onto Mountain Road. The inn is one mile up the road.

E: *Any house that has nine fireplaces needs a wood lot and a man with a chain saw.* ☛ *Four of the bedrooms here have a fireplace, so remember to request one when you reserve.*

The register of a country inn
is a treasure of the names of good people.

Olive Metcalf

The Inn at Tory Pines
Francestown, New Hampshire
03043

Innkeeper: Dick Tremblay
Telephone: 603-588-6352
Rooms: 32, 28 with private bath, and 2 suites; all with television and phone. One cottage.
Rates: Rates start at $49, double occupancy, EP. Package plans available.
Facilities: Open all year. Breakfast, lunch, dinner, bar. Swimming, tennis, golf, golf pro shop, downhill and cross-country skiing, skiing pro shop, ice skating. All major credit cards accepted.

The inn is the home of the ☞ Hall of Fame golf course, which is patterned after the best eighteen holes from famous courses all over the world. Dick Tremblay is a PGA professional golfer. The inn has carts, lessons, clinics, and a good practice range.

Skiing is also superb here. The inn is at the foot of Crotched Mountain in the Monadnock region of southern

New Hampshire. There are excellent cross-country trails on over 400 acres of the inn's own land plus ☞ guided mountain tours for the more adventurous. Complete rental equipment is available, along with waxing and repair services.

The house is old, built in 1799. It is a Georgian Colonial. Two big maples, exactly as old as the house, flank the original entrance. They are called "wedding maples." The three dining rooms are extremely well furnished and comfortable. Two have fireplaces, and one of them has those great ☞ Indian shutters on the windows that fold back completely out of sight. There is even a private dining room upstairs. The bar has a fourteen-foot-long pine top cut from one log, plus a fireplace. The lounge also has a huge fireplace.

The rooms are across the road in what once was an old barn, but today you would never know it. All the rooms are super comfortable with ☞ great views. They all have televisions and telephones.

The food here is excellent. I had broiled scallops that the chef had made more than somewhat special, as he does with almost all of his dishes. The stuffed shrimp were huge. Eating my way through New England surely is fun, even if a bit fattening.

How to get there: From Hartford, take I-91 north to Brattleboro, to Route 101 east to Peterborough. Then take Route 202 north to Bennington, New Hampshire, and take Route 47. Tory Pines is 4 miles farther on the left. From Boston, take Route 3 to 101A west to Milford, New Hampshire, then a hard right at the rotary to Route 13 to New Boston, and Route 136 to Francestown. Bear right in the village. The inn is in 4 miles, on the right, on Route 47.

ठ

E: *On the pond where you skate live a gaggle of geese and two ducks.*

Olive Metcalf

Franconia Inn
Franconia, New Hampshire
03580

Innkeepers: Richard and Alec Morris
Telephone: 603-823-5542
Rooms: 27, 21 with private bath.
Rates: $47 to $55, per person, double occupancy, MAP. EP
rates also available.
Facilities: Closed April 1 to May 25, and mid-October to December 15. Breakfast, dinner, bar, lounge. Swimming,
four tennis courts, cross-country ski center, horseback
riding, hot tub. Downhill skiing and soaring nearby. All
major credit cards accepted.

This is an inn in the fine tradition of old New England
hostelries. The rooms are simple and comfortable. Many of
the rooms connect with a bath, an ideal situation when you
bring youngsters, and this is an inn that welcomes children.
Never a dull moment any season of the year. While the children play Ping-Pong or watch a movie, you can relax in ☞ the

lounge and listen to selected classical and popular music by the glow of the fireplace.

A card room and a library are here for your enjoyment, as is a screened porch overlooking the pool and the mountains. And they have something a bit unique, a game room for children, no adults allowed. Another entertainment for you is horseback riding. There are ☞ trail rides through Ham Branch stream and around the hay fields.

The living room is paneled with old oak and, with the fireplace, is very warm and cozy. The dining rooms, too, are gracious. There is a small one with a fireplace, a nice spot for breakfast. The food is very good, veal, rack of lamb, shrimp, steak, roast duck, chicken, all prepared with a gourmet touch.

There are sixty-five miles of cross-country trails right at hand, and they also have facilities so that you can ski from inn to inn on connecting trails. Downhill skiing is but ten miles away. Do come and enjoy.

How to get there: Take I-91 north to the Wells River-Woodsville Exit. Go right on Route 302 to Lisbon, New Hampshire. A few miles past Lisbon, go right on Route 117 to Franconia. Crossing the bridge into town, go right to the Exxon station. There, take another right to Route 116, and you're 2 miles to the inn. Or, if you have a single-engine plane, the inn has its own F.A.A.-listed airfield with a 3,000-foot-long runway.

🍸

E: ☞ *Horse-drawn sleigh rides in this beautiful winter wonderland are my idea of heaven.*

Olive Metcalf

The Horse and Hound
Franconia, New Hampshire
03580

Innkeepers: Betty and Bob Larson; managers, Bob and Eric
Larson
Telephone: 603-823-5501
Rooms: 10, 6 with private bath.
Rates: $40 to $55, double occupancy, EPB.
Facilities: Open all year. Dinner, Sunday brunch. Skiing,
biking, hiking. MasterCard and Visa accepted.

The Horse and Hound is located at the base of Cannon
Mountain just north of Franconia Notch. Tucker Brook
rushes down from the top of the mountain just past the edge
of the inn's property. In winter you can set off from the door
of the inn on your cross-country skis. In other seasons, ☛ bicycling is a big thing here at the inn. There is a seven-mile
circle for you to try. Should be fun up here in these beautiful
mountains.

You also can go soaring in a plane or just take an airplane ride. What a way to enjoy the fall foliage. I did it once in a helicopter and it was sublime.

There are three fireplaces to warm you whether you are in the living room or the dining rooms. The library lounge has lots of books that are well organized in categories such as bike books, children's books, and classics. There is music in here also. They play a lot of old and new jazz and classical jazz; this is such a fine sound.

Comfortable accommodations are here. The rooms are bright and airy and have lovely views.

The menu is good and the food is excellent. Under appetizers, the Chef's Seafood Bisque is good. I like the Chef's Fancy; he comes up with interesting ideas. I also like a veal du jour where the waiter explains the day's choice. There are several beef entrees and all are tender. The lamb, as they say about their double lamb chops, is doubly delicious. It's also nice to be able to order ☞ roast Tom Turkey with all the fixings any time of the year. Too often turkey is served only on the holidays. The desserts and pastries all are made here and are so good.

How to get there: Take I-93 north, exit at Route 18, and turn left. The inn is on the left, several miles down the road. The inn is on Wells Road.

❧

E: *The terrace in summer is so lovely for Sunday brunch or just cocktails. The inn dog is Deacon, a black lab.*

Lovett's by Lafayette Brook

Franconia, New Hampshire
03580

Innkeepers: Mr. and Mrs. Charles J. Lovett, Jr.
Telephone: 603-823-7761
Rooms: 7 in main house; cottages and dorm.
Rates: $40 to $61, per person, double occupancy, MAP.
Facilities: Closed April to July, and after Columbus Day until
    after Christmas. Breakfast, dinner, bar. Swimming,
    game room. Tennis, golfing, riding, bicycling, fishing,
    and skiing nearby. American Express, MasterCard, and
    Visa accepted.

There are a lot of reasons for coming to the White
Mountains and Franconia Notch, and one of the reasons is
this inn. It was constructed circa 1784, even before a road
was built through Franconia Notch. The inn is well into its
second generation of ☞ one-family ownership, and that says
a lot.

Charlie Lovett runs a fine inn. As he says, they work
hard at having the best table and the best cellar in the North

Country. The menu changes daily. Some of the favorites are lamb served with homemade chutney, veal and mushrooms, eggplant with caviar, fresh shrimp mousse, and, at breakfast, sour cream cheddar cheese omelettes, or shirred eggs with fresh mushrooms. These are but a few of the delights that Charlie comes up with. The inn has its own herb garden. At last count there were thirty-seven different herbs at hand. No wonder the food is so good. Desserts, as you would expect, are heavenly.

There is a lovely terrace overlooking the mountins and the pool. Actually there are two pools. One is solar heated and the other fed from mountain springs. Oh, to be that hale and hearty for the latter.

A new addition to the area of Franconia Notch is the New England Ski Museum, an excellent review of a sport that goes back 5,000 years. It is important to preserve these rare artifacts.

How to get there: Take I-93 north, exit at Route 18 and turn left. The inn is on your right.

E: *The bar, the bar! From the staircase in a Newport Mansion, the marble bar is the most inviting spot I've run into in a month of Sundays.*

I never thought of business when awakened at an inn by the three o'clock chime of a nearby church.

Sugar Hill Inn
Franconia, New Hampshire
03580

Innkeepers: Carolyn and Richard Bromberg
Telephone: 603-823-5621
Rooms: 10, all with private bath; 6 cottages.
Rates: In summer, $29 to $32, per person, double occupancy,
EPB. Rest of year, $45 to $60, per person, double occu-
pancy, MAP.
Facilities: Closed in April and December. Breakfast only
meal in summer, breakfast and dinner in rest of year.
Beer and wine license. Skiing, riding, fishing, canoeing,
tennis, golfing, and hiking nearby. All major credit cards
accepted.

The White Mountains are so beautiful and majestic, it is
a joy to find the Sugar Hill Inn tucked into this loveliness. It
is a charming inn. It was built in 1789 as a farmhouse by one
of Sugar Hill's original settlers, and converted to an inn in
1929.

The Brombergs have done a careful restoration job.

They have made the most of the beautiful old beams and floors and the handsome fireplaces. They have two comfortable living areas with cozy furniture, television, and lots of magazines. In one is an old pump organ that really works. In the dining room is a neat player piano with a lot of rolls. Really fun for a sing-along.

Guest accommodations in the inn and the country cottages are lovely. Nice spreads, good mattresses, lovely antiques, and all super clean. The cottages are used from the middle of May through October.

Richard is the breakfast cook. He really does well. The blueberry pancakes I had were super. Be sure to try the fresh muffins. I had the ☞ applesauce and carrot muffins. Carolyn does the breakfast serving with help from their older daughter.

Dinner starters are Shrimp and Crab Mousse, hot crab dip, and homemade soups. Carolyn won a Smuckers' contest with her Estofado, a Greek beef dish. She also makes delicious rolled stuffed chicken and lamb curry, just to name a few. Two fresh vegetables are served with dinner. Desserts are all made here. They are delicious.

The views of the mountain range from the porch are spectacular. The Appalachian Trail is nearby for invigorating hikes. Cannon Mountain is at hand for terrific downhill skiing, and cross-country skiing is everywhere. Other sports, such as horseback riding, fishing, canoeing, tennis, and golfing, are only minutes away.

How to get there: Follow Route 18 through Franconia. Turn left on Route 117. The inn is one-half mile up the hill on the right.

E: ☞ *Hot cider on the woodburning stove for skiers is so nice.*

Bernerhof Inn
Glen, New Hampshire
03838

Innkeeper: Kim Babineau; owners, Ted and Sharon Wroblewski
Telephone: 603-383-4414
Rooms: 9, 2 with private bath.
Rates: $25 to $30 per person, EPB.
Facilities: Closed mid-April to Memorial Day, and mid-November to mid-December. Lunch July through October, dinner, bar. Sauna. All major credit cards accepted.

Fine European cuisine in the old-world tradition is what Ted and Sharon consider their outstanding food to be. Specialties include Wiener Schnitzel, Holstein Schnitzel, and even Schnitzel Cordon Bleu. Their desserts should be outlawed. Cherries Jubilee or Meringue Glacé are two of my fattening favorites, but delicious. They have an excellent wine list, and coffees for the gourmet finish.

A new, large bedroom has been added at the back of the inn. Although some of the other rooms are small, all are clean, light, airy, and have good mattresses and box springs. These things I think are important to any inn.

Another new addition is a family sitting room with television, books, and games, and a nice couch. Work never stops in a country inn. The living room has a very unusual, tall, round coal stove and a wonderful electronic machine. I hate electronics, but I make an exception for the "Piano Corder,"an ingenious tape-playing gadget that plays the inn's Steinway. It is much more clever than the old pianos that played rolls.

The bar and lounge is called the "Zumstein Room," and it is a charming place, serving some really unusual food, like cheese fondues, Delice de Gruyère, Raclette, and always a quiche du jour.

You are but a few minutes from either North Conway or Jackson, so you will not lack for something to do absolutely any month of the year.

How to get there: From North Conway take Route 16 north. At Glen, turn left onto Route 302. The inn is on your right.

E: *A free champagne breakfast in bed is yours on the third morning of your stay. It comes with eggs Benedict and fresh flowers. My, my.*

> *"The righteous minds of innkeepers*
> *Induce them now and then,*
> *To crack a bottle with a friend*
> *Or treat unmoneyed men."*
> —G. K. Chesterton

olive Metcalf

The John Hancock Inn
Hancock, New Hampshire
03449

Innkeepers: Glynn and Pat Wells
Telephone: 603-525-3318
Rooms: 10, all with private bath.
Rates: $50 to $60, double occupancy, EP.
Facilities: Closed one week in early spring, one week in late
    fall. Breakfast, lunch, dinner, Sunday brunch, lounge.
    Parking. Swimming, bicycles loaned. Skiing and tennis
    nearby. MasterCard and Visa accepted.

    Operated as an inn since 1789, the John Hancock has
been owned by Glynn and Pat since 1973. What a great job
they do.
    This is a nice old inn. Carefully preserved is ☛ The
Mural Room, believed to date back to the early years of the
inn. The Carriage Lounge is very unusual, with tables made
from giant bellows from an old foundry in Nova Scotia. Seats
are made from antique buggy seats. The name stems from
the fact that John Hancock, the founding father, once owned

most of the land that comprises the present town of Hancock. Set among twisting hills with a weathered clapboard facade, graceful white pillars, and a warm red door, the inn represents all that is good about old inns. Warm welcomes, good food, sound drinks, and good beds, set in a quiet town that hasn't changed much in the last two centuries.

The Wells have recently begun serving Sunday brunch, and it has become very popular with the townspeople as well as inn guests. They serve a variety of egg dishes, crepes, quiche, and French Toast à la Marie Antoinette (with pound cake).

Dinner is served by candlelight, and when winter storms howl through the hills the fireplace in the bar has a crackling fire to warm your heart and toes. Braided rugs cover part of the wide-board floors, and primitive paintings hang on the walls. There is a pastel of the inn, done in 1867, that the Wells were able to acquire.

Swim in summer in Norway Pond, within walking distance of the inn. Climb mountains, or just sit and listen to the church chimes during foliage time. Alpine and cross-country skiing are nearby in winter. Or browse in the antique shops on a cool spring morn.

How to get there: From Boston take Route 128, then Route 3 to 101 west. Hancock is located just off Route 202, 9 miles above Peterborough.

☀

E: *The inn dog is a Lhasa named Nay-Daak Poo, which means "little innkeeper."*

We sat together round a single table and talked and heard each other in the quiet of the inn.

Olive Metcalf

Colby Hill Inn
Henniker, New Hampshire
03242

Innkeepers: The Glover Family
Telephone: 603-428-3281
Rooms: 12, 8 with private bath.
Rates: $38 to $45, single; $58 to $65, double; EPB.
Facilities: Open all year. Dinner Tuesday through Sunday, bar. Television, swimming pool. Skiing, canoeing, fishing, ice skating, snowmobiling, and bicycling nearby. All major credit cards accepted.

This picturesque old house dates back to 1800. It leans and dips a bit here and there, but that only adds to the charm. The ☞ wide floorboards are authentic. You cannot find boards like that nowadays. Don Glover, Jr., is chief innkeeper. He supervises the cooking and everything else that needs doing in a country inn. While researching this book I have found innkeepers up in trees, down in cellars, chopping wood, and even doing dishes. Don can be found at any one of these activities.

The food is all cooked to order, and it's as fresh as can be. The 🖙 vegetables come from their garden (and, as Don says, sometimes from a neighbor's). Chicken Colby Hill varies from day to day at the chef's whim. I've had reports back to me that all his whims are delicious. There is a nice selection of wines and spirits. The meal is topped off by homemade breads and desserts. They are famous for their cheesecake. I'm not surprised.

Henniker is a small New England college town. Indeed, New England College is here. There are many things to do in this area. Canoeing on the many lakes or rivers, white-water rafting in season, hiking or biking on the many trails or back roads, swimming in the inn's pool or in nearby lakes, fishing of all kinds (fly-fishing or ice-fishing), and, of course, there is ice skating, skiing, and snowmobiling. About 🖙 forty-five miles of local trails are marked and maintained by Pole & Pedal.

How to get there: Go up I-91 to Brattleboro. Take Route 9 east into Henniker.

🖄

E: *The inn cat is Jelly Bean, and she has a few little beans around her.*

> *With its swinging sign near*
> *the hills it stands,*
> *Vine-clad and filled with cheer.*
> *'Tis a place to laze through*
> *fresh, golden days*
> *with sunlit peaks so near,*
> *So good-bye to cares,*
> *this spot is rare,*
> *and we thank kind fate*
> *for having brought us here.*

Stonebridge Inn
Hillsboro, New Hampshire
03244

Innkeepers: Nelson and Lynne Adame
Telephone: 603-464-3155
Rooms: 4, all with private bath.
Rates: $30, single; $35 to $40, double occupancy; continental
 breakfast included.
Facilities: Open all year. Closed Christmas Day. Lunch, din-
 ner, full license. Gift shop. Swimming and skiing
 nearby. MasterCard and Visa accepted.

Nelson and Lynne have owned the Stonebridge Inn for
several years. They have a good bit of experience as innkeepers behind them, including the fact that Nelson's father is
the innkeeper of the New London Inn in New London, New
Hampshire.

The inn was an old house that the Adames turned into a
small inn. There are four rooms, two large and two small, all
with private bath.

Downstairs there are three dining rooms. One is done in

wrought iron and glass, unusual and very pretty. The main dining room is a ☞ picture with ivory and chocolate napery dappled by flickering candlelight. There are a lot of windows in the inn, nice on a cloudy day.

The luncheon menu is extensive. Plenty of your favorite sandwiches, burgers, and what I like best for lunch, salads. They have a good seafood salad. Sunday brunch features eggs done many ways, Almond French Toast, and ☞ Oven Pancake with Fresh Fruit. These are a nice change. Another brunch specialty is Seafood Newburg Puff. Sounds so good.

☞ Dinner at the inn has several really popular items. Pork Tenderloin with Cherry Sauce is different and so good. Lamb with Hazelnuts is, as they say, a memorial dish, and then there's the fried chicken glazed with maple syrup. Now that's chicken with a New England difference! There is, of course, much more, and all of it delicious.

There is skiing nearby and summer swimming at Pierce Lake or Beard Brook. This is a very nice area of New Hampshire. Do try it.

How to get there: From western New England take I-91 north to Exit 3 and then follow Route 9 east for a bit better than 40 miles. You will find the inn on your left as you enter town. From the Boston area take Exit 5 off I-89 and follow Route 9 west for 17 miles to Hillsboro.

♷

E: There's a beautiful grandfather's clock in the living room.

olive Metcalf

The Manor
Holderness, New Hampshire
03245

Innkeepers: Jan and Pierre Havre
Telephone: 603-968-3348
Rooms: 21, all with private bath; one suite; 3 housekeeping
   cottages.
Rates: $39 to $110, double occupancy, EPB. Cottages rented
   by week or month.
Facilities: Open all year. Lunch, dinner, Sunday brunch,
   bar, lounge. No pets. Swimming pool, tennis, boating,
   ice skating. Downhill and cross-country skiing nearby.
   All major credit cards accepted.

From the moment you drive up the long driveway to the
inn you are enchanted with the surroundings. Then the
Manor comes into view and your enchantment is complete,
the inn is just so lovely. Built in 1903 by a wealthy
Englishman, Isaac Van Horn, the house still has its original
rich wood paneling, beautiful doors, some with mirrors, mag-

nificently carved moldings, marble fireplaces, and old pedestal sinks. Thankfully, all details have remained unscarred over the years.

There are two handsome library-living rooms with fireplaces. The Tapestry Lounge is elegant. There also is a cocktail porch overlooking the lake, so nice on a moonlit night.

The dining rooms are lovely. Beautiful stemware, courteous staff, and good food. From where I had lunch I could look down on Squam Lake, made famous as the lake in ☞ "On Golden Pond." Oh my, I do like it here. I had the ☞ best grilled corned beef and Swiss cheese sandwich I ever had. The inn's tangy dressing and homemade pumpernickel bread made the sandwich memorable. Everything on the menu sounded so good, it was hard to choose. Dinner, I wouldn't know where to begin to describe it. The menu is extensive, so even the fussiest person would find it hard to complain. I hate to mention the desserts, they are sinfully good. I think I'll lose about ten pounds and go back for a week.

The guest rooms are exceptional with handsome wallcoverings, and good beds and chairs. Some have ☞ lovely old pedestal sinks, and five have fireplaces. The cottages are elegant.

There is everything to do here; swimming pool, tennis, shuffleboard, croquet, Ping-Pong, and much more. The Manor's own canoes, sailboat, and fishing dinghy are free for your use. There are thirteen acres for you to play in and 300 feet of sandy beach frontage for you to sunbathe on. If it rains, there are many games to play inside or many places to just relax in this beautiful mansion.

How to get there: Take Route 3 into Holderness. Cross the bridge, and on the right you will see the signs for the Manor.

E: *The Lady of the Manor is a luxurious 28-foot pontoon craft, which is available for guided tours of "Golden Pond," parties, picnics, and transportation to* *Church Island for Sunday services in an outdoor setting. How I do like it here. Wow.*

The New England Inn
Intervale (North Conway),
New Hampshire
03860

Innkeepers: Linda and Joe Johnston, Chris and Julie; John
  Reed, manager
Telephone: 603-356-5541
Rooms: 26, 23 with private bath; 10 suites with fireplace in
  village houses; 4 one-room cottages with fireplace.
Rates: $28 to $43, EP; $50 to $77, MAP; double occupancy.
Facilities: Open all year. Breakfast, dinner. Entertainment
  on weekends and holidays. Conference room, three clay
  tennis courts, swimming and wading pools, skating rink,
  cross-country skiing and lighted trails for nighttime.
  American Express, MasterCard, and Visa accepted.

If you enjoy the charm of an authentic country inn
where cozy intimacy has been carefully preserved over the
centuries by conscientious innkeepers . . . if you relish the
warm feeling of a gracious country inn with a reputation for
hospitality and friendliness . . . if you enjoy savoring hearty
New England regional foods, selected wines, and hearty

drinks . . . if you like sports and outdoor recreation . . . if you prefer just plain quiet and relaxation . . . you'll love the village at the New England Inn.

Linda and Joe said it so well in their brochure, I just stole it.

When you arrive at the inn in any season, the sight is glorious, a white rambling country inn in the shadows of the White Mountains. The living rooms are gracious, with plenty of chairs and couches. Nice to curl up in with a good book, or, as I am prone to do, with needlework. The guest rooms are smashing, and all have recently been done over. After a full day they are a real pleasure to return to.

This is an all-American inn. The food and wine are as ☞ all-American as apple pie, and they have that, too. Try New England chicken and shrimp saute, New England chicken pot pie, or Shaker cranberry pot roast. I've had the pot roast, and it's glorious. The wines, all-American, are served in crockery pitchers. A nice change from the ordinary. But then ☞ Joe and Linda are not your ordinary innkeepers. Just ask Gladys, who plays the piano in the lovely large lounge area.

The Johnstons are involved with the ☞ Intervale Nordic Center. Between the inn and the Holiday Inn next door there are thirty-five kilometers of marked trails. Start off right by being outfitted in proper-fitting equipment, next take a lesson from a PSIA-certified instructor, and then go and enjoy cross-country skiing. The Intervale Tavern at the inn, with a blazing fireplace, serves skiers lunch and après-ski. A good hot chili is nice when you are cold.

Plan on a week at a time at this lovely inn. There is so much to do inside and out, and in any season.

How to get there: The inn is at the Gateway to the White Mountains, a Resort Loop, Route 16A, 3½ miles north of the village of North Conway.

E: *Brandy and Dickens are the dogs The horse named Danny, who pulled a sleigh, is gone now, but for the next few years on New Year's Eve you can see Danny and the Johnstons on Johnny Carson's show from 11:30 to midnight.*

Christmas Farm Inn
Jackson, New Hampshire
03846

Innkeepers: Bill and Sydna Zeliff
Telephone: 603-383-4313
Rooms: 23, 14 in inn, 9 with private bath; 9 in 1771 saltbox, all with private bath. Six suites in sugarhouse and barn. One log cabin, and 3 cottages.
Rates: $42 to $65, per person, double occupancy, MAP. Special weekly and package rates.
Facilities: Open all year. Breakfast, dinner, pub. Swimming pool, game room, putting green, 80 kilometers of cross-country trails, golf, tennis, sauna, complimentary movies. Downhill skiing nearby. All major credit cards accepted.

Yes, Virginia, there is a Christmas Farm Inn, and they have the Mistletoe Pub and the Sugar Plum Dining Room to prove it. The food is fit for any Santa and his helpers, from the hearty, full country breakfast, which includes ☞ homemade doughnuts, muffins, and sticky buns, to gracious dinners that include three entrees each evening, two homemade soups, a full salad bar, homemade breads, and a complete dessert menu.

The food is excellent. The ☞ Medallions of Pork MacIntosh is glorious, and it also has a hint of brandy. Veal and chicken are so tender. Treats from the seas are real treats. The desserts do indeed make visions of sugarplums dance in your head, and all are made right here. How about apple pie, carrot cake, or the Christmas Farm special sundae? From here take a quick trip to the Mistletoe Pub for a nightcap.

Separate from the main building is the Christmas Farm function center. Perfect spot for not only medium to small business meetings, but also weddings, anniversaries, and the like. At one side of the room is a twelve-foot-wide fieldstone fireplace. There are also games of all sorts, a sauna, bar, and four nice suites.

Also separate are the three new cottages, each with living room, fireplace, two bedrooms, and two baths. The rooms in the main building have Christmas names: Holly, Dasher, Prancer, Vixen, Donner, Cupid, Comet, and Blitzen.

Jackson is in the heart of the White Mountains, so bring your skis, or come in summer for the annual Christmas-in-July Week. ☞ There's a magnificent gala Christmas party Wednesday night with an outside buffet and Christmas tree, as well as live entertainment, dancing, shuffleboard, and golf tournaments. Santa must live nearby, because he never fails to arrive in a most unusual manner. And when he comes, he's eagerly greeted by the inn dogs, Freckles and Daffodil.

How to get there: Go north on Route 16 from North Conway. A few miles after Route 302 branches off to your left you will see a covered bridge on your right. Take the bridge through the village and up the hill a quarter mile, and there is the inn.

E: Making ☞ memories is something Bill and Sydna and their staff know all about.

olive Metcalf

Dana Place Inn
Jackson, New Hampshire
03846

Innkeepers: The Levine family: Harris, Mary Lou, Cheryl, and Richard

Telephone: 603-383-6822

Rooms: 15, 8 with private bath.

Rates: $35 to $75, EP; $90 to $140, MAP; double occupancy.

Facilities: Closed November to mid-December. Breakfast, picnic lunch available, dinner, bar, lounge. Hot tub. Cross-country skiing, swimming pool, two all-weather tennis courts. Golf and downhill skiing nearby. All major credit cards accepted.

The inn is nestled at the foot of magnificent Mt. Washington in a beautiful valley next to the Ellis River. The mountain alone draws hikers and climbers and skiers who brave the big spill to ski Tuckerman's Ravine each spring, and visitors who journey to the top of the mountain via the Cog Railway or the auto road. All of this plus this beautiful inn to stay in.

The inn was built in the mid–nineteenth century and surely must have been a stagecoach stop. We know it was once a farmhouse, set in an apple orchard, and built by An-twin Dana. Set your own pace along lawns, gardens, streams, meadows, and woodland trails. Walk through the orchard, pass the swimming pool, take the country road past the tennis courts along a mossy tree-shaded path, through a clearing, and you'll be at a crystal-clear, rockbound pool in the Ellis River. Peace here is beyond description. Clementine, a lovely English setter, and Muffin, the cat, help run the whole show.

The interior of the inn has been beautifully updated. The hot tub is in a room by itself. The dining rooms with pink napery and flowers are restful, and the food is good. ☞ Lobster bisque is a favorite of mine and very good here. I like unusual chicken and had their Rollintine of Chicken, rolled supremes of chicken with a cranberry walnut filling and a Riesling wine sauce. Desserts are wonderful. All baking is done right here. The breakfast menu is inventive. How about ☞ chocolate chip pancakes with Grade A maple syrup? Do come up and try this lovely inn.

How to get there: Take I-95 north to Portsmouth, then the Spaulding Turnpike to Route 16 north at Rochester. Follow Route 16 North past Jackson Village.

🌹

E: *The hammock on the lawn overlooks the Ellis River. Lovely spot.*

The Inn at Thorn Hill
Jackson, New Hampshire
03846

Innkeepers: Donald and Gail Hechtle
Telephone: 603-383-4242
Rooms: 22, 16 with private bath.
Rates: $48 to $56, per person, double occupancy, MAP.
Facilities: Closed April to mid-May, and November to mid-December. Breakfast, dinner, bar. Swimming pool, cross-country skiing. Downhill skiing nearby. No small children. All major credit cards accepted.

Mountains are everywhere you look from this inn. Relax on the porch in a ☞ New England rocking chair and enjoy the view. Even on a bad day it is spectacular. And the living room, with a generous fireplace, has ☞ a view that is unbelievable.

There are two chefs who turn out scrumptious food. The chicken is ☞ boneless breast of chicken baked with spiced bread crumbs and laced with honey and bacon bits. The Lobster Pie is something special that is ordered by those who know how good it is. And their New England Clam Chowder is so good that it has been ordered as a dessert by some people.

The rooms are loaded with fine antiques. The beds are not only beauties, but they are comfortable as well. The wallpapers are very nice. The innkeepers are really working all of the time on the inn, and it surely does show it. Gretel, the inn dog, is right there to keep them company as they work.

Winter brings skiing of all types. There are four alpine slopes in the area and 125 kilometers of good, groomed trails at all levels for cross-country skiing.

The Volvo International Tennis Tournament at the end of July is six miles away in North Conway. Also, Storyland is close by.

For skiers there is a shuttle bus service on weekends and holiday weeks that connects all Jackson inns to all of the slopes. The charge is nominal.

How to get there: Go north from Portsmouth, New Hampshire, on the Spaulding Turnpike (Route 16) all the way to Jackson, which is just above North Conway. At Jackson is a covered bridge on your right. Take the bridge, and just one block this side of the village center on the right is Thorn Hill Road, which you take up the hill. The inn is on your right.

E: *The lounge bar is a fun place to spend the evening after a day on the ski slopes.*

And now once more I shape my way
Thro' rain or shine, thro' thick or thin,
Secure to meet, at close of day
With kind reception, at an inn.
William Shenstone, 1714–1763
(written at an Inn at Henley)

Whitney's Village Inn
Jackson, New Hampshire
03846

Innkeepers: Terry and Judy Tannehill
Telephone: 603-383-6886
Rooms: 36, 30 with private bath; 2 cottages with fireplace.
Rates: $44 to $65, per person, MAP. Packages available.
Facilities: Open all year. Breakfast, lunch in season or box
lunch, dinner, bar, lounge. Skiing, ice skating, tobog-
ganing, tennis, swimming. American Express, Master-
Card, and Visa accepted.

This is an authentic mountain hideaway nestled in
among New Hampshire's White Mountains. It's pretty nice
to be able to crawl out of bed, dress, have a sumptuous
breakfast, and ☞ walk across to the lifts, trails, ski shop or ski
school, all just a snowball's throw away. It is a real treat not to
have to drive the car anywhere after you get here. Black
Mountain, with its own snowmaking equipment, is right
here. The lifts can handle about 3,000 skiers per hour, so
there is hardly any waiting. There are many trails that serve

the mountain, and all are kept in the best condition possible. A lighted skating rink is right beside the inn. Bring your own skates or borrow some here. The inn also has tobogganing.

Summer fun is the inn's own swimming pond, which is in such a pretty setting on the lovely grounds. There are also all sorts of lawn games. Inside, there is a game room, well equipped with Ping-Pong, television, and all sorts of games. One of the parlors has puzzles in the making, nice comfortable furniture, a Steinway piano, and lovely old oriental carpets. There are Hunter Fans all over the inn. Then there is the Shovel Handle Lounge for après-ski fun and entertainment. Lunch in season is served out here.

Dining is superb in a casually elegant dining room. Mauve and tan are the napery colors. One of the soups is Yesterday's (Mom always said it was better the next day). Their Jackson-style Duckling is excellent, and how nice to find a delicious stew. ☛ Roast goose is also seldom seen on a menu. There is a lobster cookout by the brook once a week in the warm weather.

The guest rooms are carpeted and have comfortable beds. Some of the rooms have nice wingback chairs. Try it here. You will like it.

How to get there: Go north from Conway 22 miles on Route 16. Take a right on Route 16A through a covered bridge into Jackson Village. Take Route 16B to the top of the hill to the inn.

ᶴ

E: ☛ *A really nice touch for families is a special children's table. Dinner at six o'clock is followed by a movie. Parents and children both can enjoy themselves.*

olive Metcalf

The Wildcat Inn
Jackson, New Hampshire
03846

Innkeepers: Pam and Marty Sweeney
Telephone: 603-383-4245
Rooms: 16, 10 with private bath.
Rates: $28 to $31, per person, EPB.
Facilities: Closed in May. Lunch, dinner, bar. Music in
    lounge. Downhill and cross-country skiing, hiking.
    American Express, MasterCard, and Visa accepted.

The Wildcat Inn is a very popular dining spot. In fact,
some years ago the big old front porch had to be converted
into a dining room to make more dining space for all the people who wanted to eat here. It is sad to lose a porch, but take
a look at the menu and you'll see why it was necessary. All
their food is ☞ interestingly different and so good. The ☞ pie
crust is the best I ever had, and the fillings they put in them
are delicious. All of the desserts are lovingly made by Pam.
There are good soups, fine quiches, and chili with a hearty

tang. Not just the same old cuisine, the food here will titillate your taste buds.

The Wildcat is a real old-time country inn, but there is nothing old-fashioned about the food or entertainment. In the big, old Tavern with two large fireplaces, you will find live musical entertainment, maybe a ☞ flautist, a lutanist, or a classical guitarist. Whatever it may be, you can count on it being good.

The inn is right next to both alpine and cross-country skiing. One-hundred-and-twenty-five kilometers of maintained, well-groomed trails start at the front door, near the touring headquarters, and end in the backyard beside the heated waxing hut. You can get touring skis, boots, alpine ski equipment, and touring instructions just a few strides from the inn's front door. And when the snows melt, you will find these trails glorious for walking or hiking. Jackson is a good spot anytime of year.

How to get there: Take Route 16 north from North Conway. Take Route 16A to your right, through a covered bridge, and into Jackson. The inn is in the center of town.

🍸

E: *Five downhill ski areas, with established ski schools only a few minutes away, are pretty nice; so are the inn dogs, Sassafras and Paco.*

olive Metcalf

Woodbound Inn
Jaffrey, New Hampshire
03452

Innkeeper: Jed Brummer
Telephone: 603-532-8341
Rooms: 33, 31 with private bath; 13 cottage units.
Rates: $55 to $65, per person, double occupancy, AP.
Facilities: Open all year. Breakfast, lunch, dinner. Play barn,
    ski school and rentals, swimming, golfing, tennis, boat-
    ing, fishing. Major ski areas nearby. American Express,
    MasterCard, and Visa accepted.

Woodbound is perfect for families, and caters rather
well also to us older folks. It has been a vacation resort since
1892. This is a self-contained country resort on the shores of
Lake Contoocook, and, as the brochure says, has over 200
acres of woodland, sandy beaches, and great hiking and
walking trails. Swimming, sailing, canoeing, boating, fishing,
a par three, 1,200-yard nine-hole golf course, a putting green,
tennis, volleyball, croquet, horseshoes, and shuffleboard are
all available on the premises. And inside the Play Barn you'll

find Ping-Pong, pool, shuffleboard, electronic games, and an intriguing music machine. The whole complex has a relaxed, informal, homey atmosphere.

The inn provides real home-cooked meals, and when the weather is right, great cookouts. All breads and pastries are homemade. The fresh vegetables and salad makings come from the inn's nearby gardens.

The cottages, each with its own fireplace or Franklin stove, vary in size accommodating two to eight people. Very attractive.

Children are well taken care of with supervised programs and activities. There is a baby-sitting service available night or day.

The Brummer family, all of them, run the inn, and all you have to do is ask and you will be taken care of speedily and nicely.

How to get there: From New York follow I-91 to Bernardston, Massachusetts. Proceed on Route 10 to Winchester, then take Route 119 to Rindge and watch for signs to the inn. From Boston follow Route 2, then Route 119 to Rindge.

E: *I just love a real family country inn.*

olive Metcalf

The Monadnock Inn
Jaffrey Center, New Hampshire
03454

Innkeeper: Sally Roberts
Telephone: 603-532-7001
Rooms: 14, 7 with private bath.
Rates: $35 to $45, double occupancy, continental breakfast included.
Facilities: Open all year. Dining room closed on Mondays, Christmas Eve, and Christmas Day. Lunch Tuesday through Friday, dinner Tuesday through Saturday, Sunday brunch, bar. Cross-country skiing. MasterCard and Visa accepted.

From the minute you set foot on the wide front porch until you sink into your comfortable four-poster at night you will be happy at this lovely inn. There is so much to do. Have you ever been to the Cathedral in the Pines? It's not far. Have you ever wanted to get really involved in maple sugaring? This is the place. It can be arranged with a snap of the fingers.

Sally does a terrific job as innkeeper. She likes to think the Monadnock Inn is capable to taking you back in time. But it was never this good.

The food is worth writing home about. The cheesecake, by their own admission, is inn-famous. Baked Oysters with Parmesan Cheese is just one appetizer. Sautéed Pork Tenderloin in Mustard Sauce or Roast Cornish Hen in Devilled Sauce are but two of the marvelous entrees. This is different food, and very good.

In brisk winter weather there is always a roaring fire in one of the fireplaces and miles of cross-country trails for skiers. Or come in the fall for wonderful, glorious foliage. Autumn in New Hampshire should have a song all its own.

How to get there: The inn is located on Route 124, southeast of Keene, a scant 2 hours from Boston.

E: ☛ *There aren't many places like this around. Cherish it.*

> *I was lost, I was tired, I was discouraged,*
> *and then I found a friendly inn.*

Beal House Inn
Littleton, New Hampshire
03561

Innkeepers: Doug and Brenda Clickenger
Telephone: 603-444-2661
Rooms: 14, 9 with private bath.
Rates: $33 to $60, double occupancy, EP.
Facilities: Open all year. Breakfast. Dinner for groups by arrangement and on holidays. Antique shop. All major credit cards accepted.

The Beal House was built in 1833 as a farmhouse and barn. Like most farms in New England, over the years the house and barn became connected into one continuous building. Ultimately it all became converted into an inn. The inn has an antique shop, but is also an antique shop in itself, for all the furnishings are for sale. You can ☞ sleep in a bed you may wind up buying. This is a good way to go antiquing; try before you buy.

All the rooms are clean and neat. The front rooms have

336

☛ glorious four-poster beds. There also is an upstairs sitting room, small but cozy.

Breakfast is bountiful. Doug is the chef, and his specialty is popovers. Of course, he does all sorts of other good things. His dining room has a fireplace, and is set with beautiful blue willow plates. Off of this room is the porch, full of wicker furniture and potted plants. Menus of all nearby restaurants are at hand for your perusal.

This is a lovely area to visit, not far from Franconia Notch and the Old Man of the Mountain. You also have Crawford Notch nearby. Do take a drive down the notch and look at the railroad they pinned to its west side. When you see it you cannot believe it.

The inn is in town so that you have the whole town of Littleton to walk about and see.

How to get there: From I-93 take Exit 42, turn right, and go one mile to the intersection of Route 18 and Route 302. This is Main Street and the inn is here.

E: *The gazebo in the back yard is charming.*

A good inkeeper, a good cook,
and an affable barkeeper
are as standard in a country inn
as a fire engine in a fire house.

Edencroft Manor
Littleton, New Hampshire
03561

Innkeepers: Laurie and William Walsh, Jr., Barry and Ellie Bliss
Telephone: 603-444-6776
Rooms: 6, 4 with private bath.
Rates: $35 to $45, double occupancy, EP
Facilities: Closed first two weeks in March. Restaurant closed Mondays. Breakfast for house guests, lunch Tuesday through Saturday every season but winter. Dinner. Cross-country skiing, snowmobiling. American Express, MasterCard, and Visa accepted.

The grand, old Victrola (and it works) sitting in the living room took me back to my childhood with nice memories of winding ours up and listening to the records. The inn has a huge collection of them. A large fireplace and plenty of books are also in this room. All in all, very charming. For you garden buffs there is a small solarium with plants and antiques just off this room.

The bedrooms have color names. The brown room has its own fireplace. The gold room is yummy with two double beds at angles to each other. Also, this is a bright, cheery room. In all the rooms are homemade quilts. One is done with old neckties and is just grand.

Sitting in the lounge-bar area you are overlooking both Cannon and Lafayette Mountains. Beautiful in winter, and equally beautiful any other season with the hanging plants overhead.

All breads, desserts, and soups are made right there. A special of theirs is a "Melt." This is an open-faced sandwich with lettuce, tomato, and melted cheese plus a wide range of ingredients you can add as you wish, tuna, ham, turkey, roast beef, or a special vegetarian mix. How about a combination? This menu is very inventive and good food results.

How to get there: Take I-93 to its very end just above Littleton, New Hampshire. Turn left on Route 18. Go halfway up the hill and turn right onto Route 135 north. Three-tenths of a mile further on, on your right, is the inn.

E: *Six appetizers, four soups, and a lovely dessert cart . . . too much.*

olive Metcalf

Lyme Inn
Lyme, New Hampshire
03768

Innkeepers: Fred and Judy Siemons
Telephone: 603-795-2222
Rooms: 15, 10 with private bath.
Rates: $55 to $75, double occupancy, with complimentary breakfast.
Facilities: Closed two weeks in late spring and the Sunday after Thanksgiving to the day after Christmas. Dining room closed Tuesdays. Dinner, bar. Near Dartmouth College, golf course, canoeing, fishing, and skiing. No children under 8. All major credit cards accepted.

This lovely inn sits at the end of the common of this quiet New Hampshire town. The inn dates back to 1809. All of the original rooms have been restored in keeping with the age of the building, and each bedroom is filled with ☛ antiques and its own unique character.

The tavern has a neat, small fireplace that makes this room a must on cold nights. Next door in the dining room do not miss the fresh spinach salad served with bacon bits and chopped egg. The house dressing is, to quote me, ☞ fantastic. But then, so is everything else from breakfast through dinner. The Wiener Schnitzel is very light, delicious. Their use of garlic is liberal and delightful. The chef really does credit to his kitchen.

There is an extensive library for guests to enjoy. You are ☞ encouraged to take home a partially read book and return it when you are finished. This is nice.

There is much to do in the area. Great walking, great hiking, and wonderful skiing. But a few miles away is Dartmouth College with its Ivy League sports competition and fine cultural events. Locally you have a golf course, and there is canoeing on the Connecticut River. There are many secluded ponds for the fisherman to try his luck. And, of course, you have antique shops all about.

And do try a hot dog at the general store just on the other side of the common. Rare treat.

How to get there: Take Exit 14 from I-91. The inn is located east of the interstate on Route 10 right at the village common.

E: *The wicker furniture on the huge screened porch is enchanting.*

> *A glass of good whiskey*
> *before an open fire in a good inn*
> *is an unspoken toast to life*
> *as it should be lived.*

olive Metcalf

Hide-Away Lodge
New London, New Hampshire
03257

Innkeepers: Lilli and Wolf Heinberg
Telephone: 603-526-4861
Rooms: 8, all with private bath.
Rates: $34 daily, $210 weekly, EP. MAP rates available.
Facilities: Closed Tuesdays and November to mid-May. Dinner, bar. Little Lake Sunapee, golf, tennis, and summer theater nearby. No credit cards accepted.

When I first discovered this inn, I knew I had found something special. A lovely old house, Wolf Heinberg and his most engaging smile, and oh, the food.

I'll always remember my first visit here. I had been hearing about the food served here, and after talking with Wolf I was sure all I had heard was true. At dinner hour I went down to the cocktail lounge, The Pipedreaming Pub. I placed a cocktail order, drooled over the menu, ordered dinner, and asked for the wine list. Wolf suggested that maybe a look in the wine cellar would help me decide. I followed him into a huge, temperature-controlled wine cellar. Fantastic, every wall was covered with wine. In the center of the room is a large table with silver candelabra and a beautiful wine book. Wolf is a very proud man, and he should be. The inn carries four stars in the Mobil Guide.

☛ The inn will, on twenty-four-hour notice, and for any number of people, prepare a gourmet feast. Included are pheasant, rack of lamb, venison, and many others. The regular menu is a dream. Crisp duckling with peach glaze is a favorite, not to mention many veal delights, fresh vegetables, and desserts about which I could write a whole chapter. As if this were not enough, there are bits of poetry all over the inn written by Wolf. You must come and read them. But call ahead, reservations are a must.

How to get there: Follow Main Street in New London past Colby-Sawyer College to the blinker light at the north end of town. Go straight ahead and follow the signs to the inn about 2 miles from town. The inn is on Little Lake Sunapee Road.

☗

E: *I wanted to stay in the wine cellar.*

New London Inn
New London, New Hampshire
03257

Innkeepers: George and Clara Adame
Telephone: 603-526-2791
Rooms: 26, all with private bath.
Rates: $25 to $35, single; $30 to $49, double; EP.
Facilities: Open all year. Breakfast, lunch, dinner. Nelson's Tavern. Skiing, theater, golf, two public beaches, and water sports nearby. MasterCard and Visa accepted.

The New London Inn, which has been serving the traveler since 1792, absolutely blooms under the direction of the Adames. It is full of beautiful antiques and good eating. It's worth a trip to stop and look and eat, even if you can't stay.

Nelson's Tavern is a favorite place to eat and to meet friends. It offers soups, salads, sandwiches, and a good array of homemade hot dishes. Cocktails are always nice in here. The main dining room features good things, such as a real favorite ☛ Beef Stroganoff. The Beef Burgundy is good and Colonial Fried Chicken is special because it is dipped in a maple syrup batter before it is fried.

The rooms are nice, large, and comfortable. Some are furnished with old-fashioned wicker pieces. Most rooms have cross-ventilation and louvered doors, and a few have air conditioners.

Located in the Mount Sunapee lake region, the inn has three lakes close by, with all the water sports. Golf is nice because there is no waiting, and there is good skiing. New London is the home of Colby-Sawyer College. There is always something going on at the college. The New London Barn Players, the oldest summer theater in New Hampshire, is famous for ☞ old Broadway hits.

This is a beautiful part of the world any time of the year, so come on up.

How to get there: Take Exit 8 at Ascutney, Vermont, from I-91. Follow signs to Claremont, New Hampshire. Take Route 11 east to Newport, Sunapee, Georges Mills, and New London. There is bus service via Vermont Transit from Boston, and from White River Junction, Vermont.

☖

E: *The inn was built in 1792. It's an oldie but a goodie.*

When the stars are lost and rain seeps coldly
upon the ground, how wonderful to find a lighted inn.

Pleasant Lake Inn
New London, New Hampshire
03257

Innkeepers: Grant and Margaret Rich
Telephone: 603-526-6271
Rooms: 13, one with private bath.
Rates: $30 to $45, double occupancy, EPB.
Facilities: Inn closed two weeks in April and two weeks in November. Dining room closed Mondays. Dinner, Sunday brunch, bar. Swimming, boating, fishing, and all winter sports. MasterCard and Visa accepted.

Pleasant Lake Inn is the oldest operating inn in this area. It began as a farm in 1790 and became an inn almost one hundred years ago.

Inn guests today are given privileges at the Slope and Shore Club on Pleasant Lake, just across the road, which offers tennis, boating, fishing, and swimming. There are ice-boating and cross-country skiing here in the winter. The inn also has a nice pond for ice skating on the property and downhill skiing is close at hand. King Ridge is five minutes away, Mount Sunapee and Whaleback fifteen minutes away, Pat's Peak is twenty-five minutes away, and many more are within an hour's drive.

The view from the inn's front windows is magnificent, and in the fall, it's ☞ spectacular. The inn looks right out onto Pleasant Lake, and beautiful Mount Kearsarge is just on the other side of the lake.

There are antique furnishings, warming fireplaces, nice views, and very comfortable guest rooms throughout the inn. Two cockatiels are here. One is gray and one is white. They surely are pretty. A nice dachsund, named Heidi, also lives here.

The food served in the pleasant dining rooms is good. Breakfast is hearty and includes a longtime favorite of mine, blueberry pancakes. Dinner appetizers include a beauty, ☞ escargots in mushroom caps with herbed garlic butter, baked in a pastry shell. All sauces and soups are prepared with fresh ingredients, ☞ no artificial agents, and sauces are thickened by natural reduction instead of with heavy starches. Entrees include steaks, chops, veal, chicken, and fish. They have nice liqueur parfaits for dessert and, as they say, if you have a favorite, they will try to make it.

How to get there: From I-89 take either New London exit. Halfway through New London, turn at the New London Trust Company. This is Pleasant Street. Go about 2 miles, and the inn is on your left.

E: *The family room has a bumper pool table, a really favorite game of mine.*

olive Metcalf

The Scottish Lion
North Conway, New Hampshire
03860

Innkeepers: John and Phyllis Morris; owners, Jack and Judy
   Hurley
Telephone: 603-356-6381
Rooms: 8, with 5 baths.
Rates: $25, per person, EPB.
Facilities: Open all year. Closed Christmas Eve and
   Christmas Day. Lunch, dinner, bar. Parking. Import
   Shop, free catalogue available. All major credit cards ac-
   cepted.

The rooms at the Scottish Lion are cozy. One has an
eyelet-trimmed canopy bed, another a spool bed with a
patchwork quilt. All are charming. The whole inn is full of
fine ☞ Scottish paintings. Do not miss any of them.
   Food, of course, features the best of Scottish touches. A
hearty Scottish breakfast is served to house guests. Dinner is
rated three stars in the Mobil Guide. Highland Game Pie,
which is venison, beef, hare, and fowl simmered in wine and

baked in puff pastry may sound strange, but a gentleman who had had it the night before reported to me, "Delicious." Hot Scottish oatcakes are served instead of bread or rolls. A marvelous dish named Rumbledethumps is one of the potato choices, what a taste. I must tell you one more: Forth Lobster Lady Tweedsmuir, tender pieces of lobster in a delicate cream and Drambuie sauce, stuffed in the shell. You must try this dish.

For dessert, Scottish Trifle or Scots Crumpets with fresh fruit and honey are but a few. The inn also serves a very special coffee. The pub has a long list of tantalizing pleasures, such as Hoot Mon cocktail, St. Andrews Hole-in-One, or Loch Ness Monster.

The Import Shop features the finest of imports from Scotland, England, and Ireland. They have over 300 different tartan ties, plus wools, cashmeres, crystal, thistle pottery, and much more. Do go and enjoy.

How to get there: Take Route 16 to North Conway. The inn is one mile north from the center of town, on the left.

E: *When you come down the road and see the magnificent flag streaming out in the wind you just can't go by. Stop for a drink, if you can't stay the night. You'll love it.*

The 1785 Inn
North Conway, New Hampshire
03860

Innkeepers: Charles and Rebecca Mallar
Telephone: 603-356-9025
Rooms: 13, 5 with private bath.
Rates: $55 to $70, double occupancy, EPB.
Facilities: Open all year. Lunch, dinner, bar, lounge. Golf,
tennis, swimming, canoeing, fishing, and skiing nearby.
American Express, MasterCard, and Visa accepted.

The 1785 Inn is one of the oldest houses in all of Mount
Washington Valley. It was built in 1785 by Captain Elijah
Dinsmore. Records indicate that Captain Dinsmore received
a license to "keep a Publik House" in 1795. In addition to
being a public house, the lovely old inn served as a stagecoach stop. The chimney and dining room fireplace with
brick oven are original to the house. They form a beehive
structure the size of an entire room in the center of the inn.

Guest accommodations are ample. The Mallars have
just completely refurbished the inn. What a large undertak-

ing! They have done such a fine job. There is a ☞ sink in all
the rooms. I find this a very nice feature in rooms with
shared baths.

There are two living areas; both have fireplaces, and one
has a television set. They are furnished with attractive chairs
and couches for your comfort. An old oak icebox is in here. It
surely makes a beautiful piece of furniture. The tavern has a
large bar, a woodburning stove, and good sitting areas. There
is light classical music here at times.

The views from the porch-dining room are just lovely.
The food is inventive and very good. I had a salad one noon,
☞ crab and shrimp served on top of spinach and alfafa
sprouts, tomatoes, and herbed dill dressing. Wow, it was
good. Dinners have dishes like Raspberry Duck, duck roasted
with a brandy-laced raspberry sauce and served on wild rice.
There are several veal selections, and, of course, fish,
chicken, and beef. The desserts are wild. ☞ Deep-fried ice
cream. Honest, and it's great. So is the chocolate velvet.

How to get there: Take Route 16 North. The inn is on the left
just before you come to Route 16A.

E: *A nice inn surrounded by many activities, good food—
what more do you want.*

olive Metcalf

Stonehurst Manor
North Conway, New Hampshire
03860

Innkeeper: Peter Rattay
Telephone: 603-356-3113
Rooms: 16 in the manor; 9 in the annex adjoining the manor;
all but two with private bath.
Rates: $55 to $95, double occupancy, EP. MAP rates available
in summer and fall.
Facilities: Open all year. Breakfast, dinner, bar. Meeting
room for up to 50 people. Pool, tennis, shuffleboard, volleyball. All major credit cards accepted.

This turn-of-the-century mansion is a fine country inn.
Set back from the highway among stately pine trees, it makes
you think you are going back in time, and in a way you are.
The front door is huge. Once inside, you see beautiful
oak wood and wonderful wall-to-wall carpet. The room to the
left is all wicker and all comfort. Ahead of you is the warm
living room, with walls full of ☞ books, and a huge fireplace.
The unusual screen and andirons were made in England. To

the right of the fireplaces is a twelve-foot, curved window seat of another era. The lounge area has a two-seat bar, just the right size.

Relax in a high-back wicker chair in the dining room and enjoy the fine, gourmet delights of steaks, seafood, chicken, or one of the ☞ six different veal dishes served here. Desserts are just spectacular.

The manor staircase is a beauty, and its large rooms are beautifully appointed. ☞ Fantastic wallpapers and beautiful carpets all add to this great inn. The third floor rooms have windows at odd angles, dictated by the roof line of the house. Some rooms have porches, and one has a stained-glass door going out to its porch. There is a lot of lovely stained glass throughout the inn. On the second floor, in one of the hall bathrooms, is a wood-enclosed steel bath tub. Be sure to take a look at it. It is quite a sight.

Their pool, the largest in the Mount Washington area, is made of ☞ wood, the only wooden one I have ever seen. You swell it in the spring, just as you would a wooden boat. Cocktails are served around the pool in the summer. There are tennis courts, and shuffleboard and volleyball courts. Plenty of things will keep you busy, or, like me, you might want to just sit and relax.

How to get there: The inn is on Route 16 just a short distance north of North Conway.

E: The inn has been awarded three stars in the Mobil Guide and has won the silver spoon award.

olive Metcalf

Follansbee Inn
North Sutton, New Hampshire
03260

Innkeepers: Sandy and Dick Reilein
Telephone: 603-927-4221
Rooms: 23, 11 with private bath.
Rates: $30 to $50, double occupancy, EP.
Facilities: Inn closed two weeks in April and two weeks in
    November. Restaurant closed Mondays. Breakfast, din-
    ner, lounge. Cross-country skiing from the inn, swim-
    ming, boating. Downhill skiing and golfing nearby.
    MasterCard and Visa accepted.

North Sutton has an old church with an old clock that
chimes out the time. What a wonderful sound to hear. Next
door is Follansbee, and you smell great things when you
enter this fine inn.

The food at the inn is superb. ☞ All soups, breads, salad
dressings, and desserts are made right here. ☞ The potato is
baked and stuffed, and it's a pleasure to get one piping hot.
There are several steaks to choose from, and hand-breaded

onion rings taste as divine as they sound. You could try the trout, or scampi, either crab or shrimp. Add to these, veal, prepared three different ways, chicken, and linguini. But you haven't had it all until you try the homemade desserts. The dining room you are in has comfortable captain's chairs and touches of chintz and crisp linen. A lovely setting for the superb food.

There is much to do in the area, such as riding, golfing, skiing, or just sitting in the living rooms with a book or needlework. The rooms are amply bright and comfortable. What more could one want? This is a lovely inn.

How to get there: Take I-91 north to Ascutney, Vermont. Follow Route 103 to Route 11 east, to Route 114. Proceed to North Sutton. The inn is behind the church.

E: *The innkeepers have traveled all over the world, and the inn reflects the treasures they accumulated.*

*A night at an inn adds a tinge to the coming day
that cannot be described, only be enjoyed.*

Home Hill Inn
Plainfield, New Hampshire
03781

Innkeeper: Roger Nicolas
Telephone: 603-675-6165
Rooms: 6, 5 with private bath. Cottage with kitchen and living room.
Rates: $45, single; $75 to $90, double occupancy; continental breakfast included. Cottage $150 to $200, per night; inquire about a weekly rental.
Facilities: Closed Sundays and Mondays, two weeks in March, and two weeks in November. Dinner, bar, lounge. Swimming pool, tennis court, cross-country skiing, fishing in Connecticut River. MasterCard and Visa accepted.

Roger's brochure said Home Hill Country Inn and French Restaurant, and I could hardly wait to get there.

Roger was born in Brittany in northwest France, and he speaks with a pleasant French accent. He has an ☞ authentic French restaurant here. The food presentation is picture perfect and the taste is elegant. No gravies, only sauces, and no flour, cornstarch, or fillers are allowed. Roger believes in innovative French cooking.

I started with a ☞ Fresh Fish Mousse with Lobster Sauce. I have never had better. Next, cream of onion soup, then veal slices, very thin and young with French mushrooms. You may have the salad before, with, or after dinner and the ☞ house dressing is gorgeous. Roger joined me at dinner and had duck prepared with white plums. I tasted it and it was very moist and delicious. Another dish served occasionally is veal stuffed with kiwi. Desserts, as would be expected, are superb. The wine list features both French and California wines.

In the kitchen is a lovely, long pine table where breakfast is served. What a homey spot at which to enjoy the continental breakfast of juice, ☞ croissants, butter, jams, and coffee.

The rooms are charming. The cottage is large enough for eight people. There are French and American antiques, reproductions, and comfort. The lounge-library is lovely; in fact, you will find it hard to find any fault with this inn.

Roger's two Great Danes are Big Mac, a black Dane, and Diane, a brindle. The inn is on 25 acres, only 500 yards from the Connecticut River. There is a swimming pool (a bar is out here), tennis courts, and cross-country skiing. Any season, any reason, head for Home Hill.

How to get there: Take I-89 to Exit 20. Follow Route 12A south to River Road and turn right. In 3½ miles you'll find the inn on the left.

ᛏ

E: *Herman, the automatic tennis ball shooter, is a neat exercize encourager.*

Philbrook Farm Inn
Shelburne, New Hampshire
03581

Innkeepers: Connie Leger and Nancy Philbrook
Telephone: 603-466-3831
Rooms: 19, 6 with private bath; 5 cottages with housekeeping
    arrangements.
Rates: $32 to $37, per person, double occupancy, MAP. Cot-
    tage $220 weekly.
Facilities: Closed April and late October to December 26.
    Breakfast, lunch, dinner, BYOB lounge. Library, pool
    table, Ping-Pong, cross-country skiing, snowshoeing, hik-
    ing. Downhill skiing nearby. No credit cards accepted.

In 1861 Philbrook Farm started as an inn. Today it is
still an inn and still has Philbrooks living here, running it in
fine New England tradition. With over 1,000 acres there is
plenty of room to roam any season of the year.

This is a very peaceful and relaxed inn. ☞ The library is
comfortably crowded with good books. Fireplaces are all over.

There is even a player piano in the dining room. A lovely Victorian living room has card tables and an old pump organ. The television lounge has walls of Currier & Ives prints plus a good fireplace.

Food is served here family-style and prepared from 🖙 scratch. The baked goods are made daily. Every Sunday features roast chicken, and Sunday morning fare is pure New England, with codfish balls and corn bread. Saturday gives another New England special, namely baked beans. The gardens provide fresh vegetables and good salads, and the home-made soups are a meal in themselves.

Bedrooms are furnished with antiques, some lovely, four-poster beds, and a collection of old bowl and pitcher sets, really the best I have ever seen.

How to get there: The inn is 1½ miles off Route 2. Going west, look for a direction sign on your right, and turn right. Cross the railroad tracks and then a bridge. Turn right at the crossroads and go a half-mile to the inn, which is on North Road.

ᛦ

E: *The playroom, with its collection of* 🖙 *old farm tools and kitchen utensils, is a nice reminder that sometimes nice things are saved.*

You cannot hide a good country inn.

Snowvillage Lodge
Snowville, New Hampshire
03849

Innkeepers: Pat and Ginger Blymyer
Telephone: 603-447-2818
Rooms: 14, all with private bath.
Rates: $75 to $85, single; $62 to $69 per person, double occupancy; MAP. Special package rates available.
Facilities: Open all year. Breakfast, dinner, bar, lounge. Cross-country skiing, ski rental and instructions, nature trail, tennis. Downhill skiing, hiking, canoeing, fishing, and riding nearby. American Express, MasterCard, and Visa accepted.

If you want to learn about Hollywood firsthand, come on up to Snowville Lodge. Pat is a good Hollywood lighting director and Ginger an award-winning hairdresser for the stars. They are still active in their professions even while they are a set of better-than-average innkeepers.

Pat has become a very good chef, doing everything just right, and when he is gone the kitchen is very well covered.

I had the best ☞ Veal Picatta here. One main course is served each night, and whatever it might be, rest assured it will be scrumptious.

The view from the inn is breathtaking. Mount Washington and the whole Presidential Range, plus the rest of the White Mountains, greet your eyes everywhere you look. In summer at the top of Foss Mountain, right at the inn, you can eat your fill of wild blueberries.

The guest rooms are comfortable and spacious, with tons of ☞ towels in luscious colors. Each room is named after a favorite author of the Blymyers'. The living room, with a huge fireplace and nice couches all around, makes this an inn for rest and relaxation. There is a service bar and lounge, and plants are everywhere. The game room has a television, and there is a very extensive library. A huge porch surrounds the inn. Sit out here and enjoy the view.

For you inveterate shoppers, fear not; North Conway is but fifteen or twenty minutes away, full of great shops, including many factory store outlets.

Ginger is everywhere you need her, and ☞ just is a natural, delightful innkeeper.

How to get there: Out of Conway on Route 153, go 5 miles to Crystal Village. Turn left, go about 1½ miles, turn right at the Snowvillage sign and go up the hill, ¾-mile to the inn.

E: *There are always new things going on up here. Bring the kids. There are planned activities for them, and you can have fun, too.*

361

Oliva Metcalf

The Homestead
Sugar Hill, New Hampshire
03585

Innkeepers: Esther Serafini and Barbara Serafini Hayward
Telephone: 603-823-5564, 603-823-9577
Rooms: 19, 10 in main house, all with running water; 9, all
 with private bath, across the street.
Rates: $45 to $50, per person, MAP.
Facilities: Closed mid-March to Memorial Day, and Novem-
 ber 1 to December 24, except for Thanksgiving week.
 Breakfast, dinner. Jacket requested for dinner. BYOB.
 No credit cards accepted.

Essie Serafini is a legend in her own time. She has been
at the inn for more than sixty years. Her first job, at the age of
ten, was to pass the relish tray. In those days her family
charged $3.00 a week for room and board.

The inn celebrated its ☛ 100th anniversary in 1981, and
good friends presented Essie with a magnificent $8,000 Gul-
bransen electric organ. Essie does not read music and does
not have to. Wow, can she play.

There are many original family antiques that furnish the rooms of the Homestead. One of the beds, a pine four-poster, came by ox cart from Richmond, New Hampshire. In the parlor is a hand-hooked rug, nine-by-five feet, all about New Hampshire that identifies dozens of landmarks, animals, and birds. This rug was done by Essie. She also wrote a delightful booklet titled, "Tales, Tours and Taste Treats," full of folklore, on sale at the inn or next door at the Sampler, a shop run by Essie's daughter, Barbara.

The rooms are spotless, what else would you expect from this lady, and the food is superb. Essie still finds time to do most of this. She is a powerhouse of a woman.

The inn has a very special thing about ☛ Thanksgiving week. People come from all over for this special treat, so make your reservations early.

How to get there: Take Exit 38 from I-93 to Route 117. The Homestead is about 3 miles up the hill on Route 117. Or coming from the west, turn east on Route 117 from Route 302.

E: Essie is such a special, warm, wonderful person, I just love her.

Olive Metcalf

Dexters
Sunapee, New Hampshire
03782

Innkeepers: Frank and Shirley Simpson; Holly and Michael Durfor
Telephone: 603-763-5571
Rooms: 17, all with private bath.
Rates: From May 1 to June 15, and all of September, $43 to $54, per person, double occupancy, EPB. Rest of year, $47 to $60, per person, double occupancy, MAP.
Facilities: Closed mid-October to December 26, and late February to May 1. Breakfast, lunch in July and August, dinner, bar. Tennis, swimming pool, recreation barn. Fresh fruit and flowers in your room. No credit cards accepted.

Your day starts with ☞ juice and coffee served in your room at a time you set the night before. Or you can try being really spoiled and have your complete breakfast served in bed, but you will miss the lovely morning view of Lake Sunapee from the dining room.

The lounge and bar are unique, with games, books, and even a little shop just outside the door. The rooms at the inn are a bit above average, with some carefully thought-out, unusual, wallpapers. ☛ The pillows are made of heavenly feathers, and plenty of them. Most of the beds are antiques that came down through the Simpson family.

The feature of the inn is tennis, and if you are a buff you will love it, for there are three fine courts. And after a game there is a large outdoor pool to cool off in.

In the spring time the lake trout and salmon are close to the surface and hungry, so come all you fishermen. Spring is always late up here, so you have a longer season. For a good summer or fall activity there are some of the loveliest walking and hiking trails right on the inn property.

There is a special recreation room in the barn for all ages, but it is keyed to those under sixteen who need a place of their own when the five o'clock cocktail hour begins.

How to get there: Take I-89 out of Concord and follow Exit 12 to Route 11, to 103B at Sunapee. Or take I-91 out of Springfield and follow Exit 8 to Claremont, New Hampshire, to Route 103. The turn to the inn is marked by a sign 200 yards south of the intersection of 103 and 11. The inn is about 1½ miles off Route 103.

E: *Frank is a special innkeeper, right on top of everything. He has an outside terrace under the trees that is used for lunch. How nice!*

Seven Hearths
Sunapee, New Hampshire
03782

Innkeepers: Charles Studen, Joseph Suszynski, and David
   Larsen
Telephone: 603-763-5657
Rooms: 10, all with private bath.
Rates: $69 to $84 per person, double occupancy, MAP. EP
   rates available.
Facilities: Inn closed in April. Restaurant closed Mondays
   and Tuesdays for dinner. Breakfast, dinner, Sunday
   brunch, full license. Swimming pool. MasterCard and
   Visa accepted.

The inn is nestled in a quiet and tranquil part of the
lovely area of Sunapee. The name Seven Hearths came about
from the fact that the inn has ☛ seven working fireplaces.
   The house was built in 1801, but thanks to the effort of
these three men, it has been carefully restored. The guest accommodations are large. ☛ Five of the working fireplaces are
in the guest rooms. Some rooms have wide-board floors and

beams in the ceiling. Two rooms downstairs have an outdoor terrace overlooking the lake. There are plants, huge ones, all over, and lots of books to read.

A massive fieldstone fireplace is in the huge living room. In one corner of the room is the smallest baby grand piano. Twin couches with interesting throw pillows provide a nice place to relax. This is the music center, and I enjoyed listening to Edith Piaf render some lively songs.

The dining room has another fireplace that is very cozy and the food served in here is very good. I had Veal Marsala with fresh mushrooms. It was delightful. They also offer grilled salmon with fresh dill butter. The herbs and vegetables are all grown here, to provide the very freshest food. A nice thing here is that the food reflects the seasons. Hearty roasts are served in the winter. Desserts are homemade. Fresh-poached peaches with a raspberry puree is just one of their specialties.

There is a nice screened porch with comfortable rockers and a lovely swimming pool with a wooden deck all around it. The smell of the tall pines is heavenly. The black labrador, Mabel, and two cats, Sara and Bubbles, love this peaceful countryside as much as you will.

How to get there: Take Exit 12 from I-89 and turn west on Route 11. In 4.2 miles, on the right, is a sign for the inn, which is in a few yards.

E: *In the living room is an album with menus going back to the 1930s. Thanksgiving dinner, five courses, $1.50. Wow.*

The Birchwood Inn
Temple, New Hampshire
03084

Innkeepers: Judy and Bill Wolfe
Telephone: 603-878-3285
Rooms: 7, all share baths.
Rates: $30 to $35, single; $35 to $40, double; EPB.
Facilities: Closed three weeks in April. Dinner served Tuesday through Saturday. BYOB. Trout fishing, hiking, hunting, golf, summer theater, and lakes nearby. No pets. No credit cards honored, but personal checks accepted.

The inn is in the Mount Monadnock region of New Hampshire, so there is plenty to do and see here. From the top of the mountain you can see four states, a nice reward for you hikers. There are trout waiting for the fisherman, much game for the hunter, plus all those good things for the quieter type such as golf, summer theater, horseback riding, and walking.

Bill and Judy are the owner-chefs and are very good at

what they do. I understand from my spies that their ☞ stuffed lobster is better than anywhere else. Chicken Piccata and Shrimp Parmesan served on green noodles are two more examples of their good food. They have She-crab Soup, which is hard to find north of South Carolina. It is excellent.

The inn has an ☞ 1878 square Steinway grand piano that is kept in perfect tune. The inn history stretches back some two centuries to circa 1775. During this time many people have come and gone, one notable personage being Henry David Thoreau. A room at the inn is named for him. Other rooms have rather different sort of names such as "The Bottle Shop"and "The School Room." The innkeepers will entertain you with the stories of how the rooms became so named.

How to get there: Take Route 3 out of Boston to Nashua, New Hampshire, Exit 7W. Follow Route 101 to Milford to Route 46 to Temple.

E: *The dining room walls are covered with Rufus Porter murals. They are beautiful.*

The chill of a wood-stove-warmed bedroom
evaporates in the crisp smell of bacon for breakfast.

olive Metcalf

Kimball Hill Inn
Whitefield, New Hampshire
03598

Innkeepers: Penny and Rick Preston
Telephone: 603-837-2284
Rooms: 8, 5 with private bath; 3 cottages.
Rates: $25 to $45, double occupancy, continental breakfast
  included.
Facilities: Closed in April. Restaurant closed to general public on Mondays and Tuesdays. Lunch, dinner, bar,
  lounge. Gift shop. Swimming, riding, golfing, and tennis
  nearby. American Express, MasterCard, and Visa accepted.

If you are looking for an inn that is comfortable, with
good food and ☞ a fantastic view, look no further. I sat in the
pub and had lunch looking out at the Presidential Range to
the east and the Green Mountains to the west. Beautiful! The
elevation of the inn is 1,390 feet.

Preston's Pub is finished inside with old barn wood. This
is real barn-board, for they took down an old barn in Lancas-

ter, New Hampshire, washed the wood, and refurbished the interior of the inn with it. The result is warm and cozy. If you look up you will see their ☞ standard gauge American Flyer train make a loop around the pub on almost 100 feet of track. I love toy trains because I never grew up, and I am glad.

The dining room with its glorious views is pretty, serving good food. The pub also serves food. They have interesting Mountain Burgers, and a good chef's salad. The sweet and sour chicken is a different delight. There are also nice weekday specials in both the dining room and the pub.

For you inveterate shoppers they have a nice little gift shop right in the inn.

The rooms are comfortable, all different shapes and sizes, and all with spectacular views.

You will find many activities to entertain you a few miles down the road, or just sit in the pub and watch the world at peace.

How to get there: Take Route 116 east out of Littleton, New Hampshire, toward Whitefield. The inn is one mile south of town on Kimball Hill Road.

🍺

E: ☞ *The Mountain Rat is a special drink, and I mean special; orange, lemon, cranberry juice, light and dark rum, apricot brandy with 151-proof rum on top. It is served in a 22-ounce brandy snifter. Wow!*

olive Metcalf

The Playhouse Inn
Whitefield, New Hampshire
03598

Innkeepers: Lucienne and Noel Lacan
Telephone: 603-837-2527
Rooms: 12, 8 with private bath.
Rates: $24 to $45, double occupancy, EP. MAP rates available.
Facilities: Closed Mondays in spring and fall, and mid-October to mid-May. Breakfast, lunch in summer, dinner. Beer Garden, cocktail lounge, cabaret show in summer. Swimming pool. Golf and tennis nearby. MasterCard, and Visa accepted.

With the Weathervane Theater just across the lawn, Lucienne and Noel Lacan have taken the playhouse theme for their delightful country inn. Noel is the chef, and the menu, from Prelude through Curtain Calls, proves it in every scene and act. There are those who hate vegetables, and then there's me. Endives Meunière, Braised Heart of Celery,

Lima Bean Bretonne, Mushrooms Sautéed Provençale. Pure heaven.

The swimming pool, with its view of the mountains, is lovely. There are six fireplaces in this comfortable old house. ☛ From the Backstage Bar to the Limelighter Restaurant, the theatrical touch is here, but with a really solid Gallic accent.

☛ Be sure to catch the enthralling cabaret held six nights a week in the Backstage Lounge. Five bouncingly talented youngsters—none are over thirty—raise the rafters with song and merriment and bring a tear to more than one eye. Each evening offers an entirely different show, so feel free to go twice, or three times or more.

How to get there: Take I-93, then Route 3 into Whitefield. The inn is 1½ miles north of town on Route 3.

♒

E: *The menu is great! Snails en Surprise have a new approach, and to finish off with Flaming Spanish coffee is indeed a switch.*

An unlit hearth in a good tavern is warmer by equators
than a blazing fire where there is no love.

Spalding Inn Club
Whitefield, New Hampshire
03598

Innkeeper: Topsy Spalding
Telephone: 603-837-2572
Rooms: 56, all with private bath and phone; 14 cottage suites.
Rates: Furnished upon request; MAP and AP.
Facilities: Closed mid-October to Memorial Day. Breakfast,
  lunch, dinner, bar, lounge. Swimming pool, four tennis
  courts, nine-hole par three golf course, 18-hole putting
  green, shuffleboard, lawn bowling. American Express,
  MasterCard, and Visa accepted.

I feel that everyone should at some time see how people
lived years ago, and only in these special New Hampshire
resorts can you live as our parents might have. I chose the
smallest of these resorts that I could find, and it is just grand.

Set on 500 choice acres, this inn has remained in the
same family for over fifty years. The service is ☞ impeccable.
Tables are set with fingerbowls, silver napkin rings, and
white linen. The food is excellent, and the choices are myr-

iad. It reminds me of a cruise ship where you also have un-
limited food. Breakfast alone is outstanding; ☞ hot from the
bakery popovers, doughnuts, and Danish pastries. I love how
they say fresh *native* eggs. The luncheon menu is superb,
and dinner, wow! Baked stuffed lobster, beef, veal, you name
it and it is here. The desserts are totally sinful, and I wish I
were back there right now.

Downstairs is the television lounge and bar. The television screen is huge. This is a good spot to relax. The main
living room has a large stone fireplace, lots of books, and
heaps of comfort. The inn also has a card room with a large
collection of jigsaw puzzles. One puzzle or another is always
being worked on by the guests.

The rooms are very comfortable with ☞ extra pillows
and blankets. The cottages have living rooms, bedrooms,
baths, and some even have their own porches. Fireplaces are
in every cottage.

There is so much to do here one need never leave the
inn's 500 acres. The lawns are magnificent. You know ☞
Topsy is an excellent innkeeper from the broad porch with
grand rockers at hand. My mother told me about such places.
It is wonderful that they are still here.

How to get there: Take I-93 north to Exit 41. Follow Route
116 through the village of Whitefield. Continue 1½ miles
north of town, turn right onto Mountain View Road.

E: *Lawn bowling tournaments in both singles and doubles
are held here. Have not seen this at any other inn.*

The Ram in the Thicket
Wilton, New Hampshire
03086

Innkeepers: Andrew and Priscilla Tempelman
Telephone: 603-654-6440
Rooms: 8, 3 with private bath.
Rates: $32.10 to $37.50, single; $37.50 to $48.15, double; tax
   and continental breakfast included.
Facilities: Open all year. Dinner, bar. Indoor swimming pool,
   horseback riding, hiking. Summer theater nearby. Mas-
   terCard and Visa accepted.

   The unusual name of the inn is taken from the old Bible
story of Abraham and Isaac. As a substitute for his son Isaac's
death, Abraham finds "a ram caught in the thicket" sent by
the Lord. Andrew and Priscilla founded the inn as a substitute for a life in the Midwest from which they wanted a
change.
   Luckily for all inn lovers the Tempelman's move has re-
sulted in another better-than-nice inn. This old Victorian
mansion has been carefully restored and now has lovely din-

ing rooms with crystal chandeliers, a hand-carved fireplace, and many other Victorian touches. One dining room has lovely blue delft tiles. The innkeepers are Dutch. The New Hampshire lounge has plants hanging from the ceilings.

Some of the dinner dish names are great. They taste good, too. How about China Garden Chicken, stir-fried chicken with fruit, or Lamb Rawalpindi, lamb in a sweet curry sauce, or Hampton Beach, seafood newburg in puff pastry. These are just an example of what you can expect. In the summer, all this good food can be savored on the screened porch.

This good inn is set in eight acres of wonderful country for roaming. Horses and sheep are in the lower pasture and you also have Fluffy, the cat, and her friends. Summer theater is close by. If you love to walk, there are many trails right at hand.

How to get there: Take Route 3 and just about Nashua take Exit 7 west on 101A to 101 about 15 miles to Wilton and watch for the inn signs.

E: ☛ *An enclosed swimming pool is my idea of heaven.*

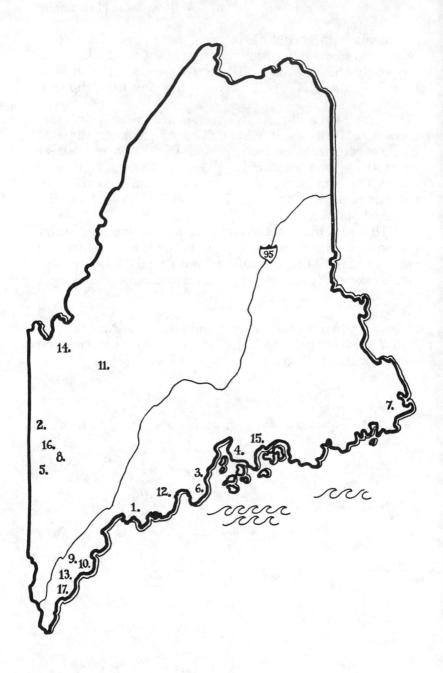

Numbers on map refer to towns numbered
on index on opposite page

Maine

Olive Metcalf

Grane's Fairhaven Inn
Bath, Maine
04530

Innkeepers: Jane Wyllie and Gretchen Williams
Telephone: 207-443-4391
Rooms: 9, 1 with private bath.
Rates: $22 to $35, single; $30 to $50, double; EP. Special
   packages for winter weekends.
Facilities: Open all year. Breakfast only meal served. BYOB
   lounge. Cross-country skiing, snowshoeing. Near restaurants. No credit cards honored, but personal checks accepted.

"Truth is never pure and rarely simple. Better to wear
out than to rust out. Remember my friend, all things must
end." These are a few of the needlepoint sayings on the 🖝
fourteen steps going up the back stairs of this lovely old inn.
The ingenious rug was done by a former owner and the top
step is "Knowledge Grows by Steps." Only in a country inn
will you find things like this.
   Rooms at Grane's are neat and very clean, with an-

tiques, good beds, and wonderful views. The front of the inn looks out on a salt tidal cove of the Kennebec River.

Breakfast is a thing of joy, with ☞ fresh fruit and souffles. I can still taste the hot bran muffins, and to top them off, the girls make their own jams and jellies. All this good eating is served in two lovely dining rooms.

The Tavern Library is a BYOB bar with fireplace, good chairs, and lots of fun. The English Bishop is a dandy hot drink for cold skiers. It is composed of port wine, oranges, cloves, honey, and brandy. If you have a cold it is just what the doctor, or kindly bartender, ordered.

How to get there: On Route 1 just short of Bath, take the exit marked New Meadows Road–West Bath. At the top of the exit, turn right for 7/10 mile. At the stop sign turn right for 10 feet and then immediately left. Go another 7/10 mile and turn right. Go 8/10 mile and turn left on North Bath Road. The inn is on the left in 5/10 mile.

E: *I have two cats, one Himalayan and one Maine Coon. At the inn is one Maine Coon, Cleo, and one bluepoint called Tuptim, and one flamepoint Himalayan called Foxie.*

When life dwindles thin and you wonder
if the sun will rise on another day.
seek perhaps an unfamiliar but rejuvenating bed
in a nearby country inn.

The Bethel Inn
Bethel, Maine
04217

Innkeeper: Dick Rasor; Manager Ray Moran
Telephone: 207-824-2175
Rooms: 65, all with private bath, telephone; 16 with fireplace.
Rates: $44 to $69, per person, double occupancy, MAP.
Facilities: Open all year. Breakfast, lunch, dinner, bar, lounge. Golf, tennis, swimming pool, lake house with sailfish and canoes, cross-country skiing, sauna, indoor games, supervised activities for children. Own walking tour guide. Downhill skiing nearby. All major credit cards accepted.

The Bethel Inn faces the village common of Bethel, Maine, which is a National Historic District complete with beautifully restored churches, public buildings, and private homes. The rear of the inn overlooks its own eighty-five acres, which include ☞ a nine-hole par thirty-six golf course.

Guest rooms have private baths and direct dial telephones. They are well done and very comfortable. A number

382

of rooms have been recently redecorated with country print wallpaper, thick carpeting, and fresh paint.

The huge living room, music room, and library are beautifully furnished for the utter comfort of the guests. The piano, by the way, is a Steinway.

Dining is a pleasure, either in the charming main dining room or on the fully screened porch overlooking the golf course. In winter dinner is served in the library, which has a generous fireplace for your comfort.

Downstairs is the Mill Brook Tavern. Jim Stoner, a blind jazz pianist, plays the piano here, June through October. Mill Brook cuts through the golf course and was the site of Twitchell's mill erected in the early 1700s in Sudbury, Canada, which is now Bethel, Maine.

Down here in the bar and lounge there is a light supper menu which is nice for the late hiker or skier. In the winter you can have hot cider, hot buttered rum, and glögg. Lunch is nice in the new screened-in terrace lounge, but the drinks are even better. They're called the Kool Krazy Bouncy and Hot drinks. I managed to taste three of them. Oh boy.

The lake house, three miles away on Lake Songo, features clambakes and barbeques. The downstairs patio on summer weekends also has a bar.

Skiing is super up here with Sunday River (I love that name) and Mount Abram right at hand. The inn has special ski packages. Do check them. And as a special special, they have over twenty kilometers of groomed cross-country trails for your pleasure.

How to get there: Bethel is located at the intersection of U.S. Route 2 and Maine Routes 5, 26, and 35. From the south take Exit 11 off the Maine Turnpike at Gray and follow Route 26 to Bethel. The inn is on the green.

E: *Friday afternoon teas, Monday punch parties, and Kool Krazy drinks. What an inn.*

The Sudbury Inn
Bethel, Maine
04217

Innkeepers: Cheri and David (Fuzzy) Thurston
Telephone: 207-824-2174
Rooms: 11, all with private bath; 2 suites.
Rates: $45 to $75, double occupancy, EPB.
Facilities: Closed April to mid-May, and end of October to
    Thanksgiving. Dinner, bar, lounge. Skiing, ice skating,
    canoeing, tennis, golfing, and hiking nearby. Master-
    Card, and Visa accepted.

This inn is located in the very pretty village of Bethel in
the mountains of western Maine. The town is home to Gould
Academy, one of Maine's foremost prep schools, which was
founded in 1836. Near the inn are miles of maintained cross-
country ski trails, downhill skiing, ice skating, canoeing (flat
and white-water), tennis, golfing, and hiking the Appalachian Trail. The inn provides easy access to the White
Mountain National Forest. The fall foliage around this area is
breathtakingly beautiful.

The whole inn has been refurbished and renovated, quite a task. When I was up here, Fuzzy was very busy finishing the lounge. The new bar is made of bird's-eye maple and is a one-of-a-kind beauty. A fireplace is in here, and on cold nights this is the place to be.

Rae is the chef, and the food she serves is good and plentiful Yankee cooking. Everything from soups and breads to desserts is homemade. Rae is famous for her chowder. I like inventive cooking and Baked Stuffed Sole stuffed with broccoli, cream cheese and walnuts is a good invention. She also serves boneless breast of chicken with this stuffing. Fuzzy's favorite is barbecue country-cut spareribs, and I love them, too.

The guest rooms are clean, neat, and comfortable. There is a gallery off the lobby where local craftspeople display their work for sale. This is a very nice touch.

How to get there: Take Exit 11 off the Maine Turnpike and follow Route 26 to Bethel. The inn is on lower Main Street.

☀

E: *Rockers on the front porch. You can sit and watch the world go by.*

A day by the fire, a hot ale in hand,
and the idiot cares of the world are as nothing.

Camden Harbour Inn
Camden, Maine
04843

Innkeepers: Jim and Laureen Gilbert
Telephone: 207-236-4200
Rooms: 21, 16 with private bath.
Rates: $45 to $115, double occupancy, EPB.
Facilities: Open all year. Dinner, Sunday brunch, bar. Television in lounge. Entertainment. Golfing, skiing, and sailing nearby: MasterCard, and Visa accepted.

Camden Harbour is one of the best-known ports in Maine, and one of the prettiest. Boats of yesteryear, both sail and power, as well as beautiful yachts of today, moor here by the rolling mountains that come right down to rocky shores. The inn sits up high above all of this and affords you a 🖝 panoramic view all year round.

All the rooms are neat as a pin. Some are rather small, but there is a first floor room with a queen-sized bed and a small deck, a twin-bedded room with a patio, and a luxury suite with sunroom with private porch, den with a wet bar, and bedroom with a fireplace. It's a beauty.

The dining room has a fireplace and a very warm atmosphere. In the summer, the enclosed porch overlooking Penobscot Bay and the mountains make a spectacular dining spot. Wherever you eat, you are sure to enjoy the food. Broiled Stuffed Mushroom Caps are a good appetizer choice for dinner. They can be followed by Crab Dijon Casserole, Maine crabmeat baked in a spicy mustard sauce, or Fresh Native Scallops broiled in butter in wine. There are also good beef choices on the menu.

With the dining room is the ☞ Thirsty Whale Tavern. Simple suppers are served in here each evening. The menu is posted on the chalkboard in the tavern. The tavern is always fun, especially if you enjoy folk music.

There are walking tours, bicycle trips, and nature walks in and around Camden. ☞ There is hardly a spot in this whole lovely Maine town that is not worth a visit. In July the Penobscot Folk Festival draws crowds to the Rockport Opera House.

This is a wonderful town to muddle about in for days.

How to get there: From Route 1, which runs through the center of town, turn up Bay View Street to #83.

🍺

E: *Andre, the famous seal, lives in Rockport Harbor all summer. He winters at the aquarium in Boston and for over 20 years has been swimming back on his own. Go see him. You will love him.*

Come back in 100 years and stay at my inn.

The Pentagöet Inn
Castine, Maine
04421

Innkeeper: Natalie F. Saunders
Telephone: 207-326-8616
Rooms: 18, 10 with private bath; one suite.
Rates: $40 to $75, double occupancy, EP.
Facilities: Closed January through March. Breakfast, dinner, bar. Extensive wine list. Fishing, sailing, and golfing nearby. American Express, MasterCard, and Visa accepted.

The Pentagöet is a lovely inn located on the unspoiled coast of beautiful Penobscot Bay. Built in 1894, this Victorian inn offers the traveler warmth and a very friendly atmosphere.

The living room holds many of Natalie's plants, has a woodburning stove and comfortable places to just relax. The dining room serves breakfast and dinner. The chef prepares one entree each evening. ☛ Dinner is served in five courses.

Seating is limited in order for you to enjoy the very best in dining.

The bedrooms are restful; some of them have little alcoves with windows that allow you a view of the town and harbor. All in all a very nice part of the world to be in.

There is good Maine fishing, as well as sailing, power boating, a nine-hole golf course, and dozens of islands nearby for delightful picnicking or just exploring. The Maine ☞ Maritime Academy is here in Castine, and their training ship, State of Maine, is open to the public.

Bear, a Maine coon cat, and Spot, a black and white general breed, help run the inn. They really are in charge.

How to get there: Take Route 95 from Portland to the "Coastal Region—Brunswick, Bath, Route 1" Exit. Follow Route 1 to Bucksport and 2 miles beyond turn right onto Route 175. Take Route 175 to Route 166, which takes you into Castine.

☒

E: *The* ☞ *porch that overlooks the town and harbor and serves lunch and tea, and sometimes dinner, is my spot in summer.*

Trifles make an inn, but an inn is no trifle.

Westways Country Inn
Center Lovell, Maine
04016

Innkeeper: Nancy Tripp
Telephone: 207-928-2663
Rooms: 7, one with private bath, 2 with half-baths; 2 cottages.
Rates: $95 to $120, double occupancy. MAP. Package plans available.
Facilities: Closed April and November. Breakfast, dinner, full license. Swimming, boating, sailing, tennis, handball, recreation building with bowling, Ping-Pong, pool, and card room. Two marinas on Lake Kezar. MasterCard and Visa accepted.

Westways was built in the 1920s as the executive retreat of the Diamond Match Company. It is a look into the past that is a pure delight.

The living room overlooking Kezar Lake is large. There is a huge stone fireplace and comfortable couches and chairs. On cool nights in winter your ☞ five-course dinner is served in here on glorious ☞ Spode china. The appetizers might be quiche or stuffed mushrooms. The soup may be stracciatella. Your salad is served with homemade dressings, and the entrees consist of two nightly choices. One day I was there one of the choices was lobster. But your choice may be Veal Cordon Bleu, or fresh red snapper, prime ribs, or steak. Great, creative desserts and coffees come next. This is indeed the way to live.

All of the rooms are gracious, most overlook the lake, and all have libraries. The president of Diamond Match was quite a reader, and his collection is here for you to enjoy. By the way, all of the rooms are different, some have wicker headboards and some have four-poster beds. All are comfortable.

The boathouse overlooks the lake and is comfortable for reading or just idle meditation. ☛ The view of the White Mountains from here is fantastic. There are over 100 acres in all that go with the inn, plus a sandy beach, and a picnic area where a seaplane once was kept.

How to get there: Coming either way on Route 302 turn north at Fryeburg, Maine, onto Route 5. Fourteen miles north the lake will appear on your left, and the inn entrance (marked with a sign) is on your left about 6 miles up the lake.

❦

E: *There is a body shower in the bath on the first floor that is unbelievable. It is certainly one-of-a-kind.*

The Craignair Inn
Clark Island, Maine
04859

Innkeepers: Norman and Terry Smith
Telephone: 207-594-7644
Rooms: 17, all share baths.
Rates: $35 to $40, per person, double occupancy, MAP.
Facilities: Open all year. Breakfast, dinner for six or more in
    winter. Special diets furnished upon reasonable notice.
    BYOB. Swimming, skiing, tennis, riding, and golf
    nearby. MasterCard and Visa accepted.

This isn't a fancy inn, but it is comfortable. It was built
about fifty years ago as a boarding house for quarry workers.
It is hung on the edge of the water, with rocks, tidal flats, an
ocean inlet, and loads of peace and quiet. The quarry has
long since been worked out, but you can swim there in the
salt water that rises and falls with the tide. If you worry about
old wooden buildings, sleep relaxed here.

There is always something to do at Craignair. If the fog
rolls in, cozy up to the fire in the sitting room. When it

snows, the Camden Snow Bowl Ski Area is a short drive away. Nearby towns and villages offer diversified activity stops, including antique shops, art galleries, museums, and specialty shops. Or you could attend a concert, play golf or tennis, ride horseback, bicycle, sail, or catch one of the numerous ☞ festivals paying homage to seafood, blueberries, chicken, sailboats, and history.

If tidal pools, clam flats, islands, meadows, and spruce forests invite you, come to Craignair in any season.

No excuse now, if you are a weight watcher, or on a salt-free diet. ☞ Terry will stick to your diet if you let her know a day or two ahead of time. There's one entree only each evening, but what variety. And on Saturday, enjoy that traditional Maine dinner, fresh lobster with steamers. The dining room is cozy, done in blue and white with lots of windows looking to the sea.

How to get there: Go to Thomaston on Route 1, then take Route 131 south for about 6 miles, and turn left on Route 73 for about a mile to Clark Island Road. Take a right, and the inn is the end of the road.

E: *The living-room library is very comfortable. This is a real Maine Coast inn with its own Maine Coast dog, a black Lab named Delia.*

Having had an excellent meal and a lovely evening,
I tucked myself in bed knowing I had sinned
but it did not seem to matter.

Olive Metcalf

Lincoln House Country Inn
Dennysville, Maine
04628

Innkeepers: Mary Carol and Gerald Haggerty
Telephone: 207-726-3953
Rooms: 6, all share 4 semi-private baths; 2 with wood stove; 2
  with fireplace.
Rates: $45 to $50, double occupancy, EP.
Facilities: Closed January through March. Breakfast for
  house guests, dinner daily by reservation. Full bar, wine
  list. MasterCard and Visa accepted.

When you walk in the side door of the inn you are in
what once was the summer kitchen and now is a library full
of books with a huge fireplace hung with old cooking equipment and one Japanese wok! On through Mary Carol's
kitchen you find two delightful dining rooms. Beyond is a
large living room with a baby grand piano. This is an inn
where you can feel totally at home.

Mary Carol's kitchen really turns out exceptional food,
including the best ☞ lamb I have ever had. It was prepared

quite differently and only Mary Carol can tell you how. Her breakfast muffins almost outdo her lamb.

The inn is a handsome, yellow, foursquare Georgian Colonial perched above the Denny River, one of the few rivers where you can find the Atlantic salmon. John Audubon once stayed here and was so impressed he named the "Lincoln Sparrow" for his hosts. The inn was built by an ancestor of President Lincoln in 1787.

Jerry is a master restorer and perfectionist. It shows all over the inn. The woodshed, a village pub, has ☞ a bar that Jerry carved from a 4,000-pound elm trunk with a bear's head carved at one end. The woodshed has fun on Thursday nights in the winter. It is "open mike" time and local amateurs come and do their thing. On Sundays it is international dart shoots with neighboring Canada. The U.S. seems to always win and whether this is their ability or Jerry's liberal beers we do not know.

You will love this inn, but it is a long way off, so do make reservations ahead.

How to get there: Route 1 goes right by Dennysville. Driving up take the second sign into Dennysville, just after you have crossed the Denny River. Turn left and you will find the inn almost immediately on your right.

E: ☞ *Bald eagles and osprey are seen here, and families of seals swim in the river. It is a long way up here but worth every mile.*

The Waterford Inne
East Waterford, Maine
04233

Innkeepers: Barbara and Rosalie Vanderzanden
Telephone: 207-583-4037
Rooms: 9, 6 with private bath.
Rates: $40 to $60, double occupancy, EP.
Facilities: Closed March 15 to May 1. Breakfast, dinner. Hiking, hunting, fishing, swimming, bird watching, and skiing nearby. No credit cards accepted.

This is a beautiful part of the world. It is secluded, quiet, and restful. The inn offers a fireplace in the parlor and a library full of books and good music for your relaxation. And when the weather is warm, you can while away your days in the rockers on the porch.

But if you're looking for activity, the Waterford Inne can offer that, too. The area provides hiking, hunting, fishing in the summer and winter, downhill and cross-country skiing, swimming, and bird watching.

This is a first for me, a mother and daughter who are the

innkeepers. They bought the inn in 1978 and have done a masterful job of restoring and renovating it. There are antiques in all the rooms, nice wallpapers, and some stencilling. For your comfort there are electric blankets in the winter, and for your visual pleasure ☞ there are fresh flowers in the summer.

Rosalie, the mother, does the cooking. The dinner is a fixed price with one entree served each evening. She is a very good and creative chef. All baking is done right here and all the vegetables are grown in the inn's garden. Barbara does the serving, and you may be seated at a table for four in the ☞ attractive dining room with fireplace, or in a secluded corner just for two.

How to get there: From Norway, Maine, take Route 118 west for 8 miles to Route 37. Turn left and go one-half mile to Springer's General Store. Take an immediate right up the hill. The inn is about one-half mile.

E: *Tansey and Teasel are the two inn cats lucky enough to live in this beautiful part of the world.*

*The crackle of an inn's hearth
can melt the chilliest of minds and bodies.*

olive Metcalf

The Kennebunk Inn
Kennebunk, Maine
04043

Innkeepers: Arthur and Angela LeBlanc
Telephone: 207-985-3351
Rooms: 35, 12 with private bath, all with air conditioning.
Rates: Off season, $26 to $38; in season, $30 to $45; double
    occupancy, EP.
Facilities: Closed Christmas Day. Full breakfast June to Oc-
    tober 15; continental breakfast off season. Lunch and
    dinner every day except Sunday. Bar, lounge. Fishing
    and swimming nearby. All major credit cards accepted.

    The inn is located right smack on Route 1 in the heart of
town, convenient to everything. Even the beaches are very
close at hand.
    Built in 1799, the inn was in total disrepair when the
LeBlancs bought it. With a tremendous amount of work and
attention to detail, they have restored the inn to its current
state of being a proper in-town country inn.
    All of the beds have ☛ new mattresses and all bedrooms

are air-conditioned. A modern touch like air conditioning in an old inn is great. There are some brass headboards, and if I know Angela, there will be more. Throughout the inn the wallpapers are ☞ French imports, and they are beautiful.

The upstairs foyer is a nice spot to gather. There are couches and chairs, television, puzzles, games, and books.

The dining room has colorful tablecloths, and the food served here is impeccable. For breakfast, among many dishes, is Omar Pacha, baked eggs on sautéed onions and topped with cheese. Another dish is King Neptune's Delight, two fresh eggs enthroned on crab meat on English muffins and crowned with hollandaise sauce. There are also ☞ crois-sants and scones baked daily. Luncheon is equally interesting. One item is a one-half-pound hamburger made of charbroiled choice beef. Delicious. For dinner do try Angela's Veal Under Glass or her husband's King Arthur's Sirloin Steak. You will love whatever you order.

How to get there: Take Exit 3 from I-95 (the Maine Turnpike) to Kennebunk. The inn is at 45 Main Street.

E: *The Saturday night feature is flambéed duck with the chef's choice of a liqueur sauce. It is served at table-side with flaming brandy.*

How good of you to have asked me in.

The Captain Jefferds Inn
Kennebunkport, Maine
04046

Innkeepers: Warren Fitzsimmons and Don Kelly
Telephone: 207-967-2311
Rooms: 11, 9 with private bath; carriage house with 3 apartments.
Rates: $65 to $73, double occupancy, EPB. Long-term rental fee for apartments.
Facilities: Open most of the year. Closed in November. Full breakfast only meal served. BYOB. No children under 12. No credit cards honored, but personal checks accepted.

The inn was built in 1804. Its style is Federal, complete with a magnificent Federal fence. It is absolutely fabulous throughout. To go along with all of this are ☞ three inn dogs whose names absolutely convulse me. Jenny Millstone, Maggie Street, and Isabelle Necessary were strays; I have never seen anything funnier than the three of them. There is also an orange and white cat, Ambrose.

Warren and Don were in the antique business before they became innkeepers and they furnished the inn from their stock, except for mattresses and box springs. There's a spectacular ☞ majolica collection of over 1,000 pieces. Cupboards overflow with antique china and pottery. The mirror in the dining room is most unusual; a landscape scene with overhanging trees is painted right on it. An unusual étagère that is made of shells and holds boxes made of shells is a work of art. There is a captain's bridge stairwell, reminiscent of a sea captain's lookout post. It is all just beautiful.

The guest rooms are color coordinated. Laura Ashley wallpapers, the ☞ finest sheets that can be obtained, extra pillows, magnificent antique bedspreads, and the furniture is as you would expect, beautiful. White wicker on the porch, a Steinway grand piano in the living room, six fireplaces, a lovely sun porch, and a brick terrace all add to the exceptional ambience of the inn. The plants remind me of home; they are trees.

Breakfast is good and it is fun. It is served at a huge mahogany table. Warren cooks and Don serves. If you stayed a week your breakfast would be different every day. Blueberry crepes, French toast with Grand Marnier, New England flannel (corned beef hash with dropped eggs), Italian eggs, and it goes on and on.

The inn provides setups for your drinks. There are plenty of restaurants nearby for lunch and dinner.

How to get there: Take Exit 3 from the Maine Turnpike. Turn left on Route 35 South to Kennebunkport. At the traffic light, turn left. Go over the drawbridge. Look for the sign for Ocean Drive. Take it one-third mile to Arundel Wharf. The next left is Pearl Street, where the inn is located.

E: *I think you can tell I sure do like it here.*

Captain Lord Mansion
Kennebunkport, Maine
04046

Innkeepers: Beverly Davis and Rick Lichfield
Telephone: 207-967-3141
Rooms: 16, all with private bath, 11 with working fireplace.
Rates: $69 to $99, double occupancy, continental breakfast included.
Facilities: Open all year. Breakfast only meal served. BYOB. Perkins Cove and Rachel Carson Wildlife Refuge nearby. No children under 12. No credit cards honored, but personal checks accepted.

For years I have been searching for a word to do justice to describing this inn. Exquisite would be the most likely, but even it is not an apt enough word. ☛ It is truly a grand inn.

Eleven of the guest rooms have working fireplaces. There are fourteen throughout the inn. Most of the rooms have padded, deep window seats, a great place to relax and daydream. One of the beds is a four-poster twelve feet high.

Rugs and wallpaper, thanks to Beverly's eye for decoration, are well coordinated, ☞ thirsty towels are abundant, and extra blankets and pillows help make your stay better than pleasant.

Throughout the inn are portraits of past owners in the Lord family. There is still some of the original Lord furniture. A handsome dining room table with carved feet and chairs belonged to Nathaniel Lord's grandson, Charles Clark, and is dated 1880. The wallpaper in one bedroom that is still beautifully intact dates also from 1880. The paper in the front bedroom goes back to 1812.

Breakfast is the only meal served, and it is a rare treat. You eat at a huge table in the center of a kitchen that has about as big a wood stove as I have seen. For other meals there are many fine restaurants in Kennebunkport.

This is a bring-your-own-bottle inn, and from the ☞ scenic cupola on its top to the parlors on the first floor, you will find many great places to enjoy a drink.

How to get there: From I-95 take Exit 3 to Kennebunk. Turn left on Route 35 and drive through Kennebunk to Kennebunkport. Turn left at the traffic light at the Sunoco station. Go over drawbridge and take first right onto Ocean Avenue. Go ³/₁₀ mile and turn left at the Mansion. Park behind the building and take brick walkway to guest entrance.

⚱

E: *Rick knows the history of the house and loves to tell it as it was, so do ask him.*

Olive Metcalf

English Meadows Inn
Kennebunkport, Maine
04046

Innkeepers: Gene, Helene, and Claudia Kelly
Telephone: 207-967-5766
Rooms: 14, 2 with private bath.
Rates $35, single; $60, double; EPB.
Facilities: Closed November 1 to April 1. Full breakfast only
  meal served. BYOB. Antique shop. One mile from ocean.
  No credit cards honored, but personal checks accepted.

This is another fine breakfast-only inn. Here in Kennebunkport there are plenty of restaurants for you to choose
from, so you'll have no problem finding a good place to eat.

English Meadows is a lovely Victorian farmhouse, circa
1840. The inn has antiques, brass and iron beds, and hooked
rugs. The carriage house is paneled and has a large fireplace
in the gracious living room. There is much wicker furniture
that has bright gray covers on the cushions. This is a nice
place to relax after a day of fun.

At English Meadows you are only five minutes from

Dock Square where you will find good restaurants, public golf courses, churches, galleries, and deep-sea fishing. ☞ A bicycle is a great piece of equipment to bring along to Kennebunkport. While the area has some gently rolling hills, you will not find backbreaking slopes to negotiate. The beach for you to use is only a mile from the inn.

At the inn is "The Whalers Antique Shop" where you will find country furniture and accessories, beautiful quilts, hooked rugs, baskets, and much interesting wicker work.

The inn is situated on six acres of land and has been operating as an ☞ inn for over eighty years.

How to get there: From the Maine Turnpike take Exit 3 to Kennebunk. Follow Route 35 south, toward the ocean. The inn is 5 miles along on the right.

E: *My heart got taken by one of the inn cats, Kee, some kind of Maltese.*

A well-run inn and a man on a diet
go together about as well as
an arsonist and a bale of hay.

Old Fort Inn
Kennebunkport, Maine
04046

Innkeepers: David and Sheila Aldrich
Telephone: 207-967-5353
Rooms: 12, all with private bath, kitchen, and television One
   suite.
Rates: $60 to $100, double occupancy, continental breakfast
   included.
Facilities: Closed end of October to May 1. Suite available all
   year. Continental breakfast only meal served. BYOB.
   Swimming pool, tennis, antique shop. Bikes for rent,
   ocean nearby. All major credit cards accepted.

   When you enter the Old Fort Inn you are in an excellent
antique shop. Next you are in a huge living room that overlooks the swimming pool. The pool has ☛ a solar cover that
enables the inn to stretch its swimming season a bit. I know
it works because I have one on my pool. This is a lovely, comfortable living room with a fireplace, a super spot to curl up
and read a book.

The rooms are charming, and all are fully equipped with a kitchen. This is so nice when you plan a longer stay than overnight. The beds have antique headboards of brass or wood along with good, comfortable mattresses. The towels are ☛ color coordinated, which I always love. There is a nice library in the foyer.

The inn provides ☛ a laundry. Until you have been on the road a week or so, you do not know how convenient such a facility is. The inn also provides a place to shower and change if you are checking out and still want to swim in the pool or the ocean that is only one block away.

There is a television in each room, and the suite has color cable. To go with these modern touches is the inn cat, Samantha. And to go with the cat is the great inn child, Shana. She is some innkeeper. You will love her.

Although you may want to prepare your own food in your fully equipped kitchen, the inn does provide you with the menus of all the area restaurants.

How to get there: Take Exit 3 from the Maine Turnpike (it is marked Kennebunk), turn left on Route 35 to Kennebunkport, and follow the signs to the inn. It is on Old Fort Avenue.

E: The spiral staircase at one end of the inn is neat.

One Stanley Avenue
Kingfield, Maine
04947

Innkeepers: Dan and Sue Davis
Telephone: 207-265-5541
Rooms: 6, 3 with private bath.
Rates; $35 to $40, double occupancy, EPB.
Facilities: Inn open all year. Resturant closed April 1 to July 4 and third week of October to Christmas. Breakfast, dinner, bar. Skiing, ice skating, golfing, mountain climbing, and white-water rafting nearby. MasterCard and Visa accepted, but personal checks preferred.

The house at Three Stanley Avenue is a lovely Queen Anne Victorian house, built in circa 1899. It is one of the three Stanley homes in Kingfield. Here are the guest rooms for the inn, neat, clean, and comfortable.

One Stanley Avenue, right next door, is the restaurant for the inn. This house is on the National Register of Historic Places. In the front hall is a ☛ beautiful old oak reach-in refrigerator that holds the inn's wine collection at perfect temperatures. There's a real beauty of a piano, a Chickering square piano, refurbished and ready to play. The small bar is also here.

The restaurant rates three stars in the Mobil Travel Guide. Dan is a rather inventive chef. ☞ Roast Duck with Rhubarb Glaze. I never would have thought of this combination in a hundred years, but it is excellent. Pork with Port Wine and Juniper Berry Sauce. Another entree is Atlantic Salmon with Dan's own sauce McIntire, named after his maternal heritage. Blackberry chicken sounds divine. I do love to cook with fruits.

The desserts are also magnificent. Rhubarb Strudel, Crème Celeste, Indian Pudding à la mode, and many more. Come on up here and enjoy Dan's fine cooking.

Sugarloaf Mountain is close by, providing superb downhill and cross-country skiing. An eighteen-hole golf course is being put in on the Sugarloaf property. White-water rafting is an exciting spring and summer sport, and many lakes surrounding the area provide other water sports. No matter what season you come, you'll always find an abundance of things to do.

How to get there: Take the Maine Turnpike to the Belgrade Lakes Exit in Augusta. Follow Route 27 through Farmington to Kingfield. In town, turn right on Route 16. Cross a bridge, and turn right to stay on Route 16. Stanley Avenue is the first street on the left.

E: *There are three charming dining rooms in which to enjoy Dan's food.*

olive Metcalf

Winter's Inn
Kingfield, Maine
04947

Innkeeper: Michael Thom
Telephone: 207-265-5421
Rooms: 12, 9 with private bath.
Rates: $55 to $65, per person, MAP. 21-day cancellation notice. EP rates and white-water rafting packages available.
Facilities: Closed after Easter to mid-June and end of foliage to before Thanksgiving. Breakfast, dinner, Sunday brunch in summer, bar, lounge. Swimming pool, tennis, cross-country skiing. Downhill skiing, hunting, fishing, hiking, golfing, white-water rafting, canoeing, and Stanley Steamer Museum nearby. MasterCard and Visa accepted.

Located in the heart of the western Maine mountains, Bigelow, Sugarloaf, and Saddleback, sits Winter's Inn on top of a ten-acre hill on the edge of town. A Neo-Georgian manor house built at the turn of the century for Amos Greene Winter, it had fallen into sad disrepair when it was rescued in 1972 by Michael Thom, a young architect. Michael has restored the house beautifully, yet every time I come up here I find something he's improved. ☞ Much to his pride, the building has now been listed on the National Register of Historic Places.

Elegant without being stiff or pretentious, the inn has been decorated with ☞ handsome wallpapers. The walls are hung with a fine collection of oil paintings and gold-framed mirrors. The view from the dining room windows of the western mountains is breathtaking. The view is the same from the swimming pool.

☞ Food served in Le Papillon is delightful, a continuing surprise in this faraway inn at the back of beyond. Guests can spend their days climbing mountains, come home to the inn for a swim and a drink, then dress for dinner and dine elegantly, savoring the best of both worlds.

Balthazar's Pub is an elegant place to have a drink, play backgammon, chat, and enjoy. There is a unique corner fireplace in here.

Hunting, fishing, hiking along the Appalachian Trail, and canoeing welcome outdoors people. Downhill skiers are especially happy here, but so is the lady guest ensconced by the pool with her needlepoint or book.

Each year, as the inn reopens in June, Michael gives a Great Gatsby Party. This is such a fun party, I'd like to attend every year. Everyone dresses in Great Gatsby-period attire for a formal garden party around the pool. The food is divine—last year poached Norwegian salmon was served—and a band plays the greatest dance music. Last year the party raised funds for the Hartford, Connecticut, Ballet. The ballet troupe performs in the area for several weeks in the summer.

How to get there: Kingfield is halfway between Boston and Quebec City, and the Great Lakes area and the Maritimes. Take the Maine Turnpike to the Belgrade Lakes Exit in Augusta. Follow Highway 27 through Farmington to Kingfield. The inn is on a small hill near the center of town.

E: *There lives here an inn cat, Balthazar. He is orange and white and as regal as his name. Once I had a look-alike cat, Alleycat, just as majestic. Balthazar turned 20 this year.*

411

The Newcastle Inn
Newcastle, Maine
04553

Innkeepers: George and Sandra Thomas
Telephone: 207-563-5685
Rooms: 20, 9 with private bath.
Rates: $29 to $49, double occupancy, EP.
Facilities: Open all year. Breakfast. Television in sitting
    room, antique shop. Swimming and cross-country skiing
    nearby. No credit cards accepted.

Found on each bed here at the inn is this greeting, ☞
"We bid you warm welcome as you enter this room. It may
not be our good fortune to come to know you this trip, but we
want you to feel this is your home while away, and that we
are eager for your comfort and happiness while our guest.
May you rest well. May you be healthy under this roof. May
your stay fulfill your every expectation. May God bless and
prosper you."

The lovely porch full of ☞ wicker furniture is always
cool in summer and a nice way to enter this charming inn.

Breakfast is the only meal being served now, but what a breakfast. On one visit I had French toast. It was superb. The dining room is charming. There is a large, comfortable living room with fireplace and another room for television viewing.

Rooms here are Maine-size small, but are well done with white bedspreads, white curtains, and they are clean, clean, clean.

At the inn you are within walking distance of the lovely town of Damariscotta and its salt-water tidal river. You are also within short driving distance of the famous Pemaquid peninsula with its lighthouse, fort, and beach. In the other direction you are not far from Boothbay Harbor. Do come up and enjoy this distinctive part of Maine.

How to get there: When going north on Route 1, take the Newcastle exit to the right. Stay to your left; the inn is about 4 blocks down the road on River Road.

E: Good cross-country skiing is all around you, so do come up.

The glowing carriage lamp beside the door
of a country inn when viewed through a cold rain
erases the rigors of the day
and promises a fine, fine evening.

olive Metcalf

The Old Village Inn
Ogunquit, Maine
03907

Innkeepers: Benjamin J. Lawlor and Catherine L. Nadeau
Telephone: 207-646-7088
Rooms: 6 suites, one double, all with private bath.
Rates: $40 to $55, double occupancy, EP. $65 to $75, suites, double occupancy, EP.
Facilities: Closed first three weeks in January. Dining room closed Tuesdays in winter. Lunch served only in September and October, dinner, bar, television, game room, entertainment in the lounge, fishing, swimming, and theater nearby. MasterCard and Visa accepted.

Ben Lawlor and Cathy Nadeau have a good in-town inn that has a history going back to 1833. Interestingly, part of its history was the August 2, 1942, issue of the ☞ *Saturday Evening Post,* which had for its cover a picture of the inn done by John Falter.

There are six very nice suites available. One of the beds has a headboard made from four ladder-back chairs.

The bar is a real, English country pub with hanging stemware glasses, small tables, and a cooking unit off to one side. The dining rooms are different and comfortable. One is enclosed in a greenhouse, with a view of the ocean and with greenery everywhere. The Bird & Bottle is another dining room, and the newest is the enclosed porch that wraps around the front of the inn.

The Ogunquit Room is a perfect spot for a private party of up to twenty people. There is a living room with a television, nice for the younger set, and also a room with piano and game tables.

Hard on the rock-bound coast of Maine, this inn has interests for all. The famous Ogunquit Playhouse is here, as is the newer off-Broadway repertory theater. There is plenty of fishing and swimming, and two unusual walking trails.

The Marginal Way winds you along the spectacular bay and sea, and the Trolley Trail follows an abandoned line through the woods. I have never gone by, or even near, Ogunquit without a stop at this good inn.

How to get there: The inn is at 30 Main Street in the middle of Ogunquit. Main Street is Route 1.

E: *The greenhouse is so nice. I have one at home, so I know.*

olive Metcalf

The Rangeley Inn
Rangeley, Maine
04970

Innkeepers: Ed and Fay Carpenter
Telephone: 207-864-3341
Rooms: 26, all with private bath.
Rates: $33 to $38, single; $39 to $44, double occupancy; EP.
   MAP available.
Facilities: Inn open all year. Dining room closed Easter to
   Memorial Day and Thanksgiving to Christmas. Break-
   fast, dinner, bar, lounge, banquet facilities. Fishing,
   boating, swimming, hiking, tennis, golfing, hunting,
   skiing, and snowmobiling nearby. American Express,
   MasterCard, and Visa accepted.

   As their brochure says, "From out of the past. Try our
old-fashioned comfort and hospitality." The Carpenters really
mean it. The Rangeley Inn is in a lovely part of the world,
1600 feet above the ocean. Two daughters help run the inn;
Susan is the chef and Janet tends the front desk and is head-
waitress. Ed and Fay are everywhere.

The bar and lounge area is quite large. Here, Ed and I enjoyed a ☛ few games of pool. A nice woodburning stove takes the chill off the air and the bar stools are really comfortable. There also is a nice television room, furnished with couches and lounge chairs and decorated with plants that add a lot of charm.

Almost all the rooms are carpeted and all are ☛ very clean. The baths have wonderful claw-footed tubs; some rooms have showers. A bath in an old bathtub is heavenly. You can be up to your neck in water; you can't do this in a modern tub.

The kitchen is new and Susan loves it. She is a fine chef. She prepared a chicken dish when I was there that was delicious. I topped it off with a favorite dessert, ☛ strawberries dipped in chocolate, served with whipped cream flavored with Kahlua.

Spring brings superb fishing for brook trout and landlocked salmon. Some brooks are open only to fly-fishing. Wildflowers and migrating birds are plentiful, so bring a camera. Summer is boating, swimming, and hiking, or tennis and golf. Fall is spectacular fall foliage and hunting. Winter, of course, brings snow activities. Saddleback is nearby for downhill skiing, and cross-country skiing and snowmobiling are everywhere.

In any season of the year, Angel Falls, twenty miles away, is impressive and worth a visit. It is a fifty-to-sixty foot fall. Beautiful!

How to get there: From the Maine Turnpike, take Exit 12 at Auburn. Pick up Route 4 and follow it to Rangeley.

♉

E: *There is organ music Memorial Day to Thanksgiving, and a dance band in ski season.*

olive Metcalf

Surry Inn
Surry, Maine
04684

Innkeepers: Sarah and Peter Krinsky
Telephone: 207-667-5091
Rooms: 13, 11 with private bath.
Rates: $42 to $48, double occupancy, EPB.
Facilities: Closed four days at Christmas. Box lunch available, dinner, bar. No pets. Swimming, canoeing, rowboats, horseshoes, croquet. Cross-country skiing and Acadia National Park nearby. MasterCard and Visa accepted.

If you take one lovely lady chef plus one handsome carpenter and put them together at an old inn that needs restoring and running, you have Sarah and Peter, the two, young, energetic innkeepers of the Surry Inn.

They have done wonders with this lovely old (1834) inn. It is a ☛ handsome, sprawling inn overlooking Contention Cove. The lawns sweep right down to the inn's private beach in the cove. The driveway, called Stagecoach Lane, dates back to the time when the stage met the Boston steamboat at the landing here at the inn.

There is a sixty-foot porch overlooking the cove. I could sit here night after night to watch the beautiful sunsets. The inn is full of good books to read, warm fireplaces, and restful couches and chairs. The guest rooms are lovely, with good beds and an abundance of charm.

Sarah is a fine chef. I had her Chicken au Moutarde. It is boneless breast of chicken and coated with almonds in a mustard cream sauce, and delicious. Her Dilly Shrimp are Gulf shrimp in a sauce of sour cream and fresh dill. The medallions of pork are sautéed with apples, onions, and herbs. Or Sarah may do them in ginger cream. She also makes her own breads and desserts.

This inn is a good find for me. These two people are good innkeepers and you will feel very comfortable here.

How to get there: Follow Route 1 North to Bucksport, Maine. Seven miles north of Bucksport, turn right onto Route 176 (Surry Road), and follow it to its end. Turn left onto Route 172 and the inn is in 2½ miles.

E: *The cat is Isabelle, a nice tiger cat.*

Hark, which are common noises
and which are the ghosts of long contented guests.

olive Metcalf

Kedarburn Inn
Waterford, Maine
04088

Innkeepers: Norma, Paula, and Doug Holt
Telephone: 207-583-6182
Rooms: 5, one with private bath.
Rates: $35 to $50, double occupancy, EPB.
Facilities: Open all year. Dinner, Sunday brunch. BYOB.
   Tennis, boating, swimming, golfing, skiing, ice fishing,
   and hiking nearby. MasterCard and Visa accepted.

Maine is such a beautiful state. I love it when I'm riding
along a scenic Maine road and come across an inn that even I
knew nothing about.

The Kedarburn Inn is a nice colonial house built in
1858 on the shores of Lake Keoka. There is so much to do
here in every season. Fall foliage is breathtaking and in
spring, when everything wakes up, it is glorious. In winter
there is skiing, both downhill and cross-country, plus ☞ ice-
fishing, snowmobiling, and ice skating. Summer brings
swimming, tennis, golfing, fishing, hiking, and antiquing. Or

you can just bring a good book and curl up in this comfortable inn.

Breakfast is a full and hearty one, consisting of Maine-style pancakes, homemade muffins, eggs, French toast, and ☞ oatmeal honey toast. How delicious. Sunday brunch features homemade ☞ sticky buns. I would drive all the way up here for these. Eggs Kedarburn, Phyllo Pie, and homemade dessert round off the brunch offerings.

Dinner consists of beef, cheese, or chicken fondue, baked chicken breast, steak, or baked stuffed sole. In summer, lobster dinners are featured every Friday and Saturday night, beginning with the inn's own homemade clam chowder. Steak and chicken are available for non-lobster eaters.

How to get there: Take Exit 8 off the Maine Turnpike. Follow Route 302 to Naples. Turn onto Route 35 and follow it to the inn.

E: *There's a very cute young Holt who lives here. Maybe a future innkeeper.*

Our sympathy for the hardships of our forbears should be somewhat mitigated by the fact that they had the best of country inns.

York Harbor Inn
York Harbor, Maine
03911

Innkeepers: Joe, Jean, and Garry Dominguez
Telephone: 207-363-5119
Rooms: 21, 9 with private bath.
Rates: $35 to $75, double occupancy, continental breakfast
included.
Facilities: Open all year. Dining room open daily in summer
and fall; after November 1, dining room open Thursday
through Sunday. Lunch May through December, dinner, Sunday brunch year round. Bar, cocktail lounge.
Entertainment on weekends. Public beach, fishing,
boating, golfing, tennis. All major credit cards accepted.

Wow! Three dining rooms with a ☞ view of the Atlantic.
This is a cozy and comfortable inn with good food and good
grog. Sitting there looking over the Atlantic should be
enough, but when you add the excellent food it is ☞ heaven.
Everything is made to order and baked right here. The appetizers are glorious. Tortelleni, an Italian classic, is oh, so

good, and there are several more. By his own words, Chef Gerry Bonsey creates incomparable homemade soups. You can imagine what the rest is like. I wish I had more space to tell you more. Do go, I know you will enjoy.

The cellar, which once was a livery stable, is the lounge. There is a friendly bartender and a beauty of a bar, made of solid unstained cherry wood joined with holly and ebony woods. The carpenter even put an inlaid tulip in a corner— out of tulip wood, of course. Happy hour is fun. The local people come in and I really enjoyed talking with them. The fireplace corner is so nice and cozy with the furniture clustered around the fireplace. There is listening-type music down here.

The inn is old; 1637 is the date for the room into which you first come. Originally a fisherman's house, it has sturdy beams in the ceiling, not for holding up the roof, but instead to hold up wet sails to dry before the large fireplace.

The rooms are comfortable and from some you can see the sea. On a quiet night you can hear the sea breaking on the generous beach below the inn. The annex next door has been beautifully remodeled. What a monumental job. All the rooms over here have a private bath. There are two working fireplaces and one room has its own patio.

When you arrive at the inn you are given a ☞ book, with information about the inn and area and a few poems, all lovingly put together. This is a really nice touch. Another one is the ☞ decanter of sherry in the hall for a thirsty guest.

How to get there: From I-95 take the Yorks Berwicks Exit. Turn right at the blinking light, left at the first traffic light (Route 1A), and go through the village about 3 miles. The inn is on the left.

E: *York Harbor and all the areas around are beautiful. Be sure to bring your camera so you can remember it all at home.*

Index

About the author

The "inn creeper" is the nickname Elizabeth Squier has earned in her almost twelve years of researching this guide to the inns of New England. And a deserved name it is, for she tours well over 200 inns every year from top to bottom, inside out, before recommending the best ones to you.

A recognized authority on fine food and lodging, Elizabeth is a gourmet cook and has written travel and food columns for many periodicals. Like you, she recognizes readily the special ingredients that make a good inn exceptional.

Guests—

Ye are welcome here,
    be at your ease
Go to bed when you're ready
    get up when you please.
Happy to share with you
    such as we've got
The leak in the roof
    the soup in the pot.
Ye don't have to thank us,
    or laugh at our jokes
Sit deep and come often
    you're one of the folks.

found in an inn, Brookline Mass

Other Globe Pequot Books
for your further traveling pleasure

Guidebooks:
Guide to the Recommended Country Inns of New York,
New Jersey, Pennsylvania, Delaware, Maryland,
Washington, D.C., Virginia, and West Virginia
Consumer's Guide to Package Travel Around the World
Factory Store Guide to All New England
Factory Store Guide to All New York, Pennsylvania,
and New Jersey
Daytrips and Budget Vacations in New England
Guide to Martha's Vineyard
Guide to Nantucket
Handbook for Beach Strollers
Guide to Eastern Canada
In and Out of Boston with (or without) Children
A Guide to New England's Landscape

Short Walks Books:
On Long Island
In Connecticut
On Cape Cod and the Vineyard

Short Bike Rides Books:
In Connecticut
On Long Island
In Greater Boston and Central Massachusetts
On Cape Cod, Nantucket and the Vineyard
In the Berkshires
In Rhode Island

Available at your bookstore or direct from the publisher. For a free catalogue of New England books or to order, call 1-800-243-0495 (in Connecticut, 1-800-962-0973). Or write: The Globe Pequot Press, Old Chester Road, Chester, Connecticut 06412.